Cooking with Patrick Clark

A TRIBUTE TO THE MAN AND HIS CUISINE

Cooking with Patrick Clark

A TRIBUTE TO THE MAN AND HIS CUISINE

CONCEIVED AND COORDINATED BY CHARLIE TROTTER

Ten Speed Press, Berkeley, California

Contents: Patrick Clark Recipes

A collection of recipes that spans Patrick Clark's career

4

SEAFOOD

POULTRY

5

51
Seared Tuna with White
Bean and Roasted Artichoke
Salad, Tomato Oil, and
Crispy Capers

52
Crab-Crusted Halibut with
Spinach and Crispy Potatoes

54
Jumbo Lump Crab Cakes
with Roasted Tomato Sauce
and Basil Mashed Potatoes

55
Roasted Rock Bass with
Oven-Dried Tomatoes,
Shallots, and Black Olives

56
Warm Escalope of Salmon
with Tomato Herb Sauce

57
Pan-Roasted Chilean Sea
Bass with Lump Crab, Sweet
Peas, and Fava Beans

59
Roasted Salmon with
Moroccan Barbecue Sauce,
Couscous, and Sautéed
Savoy Cabbage

61
Shrimp and Sweet Corn
Ravioli with Corn Coulis

62
Halibut in a Horseradish
Crust with Mashed
Potatoes, Chive Oil, and
Crispy Leeks

65
Stuffed Skate Wing
with Potato Knish, Leeks,
and Truffles

66
Chilean Sea Bass with
Zucchini, Chanterelles,
and Curry Oil

67
Pan-Seared Salmon with
Roasted Artichokes, Pearl
Onions, Oven-Dried
Tomatoes, and Vegetable-
Olive Oil Broth

68
Seared Peppered Salmon
with Gazpacho Sauce

71
Black Sea Bass with
Israeli Couscous, Wild
Mushrooms, and Shiitake
Butter Sauce

74
Roast Chicken Ravioli
with Wild Mushrooms
and Spinach

75
Grilled Jerk Chicken with
Caramelized Vidalia Onions
and Sweet Potato Cakes

76
Stuffed Squab with Barley
Risotto, Crispy Sweetbreads,
and Roasted Shallot Oil

79
Barbecued Quail with
Moroccan Barbecue Sauce,
Cinnamon-Scented
Couscous, and Grilled
Red Onion

83
Roasted Clay Pot Chicken
with Potato Pancakes

84
Barbecued Quail with Sweet
Potato and Mushroom Hash

85
Grilled Duck Breast with
Duck Spring Rolls and
Japanese Five Spice Sauce

CONTINUED

Contents: Guest Chef Recipes

Recipes contributed by many of Patrick's friends

APPETIZERS

SOUPS AND SALADS

CONTINUED

SEAFOOD

PATRICK CLARK: THE CHEF

by Charlie Trotter

The first time I had Patrick Clark's food I didn't even know who he was. It was late December in 1986, and I had somehow happened upon the Cafe Luxembourg in New York City. The dining room was absolutely buzzing (Andy Warhol was two tables over). On the surface it seemed to be more of a "scene" than a "food" place. The dishes I sampled that evening, however, would have done justice to a four-star restaurant that seated seventy-five, let alone a place that was probably serving upwards of two hundred-fifty guests. I had a striking combination of escargot with fermented black beans and herb beurre blanc, an amazing preparation of artichoke hearts and celery root in parchment paper, a meltingly soft steamed sea bass with a fennel–Italian parsley sauce, delicious red snapper with new potatoes and balsamic, and a crispy, deeply satisfying pear strudel. Not only was I blown away by the meal, but even more so when I learned that the chef, Patrick Clark, was also the chef of another restaurant, the famed Odeon, clear across town. Amazing! Running two quality restaurants is truly an incredible feat. I say that because I have my hands full with just one. So began my appreciation of this wonderful man. I later found out about his early days—his initial training at New York City Technical College and his stints in London and France—but the greatest training in the world would not have been enough to account for the food I had that night.

In my mind, to be a great cook two things have to be utterly in place: You have to absolutely love to eat, to the point where when you finish one meal you're already thinking about the next. It's what you might call an extreme case of food obsession. There are more of us out there than one might think. Second, you

The Patrick Clark that I knew was
a very happy man. His happiness and inner peace
could have only come from doing what
he loved and surrounding himself with love.

have to be completely taken by the act and art of feeding others, and usually, in our line of work, total strangers. From the moment I discovered chef Patrick Clark, I sized him up to be just this sort of individual—a born chef.

As I got to know him, I began to understand his essence. Patrick would painstakingly "work" a risotto, carefully sear sea scallops, or meticulously plate a dish of food, practically as if he were making love. That's how emotionally, physically, and mentally caught up in the moment he could be. Upon completion of a creation, or a task, a look of pure joy would spread across his face. This is an approach to food and cooking that simply cannot be taught. One must be born with the bug, and Patrick, I am convinced, was. When he surveyed a finished plate and smiled, or even just talked about food, you could feel the joy. And it was infectious! When you were around Patrick, you just felt good.

As much as I admired, respected, and even loved Patrick as a chef, however, I must admit I was even more in awe of how he was such a loving husband and a fabulous father. As passionate as he was about cuisine, he was even more so about his family. He was always talking about his family, and the same loving expression that would appear on his face when he cooked would grow larger and even more animated whenever he mentioned Lynette and the children. I must confess, aside from my own father, my role model for being a loving husband and father was Patrick Clark. And that's about the highest tribute I can pay anyone because, after all, cooking is only food, but a family is a family. The Patrick Clark that I knew was a very happy man. His happiness and inner peace could have only come from doing what he loved and surrounding himself with love. I think that you will discover a truly beautiful soul in the following pages.

PATRICK CLARK: THE HUSBAND AND FATHER

by Lynette Clark

I met Patrick in 1978 at New York City Technical College in a wine class taught by Dr. Thomas Ahrens. The first time Patrick asked me out, he told me he would not be able to pick me up because he was working. It was December 30th, and he was a chef at La Boite Restaurant in Manhattan and was preparing for New Year's Eve. He did, however, send a car for me. That was my first clue about his dedication to his profession. On that first date, he brought me a one pound box of Godiva Chocolates and took me to Gerald's Jazz Club and then to Riechlu of London (a small café). The first time he kissed me, he was leaning over a phone booth while calling into the kitchen to check on his stocks. That was my second clue.

Patrick prepared many, many dishes for me over the years. Among my favorites were gâteau of carrot, velouté of chicken soup with slivered almonds, seafood sausage, crab cakes, and a flourless chocolate cake. (He always hated for me to name those as standouts because many of them are from years ago.) None of those, however, were dishes he made to woo me. The first entrée he made for me was a veal chop with a watercress sauce. I took one look at the plate and said, "I can't eat anything with a bright green sauce." But he did get my attention with the tight checkered black and white chef's pants he used to wear. I used to think he must have poured himself into them. Now that impressed me.

I was to discover that Patrick was an intensely passionate person. He had passion for food, his children, his work, his colleagues, and a passion for me. But to live with a chef was to always come second to food. Some of our

I was to discover that Patrick was an

intensely passionate person.

He had passion for food, his children, his work,

his colleagues, and a passion for me.

biggest fights were over food. We almost didn't get married over an argument about the proper way to cook a steak! Food was the only "other woman" I ever worried about. There was Ms. Tomato with her succulent flesh, tender and sweet Ms. Scallop, Summer & Winter Squash, Shad Roe, Belgian Chocolate, Caviar, and Foie Gras, to name a few. When we lived in Virginia, Patrick would stop at the farmers' market and taunt me with his love of fresh fruits and vegetables. "Feel this, Lynette," he would say. "Touch that," or "Isn't this the most beautiful thing you've ever seen?" I would think, "Hey, what about me?"

I miss Patrick more than I have words to describe. I have loved him, and still love him, with an intensity that might only be matched by his passion for food. Our wedding song was "Always and Forever," and it became a phrase we often used in letters and cards to each other. Patrick gave me many wonderful memories that will unite us always and forever. But his most precious gifts to me are our five children—Preston, Aleia, Ashley, Brooke, and Cameron; they are always and forever a testament to Patrick's and my passion and love for life and for each other.

Acknowledgments

Patrick always wanted to write a book. He'd often tell me how he admired his friends who found time to run a kitchen and a family, and still found time to write a book. A lot of contributors to this book will remember discussions with him on how they were able to do this. On several occasions he did try to write his book. He had many recipes and an outline, but because of many obstacles (mostly time) he was unable to realize this dream.

I will always and forever be grateful to all of you who have contributed to making Patrick's dream come to fruition (a favorite word of his).

First, I must thank Charlie Trotter who spearheaded this entire project. He single handedly decided to pick up the ball and complete what Patrick didn't have the time to complete. He took Patrick's outlines, newspaper and magazine recipes, menus, notes, and memories from Patrick's sous chefs to put together this book.

Judi Carle, editor and new friend, has come to know Patrick through his friends, collegues, children, and extensive talks with me. She has been extremely kind and patient with me when I missed deadlines and just couldn't seem to get through writing about the man my whole world revolved around. I've cried to her and she was comforting, yet persistent enough to get everything she needed from me.

Donnie Masterton and Stephen Moise contributed most of Patrick's recipes. They flew into Chicago for the photo shoots and generally helped to fill in the blanks by answering Judi's many, many, many questions about how Patrick would have done this or that.

Sari Zernich coordinated everything for the photo shoots and worked with Stephen and Donnie to produce all the food for the photos.

Arlene Feltman-Sailhac from De Gustibus at Macy's contributed recipes that Patrick had prepared at various cooking demos.

Warner Leroy brought Patrick a laptop computer while he was in the hospital for him to record his recipes.

Ferdinand Metz and his team at the Culinary Institute of America, Keith Keogh and his team at the California Culinary Academy, and Marcus Samuelsson at Aquavit tested all of Patrick's recipes.

My A-Team: Valerie Thomas, Vanessa Baylor, Elaine Smith, Ketly Blaise-Sapp and Donna Shaw. These women have been my support throughout. They have been with me through my darkest hours. Without them I would not have made it through the hardest time of my life. Besides flying in from all parts of the country to be with me several times during this year, they have proofread all of my writings and remembered things that I could not.

Nancy Boyd-Franklin used all of her skills and talents to guide my children and I through the emotional minefield we faced.

Eternal gratitude to my mother, Elsa, for her goodness, sacrifices, and love.

To my special supporter (you know who you are) all I can say is thank you.

I beg your understanding if for one reason or another you were not included in this book. My mind is engulfed in a fog and it's often hard to see and remember clearly. Charlie and Judi have prompted and prodded, yet I know that I've left out some important friends. I can only ask for your forgiveness.

God has not promised that we wouldn't bear many a burden, many a care; joy without sorrow, or peace without pain. But God has promised strength for the day, unfailing sympathy and undying love. We are deeply grateful for His presence—He is the foundation from which we draw our hopes and wishes for a brighter tomorrow.

During the summer between my
sophomore and junior years, my father gave me a
job at Tavern on the Green. It was unbelievably
important to me. Just to work in a kitchen that was
so famous was thrilling. My father always
called his children by their first and middle names.
So, when it was time to leave work, you would hear
a voice booming through the kitchen...Preston Sean!
My friends got a kick out of it, but it
drove me nuts. I know I will never forget moments
like that, or my Dad, and all he was to me.

PRESTON CLARK AGE 17

Lobster Spring Rolls

For canapés, use 24 small wonton skins and serve the sauce in a small dish for dipping.

Serves 8

SPRING ROLLS

8 ounces pork, finely chopped

3 tablespoons peanut oil

1 clove garlic, finely chopped

½ teaspoon peeled and chopped fresh ginger

1 tablespoon sesame oil

6 large shiitake mushrooms, stemmed and julienned

2 leeks, julienned (white part only)

Salt and freshly ground black pepper

2 cups shredded savoy cabbage

8 spring roll wrappers

12 ounces cooked lobster, diced

1 cup julienned daikon

12 water chestnuts, chopped

6 scallions, cut on the diagonal in ¼-inch lengths

1 cup canola oil

———

1 teaspoon cornstarch

3 tablespoons soy sauce

3 tablespoons oyster sauce

4 teaspoons chives, cut into 1-inch lengths

To prepare the filling:
Sauté the pork in 2 tablespoons of the peanut oil over medium-high heat for 5 minutes, or until thoroughly cooked. Drain the grease from the pan and discard, and set the pork aside to cool. Sauté the garlic and ginger in the remaining 1 tablespoon peanut oil and the sesame oil over medium heat for 2 minutes. Add the shiitakes and leeks and cook for 5 minutes, or until the mushrooms are cooked and the leeks are softened. Remove from the heat, season to taste with salt and pepper, and set aside to cool.

To prepare the rolls:
Spread some of the cabbage toward the bottom of the spring roll wrappers. Top with some of the lobster, followed by the daikon, mushroom-leek mixture, water chestnuts, pork, and scallions. Roll up tightly, folding in the sides of the wrapper, until you have a tight, eggroll-like shape.

Heat the canola oil to 375° in a sauté pan. Add the spring rolls and cook for 30 to 45 seconds on each side, or until golden brown. Transfer to a paper towel to drain, and keep warm.

To prepare the sauce:
Place the cornstarch and 1 tablespoon of the soy sauce in a small saucepan and stir until smooth. Add the remaining 2 tablespoons soy sauce and the oyster sauce and stir until smooth. Cook over medium heat for 3 minutes, or until the mixture comes to a boil. Remove from the heat.

Cut off the ends of each of the spring rolls and cut the rolls in half on the diagonal. Stand 2 halves upright in the center of each plate. Drizzle some of the sauce around the spring rolls, and sprinkle with the chives.

Barbecued Prawns with Corn Relish

You can use prawns without the heads, but make sure you skewer them so they don't curl when they cook.

Serves 6

½ cup sour cream

½ teaspoon Tabasco sauce

2 tablespoons freshly squeezed lime juice

3 cups fresh corn kernels, cooked

1 small red onion, diced

1 jalapeño pepper, seeded and finely diced

2 plum tomatoes, peeled, seeded, and diced

2 tablespoons cider vinegar

1 cup olive oil

1 tablespoon chopped cilantro

Salt and freshly ground black pepper

18 prawns, heads on

½ cup Patrick's Barbecue Sauce (page 90)

6 cups mesclun greens

To make the dressing:
Combine the sour cream, Tabasco sauce, and lime juice in a small bowl and set aside.

To make the relish:
Toss together the corn, onion, jalapeño, tomatoes, vinegar, ¾ cup plus 2 tablespoons of the olive oil and the cilantro in a bowl and season to taste with salt and pepper.

To cook the prawns:
Remove the shell from the body of each prawn, leaving the head intact. Skewer the length of the prawn on a bamboo skewer. Season lightly with salt and pepper and brush with the remaining 2 tablespoons olive oil. Place on a hot grill for 30 seconds, brush with barbecue sauce, and grill for 30 seconds. Turn the prawns over, brush with more barbecue sauce, and grill for 1 minute. Remove the prawns from the grill and remove the skewers.

To prepare the greens:
Toss the mesclun greens with some of the liquid from the corn relish.

Place a mound of mesclun greens in the center of each plate and arrange the prawns on the lettuce. Spoon the corn relish in a band across the prawns and drizzle the dressing back and forth across the salad in a Z pattern.

Sautéed Shrimp Cakes

with Cool and Spicy Cucumber Salsa

For canapés, form 24 small shrimp cakes and top each one with a small spoonful of the salsa after they are fried.

Serves 4

1 8-ounce sole fillet, diced

1 pound cooked medium shrimp, diced

3 tablespoons thinly sliced scallions

2 tablespoons minced chives

2 tablespoons chopped fresh parsley

1 tablespoon freshly squeezed lemon juice

3 tablespoons Basic Mayonnaise (page 56)

Salt and freshly ground black pepper

Cayenne pepper

1 cup all-purpose flour

Olive oil for frying

Clarified butter for frying

Cool and Spicy Cucumber Salsa (recipe follows)

4 sprigs chervil

To prepare the shrimp cakes: Purée the sole in a food processor fitted with the metal blade until smooth. Transfer to a bowl and add the shrimp, scallions, chives, parsley, lemon juice, and mayonnaise. Season to taste with salt, pepper, and cayenne pepper. Form the mixture into 8 patties, cover with plastic, and refrigerate for at least 30 minutes.

Place the flour on a large plate and dredge each shrimp cake in the flour, brushing off any excess. Heat a large sauté pan until just hot. Pour equal amounts of olive oil and clarified butter into the pan until it is approximately 1/2 inch deep. Heat the mixture over medium-high heat for 5 minutes, or until very hot. Carefully add the shrimp cakes to the pan and sauté for 3 minutes, or until golden brown. Carefully turn the cakes over and cook for 3 minutes, or until golden brown. Remove the cakes from the pan and drain on paper towels.

Spoon a mound of the salsa in the center of each plate and lean 2 shrimp cakes against the salsa, opposite each other. Place a sprig of chervil in the center of the salsa.

Cool and Spicy Cucumber Salsa

YIELD: ABOUT 2 CUPS

1 cup peeled and diced seedless cucumbers

1 teaspoon salt

1/2 cup diced red onion

1/2 cup peeled, diced plum tomatoes

2 jalapeños, seeded and finely chopped

1/4 cup freshly squeezed lime juice

1/4 cup chopped fresh basil leaves

Put the cucumbers in a bowl, toss with the salt, and refrigerate for 1 hour. Transfer the cucumbers to a fine-mesh sieve, rinse under cold running water, and thoroughly drain. Place the cucumbers in a small bowl, add the remaining ingredients, and mix well. Refrigerate for at least 1 hour before serving.

Corn and Mushroom Ravioli

For an interesting textural variation, the ravioli can be sautéed in a little butter until golden brown.

Serves 4

6 ears sweet corn

1 stem parsley

1 teaspoon black peppercorns

1 sprig thyme

1 bay leaf

2 sweet onions, minced

1/4 cup unsalted butter

Salt and freshly ground black pepper

1/4 cup olive oil

1/2 teaspoon Madras curry powder

4 ounces fresh wild mushrooms

1 clove garlic, minced

1/2 teaspoon chopped fresh thyme

1 tablespoon chopped fresh parsley

24 21/2-inch round wonton skins

1 egg, beaten with 1 tablespoon milk

2 tablespoons 1-inch long chive pieces

To prepare the coulis:
Cut the kernels off the cob, reserving the kernels and cobs separately. Place the cobs in 11/2 quarts water in a stockpot. Tie the parsley stem, peppercorns, thyme sprig, and bay leaf in a piece of cheesecloth and add it to the pan. Bring to a simmer and cook for 30 minutes. Strain into a bowl through a fine-mesh sieve and return the liquid to the pan. Add half of the onions and two-thirds of the corn to the pan and simmer for 15 minutes. Pour the mixture into a blender, purée until smooth and strain into a saucepan. Bring to a boil, remove from the heat, and whisk in 1 tablespoon of the butter. Season to taste with salt and pepper and set aside.

To toast the corn:
Heat a nonstick sauté pan until very hot. Add 2 tablespoons of the olive oil and 2 tablespoons of the butter and cook for 15 seconds, or until the butter starts to bubble. Add 1/2 cup of the reserved uncooked corn kernels and sauté for 20 to 30 seconds, or until golden brown. Remove from the pan and drain on paper towels.

To prepare the filling:
Melt the remaining 1 tablespoon butter in a small saucepan over medium-low heat. Add the remaining onions and cook for 3 minutes, or until translucent. Add the curry powder and cook for 2 minutes, or until the curry powder becomes fragrant. Add the remaining corn, cook over medium heat for 3 minutes, and remove from the heat.

Heat the remaining 2 tablespoons olive oil in a medium sauté pan and add the mushrooms. Cook for 3 to 4 minutes, or until all of the liquid is evaporated. Add the garlic and thyme and cook for 1 minute. Remove from the heat and drain off any liquid in the pan. Coarsely chop the mushrooms and add to the corn-onion mixture. Stir in the parsley and season to taste with salt and pepper. Allow the mixture to cool to room temperature.

To prepare the ravioli:
Lay 12 of the wonton skins on a flat surface. Place a spoonful of the filling in the center of each wonton. Brush the edges of the remaining 12 wontons with the egg and place them, egg side down, on top of the filling. Firmly press together the edges of each ravioli, removing any air pockets, and completely seal the edges. Cook the ravioli in boiling salted water for 3 to 4 minutes, or until they float. Remove the ravioli from the water with a slotted spoon and drain thoroughly.

Reheat the corn coulis. Place 3 warm ravioli in the center of each plate and spoon the coulis over the ravioli and around the plate. Sprinkle the toasted corn and chive pieces around the plates.

Shrimp and Shiitake Strudel

The crispy shiitakes sprinkled around the plates echo the flavor of the strudel and provide the perfect textural foil to the creamy goat cheese.

Serves 8

FILLING

1 tablespoon olive oil

1 small onion, diced

4 large shiitakes, stemmed and julienned

Salt and freshly ground black pepper

1 clove garlic, finely chopped

2 scallions, thinly sliced

1 sprig thyme

4 ounces goat cheese

¼ teaspoon sesame seeds

12 large shrimp, peeled, deveined, and diced

4 sheets filo dough

⅓ cup clarified butter

3 tablespoons cornstarch

1 cup julienned shiitake mushrooms

Canola oil for frying

3 tablespoons finely chopped chives

To prepare the filling:
Heat the olive oil in a medium sauté pan. Add the onion and sauté over medium heat for 5 minutes, or until translucent. Add the shiitakes and sauté for 5 minutes, or until tender. Season to taste with salt and pepper. Add the garlic and scallions and cook for 1 minute. Add the thyme sprig and cook for 2 minutes, or until the fragrance of the thyme is released. Remove the pan from the heat, remove and discard the thyme sprig, and set the filling aside in a small bowl to cool. Add the goat cheese, sesame seeds and diced shrimp to the cooled filling and season to taste with salt and pepper.

To prepare the strudel:
Preheat the oven to 425°. Lay a sheet of filo on a work surface and brush with some of the clarified butter. Top with a filo sheet and brush with butter. Top with another filo sheet and brush with butter. Top with the remaining filo sheet and cut the stack in quarters.

Spread one quarter of the filling along one of the long edges of each filo stack, leaving a ¼-inch border on each side. Fold the ends in, roll up, and brush with butter to seal. Place on a baking pan, seam side down, and brush each roll with the clarified butter. Bake for 12 to 15 minutes, or until golden brown and crispy on the outside.

To prepare the shiitakes:
Put the cornstarch in a bowl, add the shiitakes, and toss together. Pour about 3 inches of canola oil into a small saucepan and heat the oil to 375°. Add the shiitakes and cook for 1½ to 2 minutes, or until crispy. Remove the shiitakes from the pan and place on paper towels to drain. Use immediately.

Cut the ends off of each warm strudel roll and cut into 6 equal slices. Overlap 3 strudel pieces in the center of each plate and sprinkle the fried shiitakes and chives around the strudel.

Serves 8

1/2 cup olive oil

1/2 cup chopped onions

1/4 cup chopped scallions

1/4 cup chopped
red bell peppers

1/4 cup chopped
green bell peppers

1 tablespoon minced garlic

3/4 cup fresh corn kernels

2 teaspoons
Old Bay Seasoning

Salt and freshly
ground black pepper

1 cup crabmeat

6 sheets filo dough

1 cup bread crumbs

Toasted Corn and
Caramelized Onion Sauce
(recipe follows)

To prepare the filling:

Heat 1 tablespoon of the olive oil in a large skillet over medium-high heat. Add the onions and cook for 5 minutes, or until translucent. Stir in the scallions, red and green peppers, and garlic and cook for 2 minutes. Add the corn and cook for 5 minutes. Add the Old Bay Seasoning and season to taste with salt and pepper. Remove from the heat, fold in the crabmeat, and set aside to cool.

To prepare the tarts:

Preheat the oven to 375°. Lay 2 sheets of the filo on a work surface and brush lightly with some of the olive oil. Sprinkle each sheet with 1/4 cup of the bread crumbs and top with another sheet of filo. Brush the filo sheets with olive oil, sprinkle each sheet with 1/4 cup bread crumbs, and top with the 2 remaining filo sheets. Cut the filo stack into quarters and lay each quarter in a 3-inch tart ring. Mound some of the filling in each tart and fold the excess filo over the filling to close the tart. Brush the tops of the tarts with olive oil and bake for 12 to 14 minutes, or until golden brown.

Carefully remove the tarts from the rings and place 1 in the center of each plate. Spoon the corn and onion sauce around the tarts.

Toasted Corn and Caramelized Onion Sauce

YIELD: ABOUT 2 CUPS

6 ears sweet corn, kernels removed, cobs and 1 cup kernels reserved

1 tablespoon olive oil

1 small onion, chopped

2 shallots, finely chopped

1 teaspoon chopped garlic

Pinch of Old Bay Seasoning

2 tablespoons butter

Salt and freshly
ground black pepper

3 tablespoons
chopped chives

Place the corn cobs in a large stockpot and add enough water to cover the cobs. Bring to a boil and then lower the heat and simmer for 30 minutes. Strain into a bowl through a fine-mesh sieve and return the liquid to the pan. Simmer for 45 minutes, or until reduced to 2 cups.

Heat the olive oil in a large saucepan over medium heat. Add the onion and cook for 10 minutes, or until the onion is a deep golden brown. Stir in the shallots and garlic and cook for 1 minute. Remove from the heat and set aside.

Toast 1/2 cup of corn kernels in a dry skillet over medium heat for 5 minutes, or until golden brown. Add the remaining 1/2 cup corn kernels, the reduced corn stock, and the Old Bay Seasoning to the onion mixture. Simmer the mixture over medium heat for 15 minutes. Purée in a blender until smooth and strain into a saucepan through a fine-mesh sieve. Return the sauce to the heat and whisk in the butter. Season to taste with salt and pepper. Stir in the chives and the toasted corn.

Crab and Corn Filo Tart

Filo dough is an interesting, yet simple substitution for traditional tart dough.

Fried Oysters with Basil Sauce

This dish has a beautiful presentation yet is amazingly simple to prepare.

Serves 4

1 cup firmly packed fresh basil, blanched and shocked

1/2 cup olive oil

Salt and freshly ground black pepper

1/2 cup milk

1 egg

1 cup Panko Japanese bread crumbs

1 tablespoon chopped fresh chervil

1 tablespoon chopped chives

1 tablespoon chopped fresh thyme leaves

1 cup all-purpose flour

16 belon or Pine Island oysters, shucked, bottom shells reserved

Peanut oil for frying

4 cups seaweed, blanched

To prepare the basil sauce:
Purée the basil with the olive oil until smooth. Season to taste with salt and pepper.

To prepare the oysters:
In a small bowl, whisk together the milk and egg and season to taste with salt and pepper. In a separate small bowl, combine the bread crumbs, chervil, chives, and thyme. Put the flour on a plate and season it with salt and pepper. Dredge the oysters in the egg and then in the flour, shaking off any excess. Dip the oysters in the egg again and dredge in the bread crumb mixture.

Heat the peanut oil to 375° to 400° in a deep pot. Fry the oysters in the oil for 2 to 3 minutes, or until they are slightly undercooked and the crust is golden brown. Remove the oysters from the oil and drain on paper towels.

Spread a layer of seaweed on each plate and top with 4 oyster shell bottoms. Spoon some of the sauce in each shell and top with a warm fried oyster.

Asparagus

with Julienned Vegetables and Chive-Crème Fraîche

This combination of different vegetables also makes an impressive side dish when served on a large platter.

Serves 6

12 ounces fresh spinach, stemmed

1 cup butter

1 cup finely julienned carrot

1 cup finely julienned turnip

30 thin asparagus spears, trimmed 3 inches below the tip

1 cup finely julienned leek (white part only)

4 ounces shiitake mushrooms, stemmed and cut in 1-inch pieces

1 1/2 teaspoons chopped fresh tarragon

1 tablespoon chopped fresh basil

1/2 teaspoon Dijon mustard

Salt and freshly ground black pepper

1/2 cup crème fraîche

3 tablespoons freshly squeezed lemon juice

Pinch of white pepper

2 teaspoons chopped chives

To prepare the spinach:
Bring a pan of lightly salted water to a boil. Add the spinach and cook for 2 minutes. Drain well, squeezing out as much water as possible. Coarsely chop the spinach and set aside.

To prepare the vegetables:
Bring 1 quart of water and 2 tablespoons of the butter to a boil. Add the carrot and cook for 3 to 4 minutes, or until just tender; remove with a slotted spoon and pat dry on paper towels. In the same boiling water, add the turnip and cook for 3 minutes, or until just tender; remove to paper towels with a slotted spoon. Add the asparagus to the pan and cook for 3 minutes, or until just tender; remove to paper towels with a slotted spoon. Add the leek to the pan and cook for 4 minutes, or until just tender; remove to paper towels with a slotted spoon. Reserve the cooking liquid and combine the leeks, carrots, and turnips in a bowl and set aside.

To prepare the mushrooms:
Sauté the mushrooms in 3 tablespoons of the butter over medium heat for 4 minutes, or until just cooked. Set aside.

To prepare the sauce:
Cook the reserved vegetable cooking liquid over low heat for 20 to 30 minutes, or until reduced to about 1 cup. Whisk in 1/2 cup of the butter, 1 tablespoon at a time. Whisk in the tarragon, basil, and mustard and season to taste with salt and pepper. Keep warm over very low heat.

To reheat the vegetables:
Bring 1 quart of water to a boil in a large saucepan. Insert a steamer basket and steam the asparagus for about 3 minutes. Sauté the spinach in the remaining 3 tablespoons butter over medium heat for 2 minutes, or until warmed through. Add the julienned vegetables and mushrooms to the sauce and place over medium heat for about 3 minutes, or until warmed through.

To prepare the crème fraîche: In a bowl, whisk together the crème fraîche, lemon juice, white pepper, and chives.

Fan 5 asparagus spears in the center of each plate. Place some of the spinach at the base of the asparagus and spoon the julienned vegetables and sauce in a straight line slightly over-lapping the base of the asparagus and the spinach. Drizzle the crème fraîche over the plates in a Z.

Crab and Corn Fritters

These crispy fritters also make great canapés.

Serves 4

1¹/₄ cups all-purpose flour

1 teaspoon baking powder

1¹/₄ teaspoons salt

¹/₄ teaspoon ground nutmeg

6 ounces crabmeat

³/₄ cup flat beer

1¹/₄ cups fresh corn kernels

1 egg white, lightly beaten

1 tablespoon chopped chives

1 tablespoon chopped
fresh parsley

1 jalapeño pepper

1 tablespoon chopped onion

Canola oil for frying

To prepare the fritters:
Combine the flour, baking powder, salt, and nutmeg in a medium bowl. Combine the crab, beer, corn, and egg white in a small bowl. Add the crab mixture to the flour mixture and stir until just combined. Add the chives, parsley, jalapeño, and onion and stir until incorporated.

Heat the canola to 375° in a large saucepan. Drop 1 tablespoon of the batter into the hot oil and cook for 1 minute. Turn the fritter and cook for 1 minute, or until golden brown. Remove the fritter from the oil and drain on paper towels. Repeat with the remaining batter.

Place the fritters on a large plate or bowl and serve immediately.

The haunting flavor of the truffles in this elegant preparation makes this a perfect first course for a special dinner party.

33

Serves 6

1 Idaho potato, peeled and diced

1 cup heavy whipping cream

3 eggs

3 egg yolks

5 tablespoons black truffle juice

1 teaspoon black truffle oil

3 stalks salsify, peeled

3/4 tablespoon olive oil

4 ounces cooked morel mushrooms

Salt and freshly ground black pepper

1 1/2 cups Chicken Stock (recipe follows)

2 tablespoons butter

2 tablespoons chopped mixed fresh herbs (parsley, basil, chervil, or tarragon)

Dash of freshly squeezed lemon juice

1 small black truffle, shaved into very thin slices

24 small sprigs chervil

To prepare the potato:
Preheat the oven to 350°. Cook the potato in boiling salted water for 15 minutes, or until soft. Pass the potato through a sieve and combine in a bowl with the cream. Whisk together the eggs and egg yolks in a separate bowl and combine with the potato mixture. Add 3 tablespoons of the truffle juice and the truffle oil and mix well. Pour the mixture into 6 buttered 3-ounce molds. Place on a sheet pan with 1/2 inch of water and bake for 25 to 35 minutes, or until firm in the center. Remove the pan from the oven and cool the custards slightly.

To prepare the sauce:
Cut the salsify into 2-inch pieces on the diagonal and then halve the pieces length-wise. Sauté the salsify in the olive oil for 3 minutes. Add the morels and season to taste with salt and pepper. Add the remaining 2 table-spoons truffle juice and the stock and bring to a boil. Add the butter and cook for 5 minutes, or until it thickens slightly. Add the herbs and lemon juice. Cut half of the shaved truffles into a fine juli-enne and add to the mixture.

Unmold a warm custard into the center of each plate. Arrange the salsify mixture around the custards and spoon some of the sauce around the plates. Top each custard with some of the shaved truffles and arrange the chervil sprigs around the plates.

Chicken Stock

YIELD: 2 QUARTS

6 pounds chicken bones

3 cups chopped onions

2 cups chopped carrots

2 cups chopped celery

1 cup chopped leeks

1 tablespoon white peppercorns

1 bay leaf

Place all of the ingredients in a large stockpot and cover three-quarters of the way with cold water. Bring to a boil, reduce the heat to low, and slowly simmer for 4 hours, skimming every 30 minutes to remove the impurities that rise to the surface. Strain and cook the stock over medium heat for 30 to 45 minutes, or until reduced to 2 quarts.

My dad used to come into my classroom
every year and serve cheesecake to my classmates.
One of the more memorable years was in the
beginning of second grade, when we first moved
to California. It was only the second week of
school and I hardly knew anyone. The cheesecake
was a great icebreaker. I remember going
home with new friends and, of course, I was
in good with the teachers. A couple of years ago he
asked me when I wanted him to come to my school.
I told him I was too old for that now. I wish
I hadn't thought I was too old.

Yellow Tomato Soup and Vegetable Timbale

This light, chilled soup can be completely prepared in advance.

Serves 10

1 large onion, chopped

2 leeks, chopped

1 carrot, peeled and chopped

2 tablespoons olive oil

4 cloves garlic

2 sprigs thyme

Salt and freshly ground black pepper

2 tablespoons curry powder

8 yellow tomatoes, chopped

3 quarts Vegetable Stock (page 67)

1 bay leaf

1 small yellow squash, cut into a fine brunoise

1 small carrot, cut into a fine brunoise

1 small zucchini, cut into a fine brunoise

1 small sweet onion, cut into a fine brunoise

1 red tomato, peeled, seeded, and chopped

1 tablespoon chopped chives

4 sprigs chervil

To prepare the soup:
Sauté the onion, leeks, and carrot in 1 tablespoon of the olive oil in a medium sauté pan over medium heat for 5 minutes. Add the garlic and thyme and cook for 3 to 5 minutes, or until the vegetables are tender. Season to taste with salt and pepper. Add the curry powder and stir until a paste forms. Add the yellow tomatoes and cook for 2 minutes. Add the vegetable stock and bay leaf and simmer for 30 minutes. Remove and discard the bay leaf, purée the soup until smooth, and strain into a bowl through a fine-mesh sieve. Cool over an ice bath and refrigerate until ready to serve.

To prepare the vegetables:
Sauté the squash, and the carrot, zucchini, and onion brunoise in the remaining 1 tablespoon olive oil over medium heat for 2 to 3 minutes, or until tender. Add the tomato and cook for 30 seconds. Remove from the heat, season to taste with salt and pepper, and cool completely. Pack the sautéed vegetables into ten 2-ounce timbale molds.

Unmold a timbale in the center of each shallow bowl. Carefully ladle the chilled soup into the bowls, sprinkle the chives around the soup, and place a sprig of chervil on each timbale.

Caesar Salad with Parmesan Crisps

You can add grilled chicken strips to this salad for a more substantial dish.

38

Serves 6

2 cups diced sourdough bread

2 tablespoons chopped fresh marjoram

1/4 cup canola oil

Salt and freshly ground black pepper

2 3/4 cups freshly grated Parmesan cheese

30 spears of hearts of romaine

Caesar Salad Dressing (recipe follows)

To prepare the croutons: Preheat the oven to 350°. Toss together the bread, marjoram, and canola oil. Add salt and pepper to taste, and place on a baking sheet. Bake, stirring occasionally, for 15 minutes, or until golden brown. Remove the pan from the oven and let cool to room temperature.

To prepare the Parmesan Crisps: Spread 2 cups of the Parmesan cheese in a non-stick sauté pan. Cook over medium heat for 5 minutes, or until the cheese is melted. Remove from the heat and slide the cheese onto paper towels. Break into pieces when cooled.

Place 5 romaine leaves in the center of each plate. Sprinkle the croutons and the remaining 3/4 cup Parmesan cheese over the romaine. Drizzle the dressing over the lettuce and arrange some of the Parmesan crisps at the base of the plate.

Caesar Salad Dressing

YIELD: ABOUT 2 CUPS

6 cloves garlic

1 1/2 cups extra virgin olive oil

1 tablespoon Dijon mustard

2 tablespoons freshly squeezed lemon juice

2 tablespoons sherry wine vinegar

Freshly ground black pepper

10 anchovies, rinsed and finely chopped

Purée the garlic and olive oil until smooth. Strain through a fine-mesh sieve, pressing on the garlic to release the juice. Put the mustard in a bowl and whisk the lemon juice and vinegar into the mustard. Season to taste with black pepper. Add the anchovies and whisk in the garlic olive oil. The dressing may be kept in the refrigerator for up to 3 days.

Serves 4

4 large sweet potatoes

6 tablespoons butter

1 leek, sliced
(white part only)

2 onions, sliced

3 quarts Chicken Stock
(page 33)

1 sprig thyme

1 stem parsley

1 bay leaf

1 teaspoon
black peppercorns

Salt and freshly
ground black pepper

Smithfield Ham and Leek
Ravioli (recipe follows)

2 teaspoons chopped chives

To prepare the soup:
Preheat the oven to 350°. Bake the sweet potatoes for 45 minutes, or until just tender. Remove the potatoes from the oven and cool to room temperature. Peel the sweet potatoes, discarding the skins, and cut the flesh into large chunks.

Heat 4 tablespoons of the butter in a large saucepan and add the leek and onions. Cook over medium heat for 8 to 10 minutes, or until translucent. Add the sweet potatoes and 2 quarts of the stock and bring to a boil over medium-high heat. Tie the thyme, parsley stem, bay leaf, and peppercorns in a piece of cheesecloth and add it to the pan. Lower the heat to medium, and simmer for 30 minutes. Remove and discard the spice bag and season to taste with salt and pepper. Purée the soup in a blender for 2 minutes, or until smooth, and pass through a fine-mesh sieve. Return the soup to the pan and slowly bring to a boil. Thin to the desired consistency with the remaining stock and season to taste with salt and pepper. Stir in the remaining 2 tablespoons butter.

Ladle some of the soup into each bowl and place 3 warm ravioli in the center. Sprinkle the chopped chives around the bowls.

Smithfield Ham and Leek Ravioli

YIELD: 12 RAVIOLI

1 leek, thinly sliced
(white part only)

1 tablespoon butter

1/2 tablespoon heavy
whipping cream

2 ounces Smithfield ham,
finely diced

Freshly ground black pepper

24 2¹/₂-inch round
wonton skins

1 egg, beaten

Cook the leek in the butter in a small sauté pan over medium heat for 5 minutes, or until translucent. Add the cream and cook for 2 minutes, or until it is completely absorbed. Set the leek aside to cool. In a bowl, combine the leek with the ham and season to taste with pepper.

Lay 12 wonton skins on a flat surface and place a spoonful of the ham mixture in the center of each wonton. Brush the edges of the remaining 12 wonton skins with the egg and place them over the filling, egg side down. Firmly press the edges of each ravioli together, removing any air pockets and completely sealing. Cook the ravioli in boiling salted water for 3 to 4 minutes, or until they float. Remove the ravioli from the water with a slotted spoon and drain thoroughly in a colander.

Roasted Sweet Potato Bisque

with Smithfield Ham and Leek Ravioli

The bisque can be prepared up to a day in advance and reheated just prior to serving.

39

Extra lobster stock can be frozen for several months.

Serves 10

4 1-pound lobsters

6 ears sweet corn

4 bay leaves

8 sprigs thyme

1 tablespoon black peppercorns

Salt and freshly ground black pepper

1¹/₂ cups heavy whipping cream

3 thick strips bacon, julienned

2 large Yukon Gold potatoes, peeled and cut in ¹/₄-inch dice

1 onion, chopped

¹/₄ cup butter

4 teaspoons chervil leaves

To prepare the lobster:
Cook the lobsters in boiling salted water for 3 to 4 minutes, or until slightly underdone. Remove from the water and let cool slightly. Remove the lobster meat from the shells, reserving the meat and the shells. Coarsely chop the lobster meat.

To prepare the corn:
Husk the corn and remove the corn from the cobs, reserving the corn, cobs, and half of the husks.

To make the bisque:
Place the lobster shells, corn cobs, husks, bay leaves, thyme sprigs, and pepper-corns in a stockpot and add enough water to barely cover. Simmer for 45 minutes and then strain through a fine-mesh sieve, discarding the solids. Place the broth in a large saucepan and simmer over medium heat for 45 min-utes, or until reduced to 1¹/₂ quarts. Season to taste with salt and pepper.

Place half of the corn kernels in a small saucepan and add the heavy cream. Cook over medium heat for 10 minutes, or until the cream is reduced to about 1 cup. Remove from the heat and purée until smooth. Season to taste with salt and pepper.

Cook the bacon over medium-low heat for 10 minutes, or until the fat is rendered but not brown. Remove the bacon from the pan and discard. Sauté the remaining corn, the potatoes, and onion in the bacon fat over medium heat for 10 minutes, or until the potatoes are tender. Drain any fat from the pan, add the puréed corn mixture, and cook over medium heat for 5 minutes, or until thick. Add the lobster stock in small additions until the desired consistency is reached. Add the lobster meat to the pan and whisk in the butter just prior to serving.

Ladle the soup into 10 bowls and sprinkle with the chervil leaves. Top with freshly ground black pepper to taste.

Grilled Lobster

with Warm Corn, Chanterelle, and Bacon Salad

This salad is hearty enough to be used as an entrée.

42

Serves 4

10 fresh basil leaves, coarsely chopped

$1/2$ cup butter, melted

4 $1^1/2$ pound lobsters

Salt and freshly ground black pepper

3 strips applewood smoked bacon, julienned

6 tablespoons olive oil

4 ounces chanterelle mushrooms

1 clove garlic, minced

1 tablespoon minced shallot

3 ears sweet corn, kernels removed

1 red onion, diced

1 yellow bell pepper, seeded, deribbed, and finely julienned

1 red bell pepper, seeded, deribbed, and finely julienned

3 cups frisée, large leaves removed

2 tablespoons sherry vinegar

8 sprigs chervil

To prepare the lobster:

Stir the basil into the melted butter and set aside. Steam or boil the lobsters for 4 minutes and immediately submerge them in ice water for 3 minutes. Remove the lobsters from the water, separate the claws from the tails, and split the lobsters in half lengthwise. Remove the meat from the claws and lightly brush all the lobster meat with the basil butter. Place the lobsters on a moderately hot grill, meat side down, and cook for 3 minutes. Turn over, brush the meat liberally with more basil butter, and cook, shell side down, for 3 minutes, or until the shells are bright red. Grill the claw meat for 3 minutes. Remove the lobsters from the grill, fill the head cavity with the claw meat, and season to taste with salt and pepper.

To prepare the salad:

Cook the bacon in a large nonstick pan over medium-high heat, for 5 minutes, or until crispy. Drain and discard the fat. Keep the bacon warm. In the same pan, heat 1 tablespoon of the olive oil and sauté the chanterelles with the garlic and shallot for 2 minutes, or until golden brown. Season the mush-rooms lightly with salt and pepper and set aside. Add 1 tablespoon of the olive oil to the pan and sauté the corn and onion for 2 to 3 minutes, or until the corn is cooked and the onion is tender. Add the yellow and red peppers and cook until just warm. Add the mushrooms and frisée to the pan and sauté for 1 minute. Add the vinegar and the remaining $1/4$ cup olive oil and season to taste with salt and pepper. Toss together until the frisée is just wilted. Add the bacon and season to taste with salt and pepper.

Place a mound of the salad in the center of each plate and arrange 2 lobster halves next to the salad.

Jumbo Lump Crab Salad

with Citrus, Ginger and Soy Vinaigrette

The Citrus, Ginger, and Soy Vinaigrette gives this salad an Asian flair.

Serves 4

¹/₂ cup wakame seaweed

1 cucumber, thinly sliced

1¹/₂ cups daikon sprouts

1¹/₂ tablespoons peeled and julienned fresh ginger

2 Dungeness crabs, cooked and cleaned (about 2 cups)

Citrus, Ginger, and Soy Vinaigrette (recipe follows)

2 teaspoons white sesame seeds, toasted

2 teaspoons black sesame seeds

3 scallions, thinly sliced on the diagonal

1 tablespoon fresh chervil leaves

1 tablespoon chopped chives

To prepare the salad:
Soak the seaweed in a bowl of warm water for 3 to 4 minutes, or until soft. Drain the seaweed and pat dry with paper towels. Chop the seaweed and toss in a large bowl with the cucumber, daikon sprouts, ginger, crabmeat, and vinaigrette.

Place a mound of salad in the center of each plate. Sprinkle the white and black sesame seeds, scallions, chervil, and chives over the salad, and serve.

Citrus, Ginger, and Soy Vinaigrette

YIELD: ABOUT 1¹/₄ CUPS

1 tablespoon chopped shallot

1 tablespoon peeled and finely chopped fresh ginger

¹/₄ cup plus 2 tablespoons rice wine vinegar

2 tablespoons soy sauce

1 tablespoon sesame oil

¹/₂ cup extra virgin olive oil

¹/₂ cup freshly squeezed orange juice

2 tablespoons freshly squeezed lime juice

Combine all of the ingredients in a jar. Cover tightly with a lid and shake vigorously. The vinaigrette may be kept in the refrigerator for up to 3 days.

This delicious variation of a traditional green salad is simple to prepare.

45

Serves 6

2 large sweet potatoes

2 teaspoons canola oil

Salt and freshly
ground black pepper

1/4 cup minced green
bell pepper

1/4 cup minced red
bell pepper

1 jalapeño pepper, seeded
and finely chopped

2 scallions, thinly sliced

1 teaspoon peeled and
chopped fresh ginger

1/4 cup rice wine vinegar

1/2 cup freshly squeezed
orange juice

1 tablespoon pure
maple syrup

3/4 cup olive oil

3 cups mesclun greens

To prepare the salad:
Place the sweet potatoes in
a large pot and cover with
cold water. Bring to a simmer
and cook for 15 minutes, or
until the tines of a fork can
be inserted about 1/2 inch into
the potato, but the centers
are still firm. Remove the
potatoes from the water
and let cool completely. Peel
and slice in 3/4-inch-thick
slices. Brush the slices with
canola oil and season to taste
with salt and pepper. Grill on
a moderately hot fire for 3 to
5 minutes on each side, or
until just cooked through.

To prepare the vinaigrette:
In a bowl, whisk together
the green and red peppers,
jalapeño, scallions, ginger,
vinegar, orange juice, maple
syrup, and olive oil. Season to
taste with salt and pepper.

Place a mound of mesclun
greens in the center of each
plate. Arrange the sweet potatoes around the greens and
drizzle the vinaigrette over
the salad and on the potatoes.

Crab, Artichoke, and Potato Salad

All of the components of this dish can be prepared in advance and then assembled at the last minute.

Serves 4

¹/₂ pound crabmeat

Salt and freshly ground black pepper

2 cups mizuna greens

1 tablespoon olive oil

Potato Salad (recipe follows)

Artichoke Salad (recipe follows)

4 teaspoons fresh basil chiffonade

Basil Vinaigrette (recipe follows)

To prepare the crabmeat: Season the crabmeat lightly with salt and pepper and set aside.

To prepare the mizuna: Toss the mizuna with the olive oil and season to taste with salt and pepper.

Oil the inside of a 2¹/₂-inch-diameter by 1¹/₂-inch-high ring mold and place it upright in the center of a plate. Fill the bottom 1 inch of the mold with Potato Salad, pressing firmly with an espresso tamper or other cylindrical object. Add an equal layer of Artichoke Salad, pressing firmly with the tamper. Add a layer of the crab, again pressing firmly with the tamper. Holding the salad in place with the tamper, slowly remove the mold. Repeat the process on the 3 remaining plates.

Top the salad with the basil chiffonade and place some of the mizuna on one side of the plate. Spoon some of the Basil Vinaigrette around the plate.

Potato Salad

YIELD: ABOUT 1 CUP

2 Yukon Gold potatoes, peeled and cut in a ¹/₄-inch dice

¹/₂ shallot, minced

3 fresh basil leaves, chopped

6 kalamata olives, pitted and diced

2 tablespoons freshly squeezed lime juice

1 tablespoon olive oil

Salt and freshly ground black pepper

Cook the potato in boiling water for 8 to 10 minutes, or until cooked through. Drain and transfer to a paper towel to dry. Place the potatoes in a bowl and toss with the remaining ingredients, seasoning with salt and pepper to taste. Refrigerate until ready to use, or for up to 8 hours.

Artichoke Salad

YIELD: ABOUT 1¹/₂ CUPS

4 large artichokes, cooked

1 tablespoon freshly squeezed lime juice

2 teaspoons olive oil

Salt and freshly ground black pepper

Remove all of the leaves from the artichokes and completely scrape away and discard any of the fuzzy center. Dice the artichoke bottoms into ¹/₄-inch pieces and toss them in a bowl with the lime juice and olive oil. Season to taste with salt and pepper and refrigerate until ready to use, or for up to 4 hours.

Basil Vinaigrette

YIELD: ABOUT 1 CUP

20 fresh basil leaves

2 tablespoons freshly squeezed lemon juice

¹/₂ cup olive oil

2 teaspoons cold water

Salt and freshly ground black pepper

Purée all of the ingredients in a blender for 1 minute, or until they are thoroughly emulsified. Season to taste with salt and pepper. Store in the refrigerator for up to 3 days.

The time I remember the most
with my Dad is when he took me and my two
sisters to the New York Liberty game.
I had the best time there. We had fun yelling,
"Good shot! Nice call!" At half-time we got hot
dogs, popcorn, and soda. Then we went
back to yelling. The end of the game came—
the Libertys won with a score of 74 to 58.
Then we went home and went to bed, but we
talked about it all the next day.

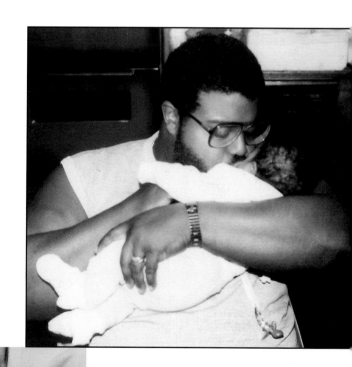

*Make sure to
get sushi-grade
tuna steaks
when serving
them rare.*

Serves 4

12 baby artichokes,
trimmed and quartered

1 1/2 cups extra virgin
olive oil

12 sprigs thyme

Sea salt and freshly
ground black pepper

1 cup small white beans
soaked overnight in water

1/4 onion

1 carrot, peeled and
coarsely chopped

1 bay leaf

8 cloves garlic

3 1/2 cups water

2 tablespoons
balsamic vinegar

2 tablespoons
red wine vinegar

3 tablespoons
minced scallions

1 cup fresh tomato juice

1/3 cup capers, drained

Vegetable oil for frying

4 6-ounce tuna steaks

To prepare the artichokes:
Preheat the oven to 375°. Toss
the artichokes with 1/4 cup of
the olive oil, 8 of the thyme
sprigs, and salt and pepper to
taste. Place in an ovenproof
pan and roast for 20 minutes,
or until golden brown.

To prepare the beans:
Place the beans, onion, carrot,
the remaining 4 thyme sprigs,
the bay leaf, garlic, and water
in a saucepan and bring to a
boil. Lower the heat and simmer for 45 minutes, or until
the beans are tender. Drain
the cooking liquid and
remove the onion, carrot,
thyme, bay leaf, and garlic.

Toss the hot beans in a bowl
with the balsamic vinegar,
red wine vinegar, and
2 tablespoons of the olive
oil. Season to taste with sea
salt and pepper. Cool to room
temperature and add the
artichokes and scallions.
Marinate at room temperature
for at least 30 minutes.

To prepare the tomato oil:
Cook the tomato juice over
low heat for 20 minutes, or
until reduced to 1/2 cup.
Strain through a fine-mesh
sieve and let cool to room
temperature. Whisk 1 cup of
the olive oil into the tomato
juice and season to taste with
salt and pepper.

To prepare the capers:
Heat the vegetable oil in a
small saucepan until very
hot. Add the capers and cook
for 1 to 2 minutes, or until
crispy. Remove from the oil
and drain on paper towels.

To prepare the tuna:
Rub the tuna with 1 tablespoon of the olive oil and
season to taste with sea salt
and pepper. Heat the remaining 1 tablespoon olive oil in a
heavy skillet over high heat
until almost smoking. Add
the tuna and sear quickly on
both sides. Remove the tuna
from the skillet and let it
rest at room temperature for
10 minutes. Cut into thin
slices across the grain.

Gently reheat the bean
mixture over medium heat.
Place a mound of beans in
the center of each plate and
fan the tuna slices to one
side of the beans. Spoon
the tomato oil on the tuna
and around the plates and
sprinkle the capers around
the plates.

Crab-Crusted Halibut

with Spinach and Crispy Potatoes

Be sure to clean the crabmeat and remove any bits of shell.

Serves 4

2 tablespoons olive oil

$1/2$ red bell pepper, seeded, deribbed, and finely diced

$1/2$ yellow bell pepper, seeded, deribbed, and finely diced

$1/4$ green bell pepper, seeded, deribbed, and finely diced

$1/4$ onion, finely diced

7 ounces peeky toe crab

1 cup Panko Japanese bread crumbs

1 cup butter, at room temperature

$1^1/2$ tablespoons Old Bay Seasoning

4 6-ounce halibut fillets

Salt and freshly ground black pepper

Canola oil for frying

1 cup peeled and diced Yukon Gold potatoes

Kosher salt

1 pound baby spinach leaves, blanched in salted water

4 sprigs chervil

To prepare the crab:
Heat a sauté pan over medium heat. Add the olive oil, the red, yellow, and green bell peppers, and the onion and cook for 2 to 3 minutes, or until soft and transparent. Transfer the vegetables to a paper towel to drain.

Put the crab, vegetables, bread crumbs, butter, and Old Bay Seasoning in a food processor fitted with a metal blade and pulse until completely mixed.

To prepare the halibut:
Preheat the oven to 375°. Put the halibut fillets on a baking sheet, season to taste with salt and pepper, and spread a $3/4$-inch layer of the crab mixture on top of the fillets. Bake for 10 minutes, or until the fish is tender. Place under a broiler and cook for 2 minutes, or until golden brown. Remove from the oven and keep warm.

To prepare the potatoes:
Heat the oil to 375° in a small saucepan. Add the potatoes and cook, stirring occasionally, for 2 to 3 minutes, or until golden brown. Transfer the potatoes to a paper towel to drain and sprinkle liberally with kosher salt.

Place a bed of spinach in the center of each plate and top with a piece of the halibut. Sprinkle the potatoes around the halibut and place a chervil sprig in the center of the fish.

Jumbo Lump Crab Cakes

with Roasted Tomato Sauce and Basil Mashed Potatoes

These crab cakes also make a great appetizer.

54

Serves 4

4 ounces whitefish

5 jalapeño peppers, halved and seeded

6 tablespoons freshly squeezed lemon juice

1 teaspoon cayenne pepper

5 scallions, thinly sliced

1 tablespoon chopped fresh parsley

1/4 cup mayonnaise

Salt and freshly ground black pepper

1 pound jumbo lump crabmeat

1 1/2 cups Panko Japanese bread crumbs

1/4 cup plus 1 tablespoon olive oil

6 plum tomatoes, cored

3 shallots, chopped

3 cloves garlic, chopped

2 cups Chicken Stock (page 33)

1 cup plus 2 tablespoons butter

2 large russet potatoes, peeled and diced

1/4 cup milk

3 tablespoons Basil Oil (recipe follows)

4 sprigs basil

To prepare the crab cakes: Purée the whitefish in a food processor. Finely dice 3 of the jalapeños. Combine the puréed whitefish, lemon juice, cayenne pepper, scallions, parsley, diced jalapeños, and mayonnaise in a large bowl and season to taste with salt and pepper. Gently fold in the crabmeat, leaving the lumps intact. Divide the mixture into 8 portions. Roll each portion in the bread crumbs and form into a cake. Refrigerate the cakes for at least 30 minutes.

Heat 1/4 cup of the olive oil in a large sauté pan and cook the crab cakes for 2 to 3 minutes on each side, or until golden brown. Transfer the cakes to a paper towel to drain.

To prepare the sauce: Preheat the oven to 350°. In an ovenproof sauté pan, toss the tomatoes, shallots, garlic, and the remaining 2 jalapeños in the remaining 1 tablespoon olive oil. Roast for 15 minutes. Remove from the oven and place on the stove over medium heat. Add the stock and cook for 15 minutes, or until reduced to about 1 cup. Place the mixture in a blender and purée, adding 1 cup of the butter a little at a time, until the mixture is smooth and all of the butter is incorporated. Season to taste with salt and pepper and keep warm.

To prepare the potatoes: Cook the potatoes in a pot of boiling salted water for 10 minutes, or until soft. Remove from the heat and drain the potatoes. Add the milk and remaining 2 tablespoons butter to the pan and whip with an electric mixer until smooth. Add 2 tablespoons of Basil Oil and whip until completely incorporated. Season to taste with salt and pepper.

Spoon the potatoes in the center of each plate and lean 2 warm crab cakes against the potatoes. Spoon the tomato sauce around the crab cakes and dot the sauce with the Basil Oil. Place a sprig of basil between the crab cakes on each plate.

Basil Oil

YIELD: 1/2 CUP

3/4 cup fresh basil leaves

Salt

1/4 cup canola oil

1/4 cup olive oil

Blanch the basil in a pot of boiling salted water for 20 seconds and immediately shock in ice water. Drain the basil, squeezing out any excess water, and coarsely chop. Purée with the canola oil and olive oil for 3 minutes, or until bright green. The oil may be stored in the refrigerator for up to 1 week.

Serves 4

2 cloves garlic, crushed

2 sprigs thyme

1 sprig rosemary

1 tablespoon freshly ground black pepper

1 cup plus 2 tablespoons olive oil

4 8-ounce rock bass fillets, skin on

12 shallots, thinly sliced

20 oil-cured kalamata olives, chopped

Salt and freshly ground black pepper

3 tablespoons chopped fresh basil

¼ cups plus 2 tablespoons extra virgin olive oil

Lemon Emulsion (recipe follows)

12 Oven-Dried Tomato halves (recipe follows)

4 chervil sprigs

2 teaspoons julienned fresh basil

To marinate the bass:
Combine the garlic, thyme, rosemary, pepper, and 1 cup of the olive oil in a glass pan. Place the bass in the pan and thoroughly cover with the marinade. Cover and refrigerate for several hours, or overnight.

To prepare the olives:
Heat the remaining 2 tablespoons olive oil in a sauté pan over medium-high heat for 3 minutes, or until just hot. Add the shallots and cook for 2 minutes, or until translucent. Add the olives to the pan, toss quickly, and remove the pan from the heat. Transfer the olives and shallots to paper towels to drain. Season lightly with black pepper.

To prepare the basil oil:
Purée the chopped basil with the extra virgin olive oil for 1 minute, or until smooth.

To prepare the bass:
Remove the bass fillets from the marinade and drain well. Heat a medium nonstick sauté pan until hot. Place the fillets in the pan, skin side down, and cover with a tight-fitting lid. Cook over medium-high heat for 7 to 8 minutes, or until the fish is just cooked through and the skin is crisp. Season to taste with salt and pepper.

Place a piece of bass in the center of each bowl and top with some of the olive-shallot mixture. Ladle some of the Lemon Emulsion around the fish and drizzle some of the the basil oil on top of the fish. Arrange 3 tomato halves around the edges of the bass and place a sprig of chervil in the center of the olives. Sprinkle the julienned basil around the bowls.

Oven-Dried Tomatoes

YIELD: 20 TOMATO HALVES

10 ripe plum tomatoes

2 teaspoons sugar

1 tablespoon kosher salt

1 tablespoon minced fresh thyme

¼ cup olive oil

Preheat the oven to 200°. Remove the stem end of the tomatoes and cut each one in half lengthwise. Place the tomatoes on a rack, cut side up, and season with the sugar, salt, and thyme. Drizzle the oil over the tomatoes and bake for 4 to 5 hours, or until the tomatoes look somewhat dry and shriveled, but still retain a little moisture. Remove from the oven and cool on the rack. Store in an airtight container in the refrigerator for up to 1 week.

Lemon Emulsion

YIELD: ABOUT 1 CUP

½ cup Fish Stock (page 56)

2 tablespoons freshly squeezed lemon juice

1½ tablespoons extra virgin olive oil

3 tablespoons butter

Bring the stock and lemon juice to a boil in a medium saucepan and remove from the heat. Drizzle in the olive oil, blending continuously with a handheld blender. Add the butter a little at a time until completely incorporated and serve immediately.

Roasted Rock Bass

with Oven-Dried Tomatoes, Shallots, and Black Olives

You can use sea bass, loup de mer, or even snapper in this dish.

55

Warm Escalope of Salmon

with Tomato-Herb Sauce

Using different colored tomatoes adds visual interest to this dish.

Serves 4

2 ripe tomatoes, peeled, seeded, and finely chopped

10 fresh basil leaves, chopped

2 tablespoons chopped mixed fresh herbs (parsley, tarragon, chives, or chervil)

1 cup Fish Stock (recipe follows)

$1/2$ cup white wine

$1/2$ cup sherry

1 cup Basic Mayonnaise (recipe follows)

1 tablespoon white wine vinegar

1 tablespoon freshly squeezed lemon juice

Tabasco sauce

Salt and freshly ground black pepper

4 3-ounce salmon fillets

2 tablespoons chopped chervil

To prepare the sauce:
Place the tomatoes in a sieve and thoroughly drain. Mix the basil and herbs in a small bowl. Simmer the fish stock over medium heat for 20 minutes, or until reduced to about $1/2$ cup. Add the wine and sherry and cook for 10 to 15 minutes, or until reduced to about $1/2$ cup. Set aside and let cool to room temperature. Combine the Basic Mayonnaise and reduced stock mixture in a small mixing bowl. Add the tomato, vinegar, lemon juice, and herb mixture and mix well. Season to taste with the Tabasco and salt and pepper and stir until combined.

To prepare the salmon:
Pound the salmon between two sheets of oiled plastic wrap until $1/8$ inch thick. Remove the plastic wrap and season to taste with salt and pepper. Sauté in a hot nonstick pan over high heat for 10 seconds on each side.

Place a piece of salmon in the center of each warmed plate. Spoon the sauce over the salmon and sprinkle with the chervil.

Fish Stock

YIELD: 1 QUART

$2^1/2$ pounds fish bones

$1/2$ cup chopped celery

$1/2$ cup chopped carrots

$1/2$ cup chopped onion

$1/4$ cup chopped leeks

$1/4$ cup white wine

$1^1/2$ teaspoons white peppercorns

Place all of the ingredients in a stockpot and cover three-fourths of the way with cold water. Bring to a boil, reduce to medium-low heat, and simmer for 40 minutes. Strain through a fine-mesh sieve, and continue cooking for 30 to 40 minutes, or until reduced to about 1 quart.

Basic Mayonnaise

YIELD: 1 CUP

1 egg yolk

$1/4$ teaspoon Dijon mustard

$1/4$ teaspoon freshly squeezed lemon juice

$1/2$ cup peanut oil

$1/2$ cup olive oil

Salt and freshly ground black pepper

In a medium bowl, beat the egg yolk and mustard together until pale yellow. Stir in the lemon juice. Add the peanut oil and olive oil drop by drop, whisking constantly, until fully incorporated and the mayonnaise is thick. (If necessary, water may be added to thin the mayonnaise.) Season lightly with salt and pepper. The mayonnaise may be stored in the refrigerator for up to 1 week.

Pan-Roasted Chilean Sea Bass

with Lump Crab, Sweet Peas, and Fava Beans

If you can't find fava beans, sugar snap peas will work well.

Serves 4

¹/₄ cup olive oil

1 onion, sliced

3 shallots, sliced

2 cloves garlic, crushed

1 cup white wine

1 quart Chicken Stock
(page 33)

Salt and freshly ground
black pepper

2 cups fresh shelled
peas, blanched

1 cup shelled fava beans

¹/₂ pound jumbo
lump crabmeat

1 tablespoon unsalted butter

1 teaspoon freshly squeezed
lemon juice

4 7-ounce sea bass fillets

1 cup fresh pea shoots

2 plum tomatoes, peeled,
seeded, and diced

8 sprigs savory

To prepare the sauce:
Heat 2 tablespoons of the
olive oil in a 3-quart saucepan. Add the onion and
sauté over medium-high heat
for 5 minutes, or until soft
and translucent. Add the
shallots and garlic and cook
for 2 minutes. Add the wine
and cook for 5 minutes, or
until the liquid is almost
evaporated. Pour in the stock
and bring to a boil. Simmer
for 10 to 15 minutes, or until
reduced by two-thirds. Season
lightly with salt and pepper
and strain through a fine-
mesh sieve. Purée the broth
with 1 cup of the peas for
2 minutes, or until smooth.
Strain through a fine-mesh
sieve and place in a small
saucepan. Add the remaining
whole peas and the fava beans
and cook until just hot. Stir
in the crabmeat and butter,
season to taste with salt
and pepper, and add the
lemon juice.

To prepare the fish:
Season the bass fillets with
salt and pepper. Place a
nonstick pan over high heat.
When hot, add the remaining
2 tablespoons olive oil. Add
the fillets to the pan and cook
for 4 minutes on each side, or
until just cooked.

Place a piece of bass in the
center of each plate. Spoon
the sauce over the fish and
sprinkle the pea shoots,
tomatoes, and savory sprigs
over the fish and around
the plates.

Serves 4

2¼ cups water or Chicken Stock (page 33)

½ cup diced carrot

½ cup diced zucchini

½ cup diced onion

¼ cup butter

1 cup couscous

2 tablespoons olive oil

Salt and freshly ground black pepper

½ head savoy cabbage, finely julienned

2 tablespoons fennel seed, toasted

4 7-ounce salmon fillets, skin removed

Moroccan Barbecue Sauce (recipe follows)

4 sprigs cilantro

To prepare the couscous:
Bring the water or stock to a boil in a medium saucepan. Add the carrot, zucchini, onion, and 1 tablespoon of the butter and cook for 30 seconds. Stir in the couscous, cover with a tight-fitting lid, and remove from the heat. Let stand for 5 to 10 minutes, or until the liquid is completely absorbed. Stir with a fork to fluff the couscous. Add the olive oil and season to taste with salt and pepper. Keep warm until ready to use.

To prepare the cabbage:
Blanch the cabbage in a pot of boiling water for 3 minutes. Immediately shock in ice water. Drain the cabbage and squeeze out the excess water. Heat the remaining 3 tablespoons butter in a saucepan and add the cabbage and 1 tablespoon of the fennel seed. Cook over medium heat for 5 minutes, or until the cabbage is hot and season to taste with salt and pepper.

To prepare the salmon:
Preheat the oven to 400°. Season the salmon to taste with salt and pepper and place in a baking dish. Roast for 10 minutes. Remove the salmon from the oven and coat each piece with some of the Moroccan Barbecue Sauce. Sprinkle the fish with the remaining 1 tablespoon fennel seed and return to the oven for 1 minute.

Press some of the couscous into a 4-inch diameter ring mold in the center of each plate and remove the ring mold. Arrange some of the cabbage on the couscous and top with a piece of salmon. Drizzle some of the Moroccan Barbecue Sauce around the plate and place a cilantro sprig on each piece of salmon.

Moroccan Barbecue Sauce

YIELD: ABOUT 1½ CUPS

2½ cups honey

1 cup rice wine vinegar

½ cup soy sauce

1 cup ketchup

2 sticks cinnamon

5 star anise

3 teaspoons garlic chile paste

1 teaspoon ground cardamom

1 tablespoon coriander seeds

1 tablespoon peeled and chopped fresh ginger

1 teaspoon whole cloves

1 teaspoon mace

1 tablespoon black peppercorns

½ cup chopped cilantro

¼ cup freshly squeezed lime juice

Combine all the ingredients in a saucepan. Bring the mixture to a boil and cook over medium-low heat for 20 to 30 minutes, or until reduced by two-thirds. The sauce should have a syrupy consistency. Strain into a container through a fine-mesh sieve and set aside. The sauce may be stored in the refrigerator for up to 1 week.

Roasted Salmon

with Moroccan Barbecue Sauce, Couscous, and Sautéed Savoy Cabbage

The Moroccan Barbecue Sauce is also great with any type of poultry.

59

Shrimp and Sweet Corn Ravioli

with Corn Coulis

This dish also makes a wonderful appetizer for eight people.

Serves 4

8 small ears sweet corn

1/4 cup plus 3 tablespoons olive oil

1 onion, finely diced

1/2 bay leaf

1 sprig thyme

10 white peppercorns

2 stems parsley

Salt and freshly ground black pepper

Pinch of cayenne pepper

1/4 cup butter

1 roasted red bell pepper, peeled, seeded, and chopped

6 ounces raw shrimp, shelled, deveined, and coarsely chopped

1/3 cup heavy whipping cream

2 tablespoons plus 2 teaspoons chopped chives

32 round wonton wrappers

1 egg, lightly beaten

24 prawns

To prepare the coulis:
Remove the corn from the cobs, reserving the kernels and 4 of the cobs. Heat 3 tablespoons of the olive oil in a sauté pan over medium heat. Add the onion and cook for 5 minutes, or until translucent. Add half of the reserved corn and cook for 7 to 10 minutes, or until very tender.

Slice the cobs into 2- to 3-inch pieces, place in a saucepan with 4 cups of water, and bring to a boil. Tie the bay leaf, thyme, peppercorns, and parsley stems in a piece of cheesecloth and add it to the pan. Simmer for 20 minutes, or until reduced to 2 cups of liquid. Strain the broth into a pan through a fine-mesh sieve, discarding the solids. Add the broth to the onion mixture and simmer for 5 minutes. Purée until smooth and strain through a fine-mesh sieve. Season to taste with salt, pepper, and cayenne, whisk in 2 tablespoons of the butter, and keep warm.

To prepare the sauce:
Purée the red pepper with 2 tablespoons of the olive oil for 2 minutes, or until smooth. Strain through a fine-mesh sieve.

To prepare the filling:
Coarsely chop the shrimp and place in a food processor fitted with the metal blade with half of the remaining corn and the cream. Pulse until fairly smooth. Add 2 teaspoons of the chives and season to taste with salt and pepper.

To prepare the ravioli:
Lay the wonton wrappers on a work surface and brush with the egg wash. Place 1 tablespoon of the shrimp mixture on one side of each wrapper. Fold each wrapper over and press firmly to seal the edges. Poach the ravioli in a pot of boiling salted water for 4 minutes. Remove from the water and sauté in the remaining 2 tablespoons olive oil for 2 minutes on each side, or until golden brown.

To prepare the corn:
Cook the remaining corn in a pot of simmering salted water for 3 minutes. Remove from the heat, drain, and keep warm.

To prepare the prawns:
Preheat the oven to 375°. Place the prawns on a baking sheet. Cut up the remaining 2 tablespoons butter and sprinkle over the prawns. Season to taste with salt and pepper and bake for 3 1/2 minutes.

Arrange 4 ravioli in a pinwheel in the center of each plate. Spoon the corn coulis around the ravioli and place 3 prawns on the ravioli. Spoon the corn kernels around the plates. Sprinkle the ravioli with black pepper and drizzle some of the red pepper sauce around the plates.

Halibut in a Horseradish Crust

with Mashed Potatoes, Chive Oil, and Crispy Leeks

The horseradish crust on the halibut gets very crispy and keeps the halibut moist inside.

62

Serves 4

Vegetable oil for frying

2 leeks, julienned

Salt and black pepper

1 1/2 pounds Yukon Gold potatoes, peeled and diced

1 cup milk, warm

1/2 cup unsalted butter

1 cup Panko Japanese bread crumbs

1/2 cup freshly grated horseradish

1 teaspoon chopped fresh thyme

1 teaspoon chopped chives

1 teaspoon chopped fresh rosemary

1 teaspoon chopped fresh parsley

1 teaspoon chopped fresh chervil

1/2 cup all-purpose flour

4 7-ounce halibut fillets

1 egg beaten with 1 tablespoon milk

1/4 cup olive oil

4 teaspoons Chive Oil (recipe follows)

4 teaspoons 1-inch long chive pieces

1 cup peeled, seeded, and diced tomato

To prepare the leeks:
Heat the vegetable oil in a medium saucepan over medium-high heat until very hot. Add half of the leeks and cook for 1 minute, or until golden brown. Remove the leeks with a slotted spoon and drain on paper towels. Repeat with the remaining leeks, and season to taste with salt.

To prepare the potatoes:
Cook the potatoes in a pot of boiling salted water for 10 minutes, or until soft. Remove from the heat and drain the potatoes. Add the milk and butter to the pan and whip with an electric mixer until smooth. Season to taste with salt and pepper.

To prepare the fish:
Combine the bread crumbs, horseradish, thyme, chopped chives, rosemary, parsley, chervil, and salt and pepper to taste in a shallow bowl. Place the flour in another shallow bowl and season to taste with salt and pepper. Dip the halibut fillets in the egg mixture and dredge in the flour. Dip each fillet in the egg mixture again and then in the bread crumb mixture. Heat the olive oil over medium-high heat in a large sauté pan. Add the halibut and cook for 3 minutes on each side.

Mound some of the potatoes to one side of each plate and lean a halibut fillet on the potatoes. Sprinkle the crispy leeks on one edge of the halibut. Drizzle some of the Chive Oil and sprinkle the chives and tomatoes around the plates.

Chive Oil

YIELD: 1 CUP

1/4 cup chives

1 cup canola oil

Blanch the chives in a pot of boiling water for 30 seconds, and drain. Coarsely chop the chives and purée with the oil for 2 minutes, or until smooth. Strain through a fine-mesh sieve. The oil may be stored in the refrigerator for up to 1 week.

Serves 4

1/2 cup olive oil

1 onion, diced

2 shallots, peeled
and chopped, plus
2 shallots, sliced

2 large leeks, white
and light green only

1 clove garlic, minced

2 tablespoons chopped
fresh parsley

2 tablespoons black
truffle oil

1/2 black truffle, thinly sliced

Salt and black pepper

2 Idaho potatoes, baked

2 tablespoons
chopped chives

3 sheets filo dough

1/4 cup clarified butter

1/4 cup bread crumbs

3 pounds button
mushrooms, quartered

2 sprigs thyme

1/4 cup plus
2 tablespoons butter

8 cups spinach,
cleaned and blanched

4 7-ounce skate wing fillets

1/2 cup flour

4 sprigs chervil

To prepare the skate filling:
Heat 2 tablespoons of the
olive oil in a medium sauté
pan over medium heat.
Add the onion and cook for
3 minutes. Add the chopped
shallots and leeks and cook for
8 to 10 minutes, or until the
leeks are tender. Stir in the
garlic, parsley, and truffle oil.
Chop half of the truffle slices,
add the chopped pieces to the
onion mixture, and season
to taste with salt and pepper.
Remove from the heat and
set aside.

To prepare the knish:
Scoop the potato flesh out of
the skin, place in a bowl, and
mash with a fork. Stir in
1 tablespoon of the olive oil
and the chives and season to
taste with salt and pepper.

Preheat the oven to 375°.
Lay out a sheet of filo on a
work surface. Brush with
some of the clarified butter
and sprinkle with half of the
bread crumbs. Top with
another sheet of filo. Brush
the filo with butter, sprinkle
with the remaining bread
crumbs, and top with the
final sheet of filo. Cut the filo
into quarters and divide the
potato mixture between the
squares. Roll each square into
a cigar shape. Brush the rolls
with the remaining butter,
place on a baking sheet, and
bake for 15 minutes, or until
golden brown. Cut each knish
in half.

**To prepare the mushroom
sauce:** Sauté the mushrooms
in 1 tablespoon of the olive
oil for 10 to 12 minutes, or
until deep golden brown. Add
2 quarts of water, the sliced
shallots, and the thyme sprigs
and simmer for 20 minutes.
Strain through a fine-mesh
sieve, return the liquid to the

pan, and simmer for 45
minutes, or until reduced
to about 1/2 cup. Whisk in
1/4 cup of the butter and
season to taste with salt
and pepper.

To prepare the spinach:
Sauté the spinach in the
remaining 2 tablespoons
butter for 3 minutes, or until
tender. Season to taste with
salt and pepper and drain
off any excess butter.

To prepare the skate:
Preheat the oven to 350°.
Season the skate with salt
and pepper. Place 2 tablespoons of the leek filling on
each fillet and fold in half to
form a triangle. Dredge the
fillets in flour, shaking off
any excess. Sauté the skate
in an ovenproof pan in the
remaining 4 tablespoons
olive oil over high heat for
2 to 3 minutes on each side.
Remove from the heat and
place the pan in the oven
for 5 minutes. Remove
the pan from the oven and
keep warm.

Place some of the spinach
in the center of each plate
and top with a piece of
stuffed skate wing. Place 2
knish halves upright behind
the skate wing and sprinkle
the remaining truffle slices
over the fish. Drizzle the
reduced mushroom sauce
around the plates and
arrange the chervil over
the skate.

Stuffed Skate Wing

with Potato Knish,
Leeks, and Truffles

*This elegant
presentation is
perfect for a
special dinner
party.*

65

Chilean Sea Bass

with Zucchini, Chanterelles, and Curry Oil

The fragrant Curry Oil gives this dish an interesting Indian flavor.

Serves 4

1/2 cup olive oil

8 ounces chanterelle mushrooms, sliced

1 tablespoon chopped shallot

1/2 teaspoon chopped garlic

8 fresh thyme leaves

Salt and freshly ground black pepper

4 7-ounce sea bass fillets

8 fresh basil leaves

16 thin lengthwise slices of zucchini

1/2 cup all-purpose flour

Curry Oil (recipe follows)

1/4 cup fresh chervil leaves

To prepare the mushrooms:
Heat 1/4 cup of the olive oil in a sauté pan over medium heat, add the mushrooms and cook for 5 to 7 minutes, or until golden and all of the liquid is evaporated. Add the shallot, garlic, and thyme and toss for 1 minute. Season to taste with salt and pepper. Remove from the heat and keep warm.

To prepare the fish:
Season the bass to taste with salt and pepper and place 2 basil leaves on each fillet. Blanch the zucchini slices in a pot of boiling water for 20 seconds, drain on a paper towel, and pat dry. Wrap 3 or 4 strips of the zucchini around each fillet and season to taste with salt and pepper.

Heat the remaining 1/4 cup olive oil in a nonstick sauté pan until hot. Dredge the fish in the flour, shaking off any excess. Sauté the fish over medium-high heat for 3 1/2 minutes on each side, or until the zucchini is golden brown.

Place a bass fillet in the center of each plate and drizzle some of the Curry Oil on the fish and around the plate. Spoon some of the mushrooms around the fish and sprinkle the chervil around the plates.

Curry Oil

YIELD: 1/2 CUP

1/2 cup chopped onion

3/4 cup canola oil

2 tablespoons curry powder

Sauté the onion in 2 tablespoons of the canola oil over medium heat for 5 minutes, or until translucent. Add the curry powder and simmer for 3 minutes. Purée the onion mixture with the remaining oil for 3 minutes, or until smooth. Refrigerate for 24 hours. Strain through a fine-mesh sieve and refrigerate for 3 hours. Carefully decant the oil, discarding any solids that have settled on the bottom. The oil may be stored in the refrigerator for up to 4 days.

Serves 4

2 sprigs rosemary

3 sprigs thyme

3 cloves garlic, crushed, plus 1 clove garlic, halved lengthwise

1½ teaspoons freshly ground black pepper

¾ cup olive oil

4 7-ounce salmon fillets, skin scaled and scored

24 pearl onions, peeled

16 baby artichokes, pared to hearts and bottoms

¼ bay leaf

2 cups Vegetable Stock (recipe follows)

Salt and freshly ground black pepper

⅓ cup extra virgin olive oil

2 tablespoons butter

8 Oven-Dried Tomato halves (page 55)

1 tablespoon chopped fresh parsley

To marinate the salmon:
Combine the rosemary, 2 of the thyme sprigs, the crushed garlic, black pepper, and ½ cup of the olive oil in a small bowl. Rub the mixture onto the salmon and marinate in the refrigerator for 3 to 4 hours.

To prepare the onions and artichokes: Preheat the oven to 375°. Heat the remaining ¼ cup olive oil in a large, ovenproof pan over medium-high heat. Add the onions and cook for 2 to 5 minutes, or until lightly browned. Add the artichokes and cook for 3 minutes, or until lightly browned. Add the remaining thyme sprig, the bay leaf, and sliced garlic and toss together. Cook for 1 minute and then add 1 cup of the stock to the pan. Place the pan in the oven for 20 minutes, or until the onions are tender. Season to taste with salt and pepper and keep warm until ready to use.

To prepare the broth:
Bring the remaining 1 cup stock to a boil. Purée the extra virgin olive oil and butter for 1 minute, or until smooth. Add the hot stock and blend for 30 seconds. Season to taste with salt and pepper and keep warm.

To prepare the salmon:
Heat a large nonstick pan over medium-high heat. Place the salmon in the pan, skin side down, and cover with a tight-fitting lid. Cook for about 8 minutes for medium.

Ladle the broth into shallow bowls. Place a piece of salmon in the center of each bowl, skin side up. Arrange the roasted onions, artichokes, and tomato halves around the salmon and sprinkle the chopped parsley over the salmon.

Vegetable Stock

YIELD: ABOUT 1½ QUARTS

3 tablespoons olive oil

1 onion, chopped

4 shallots, chopped

1 small fennel bulb, chopped

1 carrot, peeled chopped

1 celery stalk, chopped

1 clove garlic, chopped

1 tomato, quartered and seeded

6 button mushrooms, sliced

1 stem parsley

1¼ bay leaves

1 tablespoon black peppercorns

1 sprig thyme

3 quarts cold water

1 teaspoon salt

1 1 by 2-inch-strip orange zest

Put the olive oil in a hot stockpot. Add the onion and shallots and cook over medium heat for 2 to 3 minutes, or until translucent. Add the fennel, carrot, celery, garlic, tomato, and mushrooms and cook for 10 minutes, or until lightly browned. Tie the parsley stem, bay leaves, black peppercorns, and thyme sprig into a piece of cheesecloth and add it to the stockpot. Add the water, salt, and orange peel and simmer for 1 ½ hours. Strain the stock through a fine-mesh sieve, without pressing on the solids.

Pan-Seared Salmon

with Roasted Artichokes, Pearl Onions, and Oven-Dried Tomatoes

Marinating the salmon adds the subtle flavors of the herbs to the fish.

67

Seared Peppered Salmon

with Gazpacho Sauce

The cucumber and tomato in the sauce help to cut the richness of the salmon in this dish.

Serves 4

2 cucumbers, peeled

1¼ cups Basic Mayonnaise (page 56)

2 tablespoons freshly squeezed lime juice

1 cup tomato juice

¼ cup chopped chives

¼ cup mineral water (non-sparkling)

Salt and freshly ground black pepper

Cayenne pepper

1 teaspoon kosher salt

2 tablespoons freshly ground black pepper

1 pound center-cut salmon fillet, boned and skin removed

3 tablespoons peanut oil

4 tablespoons salmon caviar

1 small tomato, peeled, seeded, and diced

To prepare the sauce:
Juice 1 of the cucumbers and combine with the mayonnaise, lime juice, tomato juice, 2 tablespoons of the chives, and the mineral water in a small bowl. Season to taste with salt, pepper, and cayenne pepper. Place the bowl over ice, cover, and refrigerate for at least 2 hours.

To prepare the salmon:
Sprinkle the kosher salt and black pepper on the salmon and press the pepper into the flesh. Roll the salmon into a log shape and wrap in a double thickness of aluminum foil, twisting the ends tightly.

Heat the peanut oil in a sauté pan over high heat. Add the salmon in the foil and cook for 1 minute, rolling constantly in the oil. Remove the salmon from the pan and let it cool to room temperature inside the foil. Remove the foil, retaining the log shape, and cut the salmon into 4 slices. (The salmon should be seared on the outside and very rare on the inside.)

To prepare the cucumber:
Seed and dice the remaining cucumber and blanch in a pot of lightly salted water for 1 minute. Drain and shock briefly in ice water.

Arrange a salmon slice in the center of each shallow bowl. Spoon the chilled gazpacho sauce around the salmon and top each piece with 1 tablespoon of the salmon caviar. Sprinkle the diced cucumber and tomato around the bowls. Sprinkle the remaining 2 tablespoons chives on the caviar and around the bowls.

Black Sea Bass

with Israeli Couscous, Wild Mushrooms, and Shiitake Butter Sauce

The crispy skin on the sea bass is the perfect foil to the chewy couscous and mushrooms.

Serves 4

Salt and freshly ground black pepper

5 tablespoons chopped fresh thyme leaves

4 4-ounce black sea bass fillets, skin on and scored

2 tablespoons peanut oil

3 1/3 cups sliced shiitake mushrooms

6 tablespoons olive oil

1/2 cup butter

1 shallot, chopped

1 tablespoon minced shallots

1 teaspoon minced garlic

3/4 cup Pinot Noir

1 1/2 quarts Chicken Stock (page 33)

1 1/3 cups quartered cremini mushrooms

1 1/3 cups sliced chanterelle mushrooms

2 shallots, sliced

2 cloves garlic, sliced

2 cups cooked Israeli couscous

2 tablespoons chopped fresh parsley

16 asparagus spears, blanched

12 young sprigs thyme

To prepare the bass:
Sprinkle salt, black pepper, and 4 tablespoons of the chopped thyme on the flesh side of each bass fillet. Place the fish skin side down in a hot sauté pan with the peanut oil and cook over medium-high heat for 3 minutes, or until golden brown. Turn over the fish and cook for 2 minutes, or until just done. Remove from the heat and keep warm until ready to use.

To prepare the sauce:
Sauté 2 cups of the shiitake mushrooms in 2 tablespoons of the olive oil and 1 tablespoon of the butter in a large sauté pan over medium-high heat for 6 to 8 minutes, or until soft and all of the liquid is evaporated. Add the chopped shallot and cook for 1 minute. Season to taste with salt and pepper, remove from the heat, and let cool to room temperature.

Drain any liquid from the mushroom mixture and place the mixture in a food processor with 5 tablespoons of the butter. Process until smooth, transfer to a container, and refrigerate.

Sweat the minced shallots and minced garlic in 1 tablespoon of the olive oil in a large saucepan over medium heat for 3 minutes, or until translucent. Add the wine and cook for 20 minutes, or until reduced to about 3/4 cup. Add the stock and cook for 45 to 50 minutes, or until reduced to about 1 cup. Strain into a large bowl through a fine-mesh sieve and whisk in the cold shiitake-butter mixture.

To prepare the couscous:
Sauté the remaining 1 1/3 cups shiitake mushrooms in 1 tablespoon of the olive oil and 1 teaspoon of the butter for 5 minutes, or until soft and all of the liquid is evaporated. Remove from the pan and set aside.

Sauté the cremini mushrooms in 1 tablespoon of the olive oil and 1 teaspoon of the butter for 5 minutes, or until soft and all of the liquid is evaporated. Remove from the pan and set aside.

Sauté the chanterelle mushrooms in the remaining 1 tablespoon olive oil and 1 teaspoon butter for 5 minutes, or until soft and all of the liquid is evaporated. Add the sliced shallots, sliced garlic, and remaining 1 tablespoon thyme and cook for 1 minute.

Put the mushrooms, Israeli couscous, and parsley in a large saucepan and stir until thoroughly combined. Warm on low heat and season to taste with salt and pepper.

To prepare the asparagus:
Trim the asparagus spears 3 inches below the tip and discard the stems. Sauté the asparagus in a small pan with the remaining 1 tablespoon butter and season to taste with salt and pepper.

Place a mound of couscous in the center of each plate and top with a piece of the bass, skin side up. Pour some of the sauce around the plate and arrange the asparagus around the couscous. Press 3 of the thyme sprigs in the center of each fillet.

My favorite memory of my

Dad is when we went to Six Flags Magic

Mountain. It was so much fun.

We went on the newest ride in the park,

Skull Mountain. Dad and I went on twenty

times in a row. When we went on

the first time I was grabbing his arm.

It was really scary.

We had a great time together.

Roast Chicken Ravioli

with Shiitakes and Spinach

Try using smoked chicken for an interesting flavor variation.

Serves 4

3 cups diced roasted chicken

10 ounces spinach
leaves, blanched

3 slices bread, crust removed

1/2 cup milk

2 shallots, chopped

12 ounces
shiitake mushrooms

3 tablespoons plus
1 teaspoon butter

2 tablespoons fresh
pork fat, chopped

1/4 cup heavy
whipping cream

1 tablespoon chopped
mixed fresh herbs (chervil,
parsley, or thyme)

Salt and freshly
ground black pepper

16 round wonton skins

1 egg, beaten

2 cups Chicken Stock
(page 33)

1/4 cup olive oil

8 sprigs chervil

To prepare the ravioli:
Grind the chicken in a meat grinder or food processor and set aside. Coarsely chop 1/4 cup of the spinach and place in a large bowl. In a separate large bowl, soak the bread in the milk. Squeeze the excess milk from the bread and add the bread to the spinach. Sauté the shallots and 1/2 cup of the mushrooms in 1 tablespoon of the butter in a medium sauté pan over medium heat for 5 minutes, or until the mushrooms are tender. Add the chicken and cook for 3 minutes, or until warmed through. Add the chicken mixture to the spinach and mix well. Stir in the pork fat, cream, and herbs, and add salt and pepper to taste. Set aside and let cool to room temperature.

Spoon some of the filling into the center of each wonton skin. Brush the edges of the wonton with the egg, fold the wontons in half, and press tightly to seal. Poach the ravioli in boiling salted water for 5 minutes and remove from the pan with a slotted spoon.

To prepare the sauce:
Cook the stock in a small saucepan for 15 minutes, or until reduced to about 1 cup. Whisk in 2 tablespoons of the butter and 3 tablespoons of the olive oil and season to taste with salt and pepper.

To prepare the mushrooms:
Sauté the remaining mushrooms in the remaining 1 tablespoon olive oil and 1 teaspoon butter for 5 minutes, or until tender.

Divide the remaining blanched spinach among 4 warm, shallow soup bowls. Place 4 ravioli on top of the spinach and ladle some of the sauce into each bowl. Sprinkle the mushrooms and chervil sprigs around the bowls.

Serves 6

2 pounds chicken thighs

1/4 cup plus 2 tablespoons olive oil

Salt and freshly ground black pepper

Jerk Spice (recipe follows)

3 tablespoons canola oil

2 tablespoons butter

6 large Vidalia onions

1 pound sweet potatoes, grated

3 tablespoons all-purpose flour

1 teaspoon baking powder

1/4 cup minced onion

1 egg, beaten

To prepare the chicken:
Rub the chicken thighs with 1/4 cup of the olive oil and season to taste with salt and pepper. Toss the chicken with the Jerk Spice in a resealable bag until completely coated and refrigerate overnight.

Cook the chicken on a hot grill for 10 minutes, turn the chicken over and cook for 10 minutes more, or until completely cooked. Keep warm until ready to serve.

To prepare the onions:
Heat a large sauté pan over medium-high heat. Add the canola oil, 1 tablespoon of the butter, and the onions. Cook for 10 minutes, add the remaining 1 tablespoon butter, and cook for 6 to 9 minutes more, or until the onions are golden brown and caramelized. Season to taste with salt and pepper.

To prepare the sweet potatoes: Combine the sweet potatoes, flour, baking powder, minced onion, egg, and salt and pepper to taste in a large bowl. Form the mixture into 12 cakes. Heat a sauté pan over medium-high heat. Add the remaining 2 tablespoons of olive oil and cook the sweet potato cakes for 3 to 5 minutes on each side, or until golden brown and crisp. Season to taste with salt and pepper.

Spoon some of the onions on one side of each plate. Place 2 sweet potato cakes next to the onions and lay the chicken pieces on the onions and leaning against the cakes.

Jerk Spice

YIELD: ABOUT 3/4 CUP

1/2 teaspoon coriander seeds

5 whole cloves

6 cardamom pods

10 allspice berries

1/2 teaspoon black peppercorns

2 bay leaves, crumbled

1/2 stick cinnamon, crushed into small pieces

4 cloves garlic

8 jalapeño peppers, toasted and seeded

1-inch length of fresh ginger, peeled

Preheat the oven to 350°. Combine all of the dry spices on a small baking pan and toast in the oven for about 10 minutes, or until their aromas are released. Purée the spices with the garlic, jalapeños, and ginger, adding small amounts of water to form a paste. Remove the mixture from the blender and refrigerate in an airtight container for up to 1 week.

Grilled Jerk Chicken

with Caramelized Vidalia Onions and Sweet Potato Cakes

You can minimize the heat of the Jerk Spice by patting the chicken dry after marinating.

75

Stuffed Squab

with Barley Risotto, Crispy Sweetbreads, and Roasted Shallot Oil

For easier preparation, ask your butcher to bone the squab for you.

76

Serves 4

4 squabs, with giblets

6 ounces sweetbreads

1 cup barley

2 tablespoons olive oil

¼ cup finely diced carrot

¼ cup finely diced celery

½ cup finely diced onion

3 cups Chicken Stock (page 33)

2 tablespoons freshly grated Parmesan cheese

1 tablespoon chopped fresh parsley

1½ teaspoons chopped fresh thyme

Salt and black pepper

4 ounces wild mushrooms

1 shallot, chopped

1 clove garlic, chopped

3 tablespoons butter

3½ ounces foie gras terrine (liver pâté), diced

4 egg yolks

¼ cup all-purpose flour

¼ cup peanut oil

4 sprigs rosemary

1 cup Squab Reduction (recipe follows)

Roasted Shallot Oil (recipe follows)

To bone the squabs:
Remove and reserve giblets. Cut off the wing tips at the second joint. Place the squab breast down and make an incision down the back of the bird. Cut down to the tail and remove the tail. Peel and cut the meat and skin on the back away from the bone, first working down one side and then the other. Twist and cut through the joints, holding each of the thighs and wings to the carcass. Turn the bird over and carefully separate the breast meat and from the bone. Remove the carcass from the bird and reserve for making squab reduction. Cut along the back side of each wing and thigh all the way to the bone. Scrape the meat away from the bones and remove and discard the bones. Wrap the meat in plastic wrap and refrigerate until ready to use.

To prepare the sweetbreads:
Cook the sweetbreads in pot of boiling salted water for 1 minute. Lower the heat and simmer for 20 minutes. Place in a colander and top with a bowl large enough to cover the sweetbreads. Place a weight in the bowl to press out any excess liquid and allow the sweetbreads to drain for 30 minutes.

To prepare the risotto:
Toast the barley in a large sauté pan with 1 tablespoon of the olive oil over medium heat for 5 minutes. Add the carrot, celery, and onion and cook for 5 minutes, or until the onions are translucent. Add ½ cup of the stock and cook, stirring continuously, until all of the liquid has been absorbed. Add the remaining stock, ½ cup at a time, stirring continuously after each addition, until all of the stock is used and the barley is tender. Add the Parmesan, parsley, thyme, and salt and pepper to taste and mix well.

To prepare the filling:
Coarsely chop the mushrooms and sauté with the shallot and garlic in 2 tablespoons of the butter in a nonstick pan, over medium-high heat for 5 minutes. Add the giblets and cook for 1 minute. Season to taste with salt and pepper and set aside to cool.

Purée half of the mushroom mixture with half of the diced foie gras for 1 minute, or until smooth. Transfer the mixture to a medium bowl and stir in the remaining

CONTINUED ON PAGE 78

mushroom mixture, foie gras, and the egg yolks. Season to taste with salt and pepper.

To prepare the squab:
Lay out the squab on a work surface skin side down. Place one quarter of the filling in the center of each breast. Pull each of the 2 bottom corners of the skin up to the center of the top of the breast to form a V. Bring the top flap down to form a triangle and secure it in place with skewers.

Preheat the oven to 450°. Sear the squab in the remaining 1 tablespoon olive oil in an ovenproof pan over high heat for 1 to 2 minutes on each side, or until golden brown. Place the pan in the oven and roast for 10 minutes. Remove from the oven and keep warm.

To cook the sweetbreads:
In a large bowl, season the flour to taste with salt and pepper. Dice the sweetbreads and toss them in the flour. Heat the peanut oil in a sauté pan, add the sweetbreads, and cook for 3 to 4 minutes, or until light golden brown and crispy. Remove from the heat and keep warm until ready to use.

To prepare the giblets:
Skewer the giblets on the rosemary sprigs and sauté in the remaining 1 tablespoon butter for 2 minutes on each side, or until browned.

Spoon some of the barley in the center of each plate. Cut each squab breast in half and arrange the 2 halves on top of the barley. Place a giblet skewer next to the squab and spoon the Squab Reduction around the plates. Arrange the sweetbreads and drizzle the Roasted Shallot Oil around the barley.

Squab Reduction

YIELD: 1 CUP

15 pounds squab bones

2 onions, chopped

2 carrots, peeled and chopped

4 stalks celery, chopped

1 celery root, peeled and chopped

1 head garlic, cut in half

2/3 cup diced carrot

2/3 cup diced onion

2/3 cup diced celery

2/3 cup diced red bell pepper

4 cloves garlic, minced

4 tablespoons olive oil

4 tablespoons sherry wine vinegar

1 cup white wine

1/2 cup chopped tomato

Preheat the oven to 375°. Place the bones in a large roasting pan and cook for 30 minutes, or until the bones are browned. Place the bones in a large stockpot with the chopped onions, carrots, celery, celery root, and the halved garlic head. Add enough cold water to completely cover, and bring to a boil. Reduce the heat and simmer for 4 hours, skimming away any impurities that rise to the surface. Strain through a fine-mesh sieve, discarding the solids. Cook the stock over medium-high heat for 60 minutes, or until reduced to about 1 1/2 quarts stock.

In a medium saucepan, cook the diced carrot, onion, celery, red bell pepper, and minced garlic in the olive oil over medium heat for 10 minutes, or until the onion is translucent. Add the sherry vinegar and cook for 3 minutes, or until reduced to a glaze. Add the wine and cook for 5 minutes, or until reduced to a glaze. Add the tomato and squab stock and cook over medium heat for 30 to 45 minutes, or until reduced to about 3 cups. Strain through a fine-mesh sieve and return to the pan. Cook over medium heat for 30 to 45 minutes, or until reduced to about 1 cup.

Roasted Shallot Oil

YIELD: ABOUT 1 1/2 CUPS

4 shallots, peeled

1 cup canola oil

Preheat the oven to 400°. Place the shallots in a small roasting pan and pour in the oil. Cover with aluminum foil and bake for 35 minutes, or until the shallots are golden brown and caramelized. Remove the shallots from the oil, finely chop, and fold them into the canola oil. Use immediately, or refrigerate for up to 1 day and reheat prior to use.

Barbecued Quail

with Sweet Potato and Mushroom Hash

The crispy sweet potatoes add a nice textural contrast to the hash.

Serves 8

12 quail, boned except for legs

Kosher salt and freshly ground black pepper

1/4 cup firmly packed dark brown sugar

1/4 cup rice wine vinegar

2 tablespoons Dijon mustard

1 teaspoon lemon juice

1 1/2 teaspoons chopped fresh thyme

1/4 cup plus 2 tablespoons peanut oil

3 tablespoons olive oil

1/4 cup walnuts

2 tablespoons unsalted butter

1 pound assorted fresh mushrooms, stemmed and sliced 1/3 inch thick (portobello, shiitake, cremini, etc.)

1 1/2 shallots, finely chopped

1 clove garlic, finely chopped

3 Yukon Gold potatoes, peeled and cut into 1/2-inch cubes

3 sweet potatoes, peeled and cut into 1/2-inch cubes

1/2 large red onion, finely chopped

1/4 teaspoon finely grated orange zest

Pinch of nutmeg

Canola oil for frying

2 cups finely julienned sweet potatoes

8 sprigs thyme

3 tablespoons balsamic vinegar

To prepare the quail:
Season the quail with kosher salt and pepper and arrange in a single layer in a glass baking dish. Whisk together the brown sugar, vinegar, mustard, lemon juice, 1 teaspoon of the thyme and 1/4 cup of the peanut oil in a small bowl. Pour over the quail and marinate in the refrigerator for at least 4 hours, or overnight.

Preheat the grill until very hot. Remove the quail from the marinade and drain well, reserving the marinade. Brush the quail with 1 tablespoon of the olive oil and grill for 3 minutes on each side, brushing with the marinade as the quail cooks. Remove from the grill and cut each quail in half.

CONTINUED ON PAGE 80

Barbecued Quail
CONTINUED

To prepare the hash:
Preheat the oven to 375°.
Spread the walnuts on a
baking sheet and toast for
7 minutes, or until fragrant.
Remove from the oven
and let cool slightly, then
coarsely chop the nuts.

Melt 1 tablespoon of the butter and 1 tablespoon of the
olive oil in a large skillet.
Add half of the mushrooms
and sauté over high heat for
5 minutes, or until golden
and all of the liquid has
evaporated. Transfer to a
large plate and repeat the
process with the remaining
1 tablespoon butter, 1 tablespoon olive oil, and mushrooms. Add the shallots
and garlic to the skillet and
cook over medium-high
heat, stirring occasionally,
for 2 to 3 minutes, or until
the shallots are translucent.
Stir in the mushrooms and
the remaining $1/2$ teaspoon
thyme and season to taste
with kosher salt and pepper.

Bring 2 medium saucepans of
salted water to a boil. Cook
the Yukon Gold potatoes for
3 minutes, or until just tender. Cook the sweet potatoes
for $1^{1}/_{2}$ to 2 minutes, or until
just tender. Drain and transfer
the potatoes to a large bowl.

Heat 1 tablespoon of the
peanut oil in a large nonstick
skillet. Add the red onion
and cook over medium-high
heat, stirring frequently, for
5 minutes, or until softened.
Add half of the potatoes and
cook over high heat, stirring
occasionally, for 3 to 5 minutes, or until tender and gold-
en brown. Transfer the potatoes to a large bowl. Add the
remaining 1 tablespoon
peanut oil to the pan and
repeat the process with the
remaining potatoes. Add the
orange zest to the potatoes
and season to taste with
kosher salt, pepper, and nutmeg. Add the mushrooms
and toasted walnuts and
mix gently.

**To prepare the fried sweet
potatoes:** Heat the canola oil
in a saucepan to 350°. Drop
some of the julienned sweet
potatoes into the oil and stir.
Cook for 1 to 2 minutes, or
until golden brown. Transfer
to paper towels to drain, and
repeat with the remaining
sweet potatoes.

Spoon some of the hash
in the center of each plate
and top with a mound of the
fried sweet potatoes. Arrange
3 quail pieces upright around
the hash and top with a
thyme sprig. Place 5 circles
of the balsamic vinegar in
front of the quail.

Roasting in a clay pot helps keep the chicken moist and juicy.

83

Serves 2

2 bulbs garlic, tops removed

1 onion, cut in eighths

8 large sprigs rosemary

1 2½-pound chicken

Salt and freshly ground black pepper

2 bay leaves

¼ cup freshly squeezed lemon juice

2 Idaho potatoes, peeled and grated

2 tablespoons minced onion

1 egg, beaten

1½ tablespoons all-purpose flour

½ teaspoon baking powder

½ cup clarified butter

To prepare the chicken: Soak a clay pot in water for at least 15 minutes. Place 1 of the garlic bulbs, half of the onion, and 2 of the rosemary sprigs in the cavity of the chicken. Truss the chicken and season liberally with salt and pepper. Place the chicken in the clay pot and add the remaining garlic, onion, 2 of the rosemary sprigs, and the bay leaves to the pot. Place the pot in a cold oven and turn on the heat to 450°. Cook for 1 hour, or until the chicken is completely cooked. Remove from the oven and cut the chicken in half.

To prepare the potato pancakes: Place the lemon juice in a saucepan of water and bring to a boil. Blanch the potatoes for 2 minutes, transfer to paper towels, and dry completely. Combine the minced onion, potatoes, egg, flour, and baking powder in a small bowl. Form the mixture into 6 pancakes. Heat the clarified butter in a large sauté pan and cook the pancakes for 3 minutes on each side, or until golden brown. Remove to paper towels to drain and season to taste with salt and pepper.

Place half of a chicken in the center of each plate. Arrange 3 potato pancakes next to the chicken and spoon some of the pan juices around the chicken. Place 2 sprigs of rosemary standing upright on the chicken on each plate.

Barbecued Quail

with Moroccan Barbecue Sauce, Cinnamon-Scented Couscous, and Grilled Red Onion

The Moroccan Barbecue Sauce can also be used as marinade for meat or other poultry.

Serves 6

2 sprigs thyme

2 sprigs rosemary

1 teaspoon cracked black pepper

1/2 cup olive oil

2 cloves garlic, crushed

6 boneless quail

Moroccan Barbecue Sauce (page 59)

3/4 cup couscous

1 tablespoon butter

1 teaspoon ground cinnamon

Salt and freshly ground black pepper

1 red onion

1 tablespoon olive oil

6 sprigs cilantro

To prepare the quail:
Combine the thyme, rosemary, pepper, olive oil, and garlic in a bowl and rub on the quail. Put the quail in a glass bowl or pan, cover, and refrigerate for at least 4 hours, or overnight.

Prepare a hot wood grill. Drain the marinade from the quail. Place the quail on the grill and cook for 3 minutes on each side. Brush with the barbecue sauce and cook for 1 minute.

To prepare the couscous:
Place the couscous, butter, cinnamon, and salt and pepper to taste in a medium bowl. Stirring continuously, pour in boiling water until it slightly covers the couscous. Immediately cover the bowl tightly with plastic wrap. Let the couscous stand for 5 minutes and then remove the plastic wrap and fluff with a fork.

To prepare the onion:
Cut the onion into 1/4-inch-thick slices and rub each slice with some of the olive oil. Place the onions on a medium-hot grill and cook for 2 minutes on each side, or until slightly soft. Remove from the grill and separate the rings.

Press the couscous into 3-inch-diameter ring molds in the center of each plate. Arrange the red onions on the couscous and top with a quail. Arrange the cilantro sprigs on the plates.

Grilled Duck Breast

with Duck Spring Rolls and Japanese Five-Spice Sauce

If you can't find Japanese Five-Spice, combine equal parts of cinnamon, cloves, fennel seed, star anise, and Szechwan peppercorns.

Serves 8

3 cups oyster sauce

¹/₂ cup brandy

2 cloves garlic, crushed

2 teaspoons chopped jalapeño peppers

2 cups soy sauce

1 cup hoisin sauce

3 cups water

8 duck breasts, seared

¹/₂ cup diced bacon

1 shallot, minced

1 pound mixed Asian greens

Salt and freshly ground black pepper

Canola oil for frying

¹/₄ cup peeled and finely julienned fresh ginger

Duck Spring Rolls (recipe follows)

Japanese Five-Spice Sauce (recipe follows)

To prepare the duck:
Combine the oyster sauce, brandy, garlic, jalapeño, soy sauce, hoisin sauce, and water in a large bowl. Add the duck and refrigerate for 12 hours to marinate.

Remove the duck from the refrigerator and discard the marinade. Heat a grill until hot and grill the duck for 12 minutes, or until cooked to medium, turning often to avoid burning. Remove the duck from the grill, let rest for 2 minutes, and thinly slice.

To prepare the greens:
Cook the bacon in a medium sauté pan for 5 minutes, or until the fat has been rendered and the bacon is just starting to brown. Add the shallot and cook for 2 minutes, or until translucent. Add the Asian greens and cook for 1 minute, or until wilted. Season to taste with salt and pepper.

To prepare the ginger:
Heat the canola oil in a small saucepan until very hot. Add the ginger and fry for 2 minutes, or until crisp.

Place a mound of greens in the center of each plate and

CONTINUED ON PAGE 86

Grilled Duck Breast
CONTINUED

top with several of the duck slices. Arrange 3 spring roll halves upright next to the duck on each plate and spoon the Five-Spice sauce around the greens. Place a mound of the crispy ginger on the duck.

Duck Spring Rolls

SERVES 8

1 clove garlic, chopped

1/2 teaspoon peeled and chopped fresh ginger

2 tablespoons peanut oil

1 cup julienned carrots

1 cup julienned celery

6 large shiitake mushrooms, stemmed and julienned

2 leeks, julienned (white part only)

12 small wonton skins

8 ounces roasted duck leg and thigh meat, finely chopped

1 cup julienned cabbage

6 scallions, thinly sliced on the diagonal

2 tablespoons toasted sesame seeds

Canola oil for frying

To prepare the filling:
Sauté the garlic and ginger in the peanut oil over medium heat for 2 minutes. Add the carrots and celery and cook for 2 minutes. Add the shiitakes and leeks and cook for 5 minutes, or until the mushrooms are cooked and the leeks are softened. Remove from the heat and set aside to cool.

To assemble the rolls:
Lay the wonton skins on a work surface and spread some of the duck meat in a rectangle toward the bottom of the wonton skins. Top with some of the cabbage, mushroom mixture, scallions, and sesame seeds. Roll up tightly, folding in the sides of the wonton skins, to form tight, egg roll shapes.

Heat the canola oil in a sauté pan or wok and add the spring rolls. Fry the rolls, turning often, for 3 to 4 minutes, or until golden brown on all sides. Transfer the rolls to paper towels to drain. Cut the ends off each roll and cut each roll in half on the diagonal. Serve immediately.

Japanese Five-Spice Sauce

YIELD: ABOUT 2 CUPS

2 teaspoons chopped garlic

4 teaspoons peeled and chopped fresh ginger

1 tablespoon canola oil

1 bottle red wine (750 ml)

1 quart Chicken Stock (page 33)

1/3 cup hoisin sauce

2 star anise, crushed

2 teaspoons five-spice powder

3/4 cup diced dried apricots

Sauté the garlic and ginger in the canola oil for 1 minute. Add the red wine, and cook over medium heat for 40 to 50 minutes, or until reduced to 1/4 cup. Add the stock and cook for 1 hour, or until reduced to 1 cup. Add the hoisin sauce, star anise, and five-spice powder and cook for 10 minutes, or until thickened. Add the dried apricots and cook for 3 to 4 minutes, or until the apricots are tender. Remove the star anise and serve.

I had fun with my Dad

when we played football in the backyard.

We used to play catch. Sometimes

I would catch the ball and sometimes

I would miss it. He didn't get mad at all.

He just showed me how to catch.

Sometimes he was cooking on the grill

while he was playing.

I loved the shrimp and steak the best.

CAMERON CLARK AGE 7

Barbecued Ribs

with Spicy Coleslaw and Buttermilk-Chile Corn Muffins

The extra barbecue sauce may be kept in the refrigerator for up to one month.

Serves 6

1/4 cup paprika

2 tablespoons Old Bay Seasoning

1 teaspoon cayenne pepper

2 tablespoons chile powder

2 teaspoons garlic powder

2 teaspoons salt

1 tablespoon sugar

1/2 cup cider vinegar

2 slabs of pork ribs (3 pounds or less), underflap removed

Patrick's Barbecue Sauce (recipe follows)

Spicy Coleslaw (recipe follows)

Buttermilk-Chile Corn Muffins (recipe follows)

2 tablespoons chopped chives

To prepare the ribs:
Sift the spices, salt, and sugar together into a bowl. Combine the spice mixture and vinegar to make a paste. Rub the paste into the meat, cover, wrap in plastic, and refrigerate overnight.

Preheat the oven to 250°. Unwrap the ribs and place on an aluminum foil–lined sheet pan. Bake for 3 1/2 hours. Do not turn the meat.

Heat a grill until very hot. Remove the ribs from the oven and allow to rest for 10 minutes. Place the ribs on the grill top side down for 2 to 3 minutes, or until the fat starts to sizzle. Turn the ribs over and brush with the barbecue sauce. Cook for 1 minute. Turn the ribs over and brush with barbecue sauce. Remove the meat from the grill and cut the ribs into 3- to 4-rib pieces.

Place a mound of coleslaw on the side of each plate. Arrange a piece of the ribs leaning against the coleslaw and place 2 muffins next to the ribs. Place a ramekin of barbecue sauce on each plate and sprinkle the coleslaw with the chives.

Patrick's Barbecue Sauce

YIELD: ABOUT 1 QUART

1 onion, chopped

2 cups freshly squeezed orange juice

4 cups ketchup

1/2 cup freshly squeezed lime juice

1/2 cup cider vinegar

1/4 cup firmly packed brown sugar

1 tablespoon salt

1 tablespoon black pepper

2 tablespoons dry mustard

2 tablespoons paprika

1 tablespoon crushed red pepper

1 teaspoon garlic powder

1 teaspoon chile powder

2 tablespoons Tabasco sauce

2 tablespoons tamarind paste

2 tablespoons honey

3/4 cup butter

Purée the onion and 1/2 cup of the orange juice for 2 minutes, or until smooth. Combine the remaining ingredients in a saucepan and stir in the onion purée.

CONTINUED ON PAGE 92

Bring the mixture to a boil and simmer for 25 minutes. Remove from the heat and let cool.

Spicy Coleslaw

YIELD: ABOUT 6 CUPS

3 cups shredded green cabbage

1¹/₂ cups julienned carrots

1 cup julienned jicama

1 sweet onion, julienned

Salt and freshly ground black pepper

1 cup cider vinegar

2 cloves garlic, sliced

3 shallots, chopped

10 black peppercorns

1 jalapeño pepper, sliced

3¹/₄-inch slices peeled fresh ginger

1 cup olive oil

Combine the cabbage, carrots, jicama, and onion in a large bowl and season lightly with salt and pepper.

Combine the vinegar, garlic, shallots, peppercorns, jalapeño, and ginger in a saucepan and simmer for 5 minutes. Remove from the heat and let cool. Strain through a fine-mesh sieve and whisk in the olive oil. Pour the liquid over the cabbage mixture and toss well. Season to taste with salt and pepper.

Buttermilk-Chile Corn Muffins

YIELD: ABOUT 24 MINI MUFFINS

1¹/₂ cups yellow cornmeal

¹/₂ cup all-purpose flour

1 tablespoon sugar

1 teaspoon baking soda

1 teaspoon salt

2 eggs

1 cup buttermilk

1¹/₂ teaspoons minced jalapeño pepper

Preheat the oven to 350°. Combine the cornmeal, flour, sugar, baking soda, and salt in a large bowl. Beat the eggs and buttermilk in a small bowl and add the jalapeño. Pour the egg mixture over the flour mixture and fold in with a rubber spatula until well mixed. Scoop the batter into mini muffin molds and bake for 20 to 25 minutes, or until firm to the touch in the center. Remove from the oven and let cool for 5 minutes before serving.

Individual Meat Loaves

with Chile Mashed Potatoes and Haricots Verts

The roasted poblanos in the mashed potatoes add a fragrant smokiness that complements the meat loaf.

Serves 6

1 small onion, minced

1 green bell pepper, minced

2 tablespoons canola oil

Salt and freshly ground black pepper

1 clove garlic, minced

3/4 cup milk

2 slices bread, crust removed

1/2 pound ground beef

1/2 pound ground pork

1/2 pound ground veal

1 egg

2 tablespoons ketchup

1 tablespoon freshly grated Parmesan cheese

6 Idaho potatoes, peeled

1/2 cup plus 1 teaspoon butter, at room temperature

1 cup heavy whipping cream, warm

2 roasted poblanos, peeled, seeded, and diced

3 cups haricots verts, blanched

1 shallot, finely diced

6 sprigs rosemary

To prepare the meat loaf:
Sauté the onion and pepper in the oil for 4 to 5 minutes, or until tender but not browned. Season to taste with salt and pepper and stir in the garlic. Cook for 1 minute and set aside to cool.

Preheat the oven to 350°. In a bowl, pour the milk over the bread and let soak for 5 minutes. Squeeze the excess milk from the bread and combine with the beef, pork, veal, egg, ketchup, Parmesan cheese, and onion mixture. Season to taste with salt and pepper. Divide the mixture into 6 even portions and shape into mini loaves. Bake for 20 minutes, or until done.

To prepare the potatoes:
Preheat the oven to 350°. Boil the potatoes in salted water for 15 minutes, or until tender. Drain, place on a sheet pan, and bake at 350° for 10 minutes. Remove the potatoes from the oven and transfer to a large bowl. Add 1/2 cup of the butter to the bowl and mix with an electric mixer until smooth. Add the cream until it reaches the desired consistency. Stir in the poblanos and season to taste with salt and pepper.

To prepare the haricots verts:
Heat a sauté pan with the remaining 1 teaspoon butter. Add the haricots verts and cook for 1 minute. Add the shallot and cook for 1 minute. Season to taste with salt and freshly ground black pepper and remove from the heat.

Place a quenelle of mashed potatoes on the upper right side of the plate. Place the haricots verts to the left of the potatoes. Place the meat loaf at angle leaning against the potatoes and haricots verts and place a sprig of rosemary in the potatoes.

Beef Medallions

with Roasted Balsamic Portobello Mushrooms, Caramelized Shallot Rosti, and Zinfandel Sauce

If you have trouble turning the rosti, flip it out onto a plate and slide it back into the pan.

Serves 6

30 shallots, thinly sliced

1/2 cup clarified butter

2 1/2 large russet potatoes, grated

Salt and freshly ground black pepper

6 portobello mushrooms, stems and gills removed

1/4 cup balsamic vinegar

1/2 cup olive oil

6 sprigs thyme

6 4-ounce filet mignons

1 pound baby spinach leaves, blanched

1 tablespoon butter

Roasted Garlic Cloves (recipe follows)

Zinfandel Sauce (recipe follows)

6 sprigs chervil

To prepare the rosti:
Cook the shallots in 2 tablespoons of the clarified butter over medium-high heat for 15 minutes, or until golden brown and caramelized. Wrap the potatoes in a towel and twist the ends tightly to remove the starch from the potatoes.

Heat an 8-inch nonstick sauté pan over medium heat until very hot. Add 1/4 cup of the clarified butter and place half of the potatoes in the pan. Pat down the potatoes and season to taste with salt and pepper. Spread the shallots over the potatoes, leaving a 1/2-inch border around the edge of the pan. Top with the remaining potatoes, pat down, and season to taste with salt and pepper. Run a spatula around the pan to smooth the edge of the potatoes. Cook for 5 to 6 minutes, or until golden brown. Turn the potatoes and drizzle the remaining 2 tablespoons clarified butter around the edges of the pan. Cook for 5 to 6 minutes, or until golden brown. Remove from the pan and cut into 6 wedges.

To prepare the portobellos:
Preheat the oven to 350°. Toss the portobellos with the balsamic vinegar, olive oil, thyme, and salt and pepper to taste. Place on a baking sheet and roast for 6 to 8 minutes, or until tender. Pat dry with paper towels, slice on the diagonal, and keep warm.

To prepare the beef:
Preheat a grill until hot. Season the filets with salt and pepper and cook over a hot grill for 3 minutes on each side, or until medium-rare.

To prepare the spinach:
Sauté the spinach in the butter for 3 minutes, or until warm.

Place a mound of spinach on one side of each plate. Fan the portobello slices next to the spinach and place a piece of the rosti on one side of the mushrooms with the point resting on the spinach. Place a beef medallion in the center of the mushrooms. Sprinkle the garlic cloves and spoon the Zinfandel Sauce around

CONTINUED ON PAGE 96

the mushrooms. Arrange a chervil sprig between the rosti and the beef medallion.

Roasted Garlic Cloves

YIELD: 30 CLOVES

30 cloves garlic, peeled

3 cups milk

2 tablespoons sugar

1/2 cup olive oil

Salt and freshly ground black pepper

Preheat the oven to 350°. Blanch the garlic in 1 cup of boiling milk. Drain the cloves, discard the milk, and repeat the process 2 more times. Place the garlic in an aluminum foil–lined baking pan and toss with the sugar, olive oil, and salt and pepper to taste. Seal the garlic inside the foil and roast the garlic for 20 to 25 minutes, or until golden brown.

Zinfandel Sauce

YIELD: ABOUT 2 CUPS

2 tablespoons canola oil

1 cup sliced button mushrooms

1 shallot, minced

1 bottle Zinfandel (750 ml)

2 cups Veal Stock (recipe follows)

1/3 cup butter

Salt and freshly ground black pepper

Heat a large sauté pan over medium-high heat. Add the canola oil and mushrooms and cook for 2 minutes. Add the shallot and cook for 1 minute, or until the mushrooms are golden brown. Add the wine to the pan and cook for 15 minutes, or until reduced to about 1/2 cup. Add the stock and cook for 10 to 15 minutes, or until reduced to 1 1/2 cups. Whisk in the butter and season to taste with salt and pepper.

Veal Stock

YIELD: 2 QUARTS

6 pounds veal bones

3 cups chopped onions

2 cups chopped carrots

2 cups chopped celery

1 cup chopped leeks

1 tablespoon white peppercorns

1 bay leaf

Preheat the oven to 375°. Put the bones in a baking pan and roast for 30 minutes, or until the bones are browned. Remove the bones from the oven and place in a large stockpot. Add the remaining ingredients and cover three-quarters of the way with cold water. Bring to a boil, reduce the heat to low, and slowly simmer for 4 hours, skimming every 30 minutes to remove the impurities that rise to the surface. Strain and cook the stock over medium heat for 30 to 45 minutes, or until reduced to 2 quarts.

To prepare the sauce:

Mash the garlic, bay leaves, chiles, and salt with a mortar and pestle until a smooth paste forms. Mix in the vinegar, ketchup, brown sugar, and mustard and refrigerate overnight.

To prepare the steak:

Combine the cilantro, cumin, oregano, thyme, onion, garlic, and oil in a glass bowl. Add the flank steak, cover, and refrigerate overnight.

Preheat a grill until very hot. Cut the steak into 4 pieces and season to taste with salt and pepper. Baste both sides of the steak with the sauce and grill for 4 minutes on each side. Slice the flank steaks against the grain of the meat.

Spoon the baked beans over half of each plate and overlap the flank steak slices over the beans. Spoon the warm spoon bread to the side of the beans.

Baked Beans

YIELD: ABOUT 2 QUARTS

3 strips applewood smoked bacon, julienned

2 onions, finely chopped

2 cloves garlic, chopped

1 cup dark brown sugar

¹/₂ cup ketchup

¹/₄ cup molasses

¹/₂ cup apple cider vinegar

1 tablespoon chile powder

1 teaspoon dry mustard

1 pound Great Northern beans, soaked overnight in water, and drained

2¹/₂ quarts water

Sauté the bacon in a Dutch oven for 5 minutes, or until the fat is rendered. Add the onions and cook for 7 min-

utes, or until translucent. Add the garlic, cook for 2 minutes, and remove from the heat.

Preheat the oven the 350°. Combine the sugar, ketchup, molasses, vinegar, chile powder, and mustard in a small bowl. Add the mixture to the bacon pan and stir in the beans and water. Bring to a boil and remove from the heat. Season to taste with salt and pepper and bake for 3¹/₂ to 4 hours, or until the beans are tender.

Spoon Bread

YIELD: 12 SERVINGS

3 cups water

3 cups milk

³/₄ cup butter

3 teaspoons kosher salt

1¹/₂ teaspoons black pepper

2¹/₄ cups cornmeal

3 cups buttermilk

9 egg yolks

6 egg whites

1¹/₂ cups fresh corn kernels

Preheat the oven to 400°. Bring the water, milk, and butter to a boil. Add the salt and pepper and whisk in the cornmeal until smooth. Cook for 2 minutes, stirring continuously. Remove from the heat and stir in the buttermilk. Let cool, and whisk in the egg yolks. Beat the egg whites until soft peaks form. Fold the egg whites and corn kernels into the cornmeal mixture until just combined. Pour the mixture into a 9 by 13-inch baking dish and place in a larger pan filled with ¹/₂ inch water. Bake for 20 minutes, or until set in the center.

Serves 4

6 cloves garlic, peeled

3 bay leaves

2 serrano chiles, coarsely chopped, with seeds

1 tablespoon salt

¹/₃ cup rice wine vinegar

1 cup ketchup

¹/₃ cup firmly packed brown sugar

¹/₄ cup Dijon mustard

1¹/₂ cups cilantro (leaves and stems)

2 teaspoons ground cumin

2 teaspoons dried oregano

2 teaspoons chopped fresh thyme

¹/₂ onion, chopped

¹/₄ cup coarsely chopped garlic

¹/₂ cup canola oil

1¹/₂ pounds flank steak

Salt and freshly ground black pepper

Baked Beans (recipe follows)

Spoon Bread (recipe follows)

Barbecued Flank Steak

with Baked Beans and Spoon Bread

This hearty meal is perfect for a cold winter day.

Rack of Pork

with Cider-Pepper Glaze,
Braised Red Cabbage,
and Vanilla-Scented
Sweet Potato Purée

This recipe

could also be

made with

thick-cut

pork chops.

Serves 4

1/2 cup olive oil

1 teaspoon minced garlic

1 teaspoon minced
fresh rosemary

1 teaspoon minced
fresh thyme

1 teaspoon minced
fresh sage

1 teaspoon minced
fresh savory

1 Frenched rack of pork,
with 8 ribs (about 4 pounds)

Salt

1 onion, coarsely chopped

2 shallots, coarsely chopped

Cider-Pepper Glaze
(recipe follows)

2 cups Chicken Stock
(page 33)

3 tablespoons unsalted
butter, at room temperature

1 tablespoon
all-purpose flour

Pulp of 1 vanilla bean

1/2 cup butter

2 sweet potatoes,
peeled and boiled

1 Granny Smith apple

Freshly ground black pepper

1 teaspoon
ground cinnamon

1/4 teaspoon ground nutmeg

Braised Red Cabbage
(recipe follows)

8 small sprigs rosemary

To prepare the roast:
Combine the olive oil, garlic,
rosemary, thyme, sage, and
savory in a glass baking dish.
Add the pork rack and turn
to thoroughly coat. Cover,
and refrigerate overnight.

Remove the meat from the
refrigerator and let stand at
room temperature for 1 hour.
Remove the rack of pork from
the marinade, discarding the
marinade, pat dry with paper
towels, and season to taste
with salt. Place the rack in
a hot skillet, fat side down,
and cook over high heat for
10 minutes, or until browned
on all sides. Remove the rack
and place fat side up in a
large roasting pan. Drain and
discard the fat from the skillet
and set the skillet aside.

Preheat the oven to 325°.
Sprinkle the onion and shallots around the pork in the
roasting pan. Roast for 40
minutes. Increase the heat to
350°. and cook for 1 hour,
basting generously with the
Cider-Pepper Glaze, until a
thermometer inserted in the

thickest part of the meat
registers 140°. Transfer the
rack to a carving board, cover
with aluminum foil, and let
rest for 30 minutes. Carve
the rack into 4 chops.

To make the sauce:
Add the stock to the skillet
used for the pork and cook
over high heat for 20 minutes, or until reduced by half,
scraping up any browned bits
and skimming off and dis-
carding any fat. Strain the
drippings from the roasting
pan and return them to the
pan. Add the reduced stock
and bring to a boil, scraping
up any brown bits. Strain
into a small saucepan and
bring to a boil over medium-
high heat. In a bowl, combine 1 tablespoon of the
unsalted butter with the flour
to make a smooth paste.
Whisk the paste into the
sauce and boil, whisking
continuously, for 3 minutes,
or until thickened. Season to
taste with salt and pepper.

**To prepare the sweet pota-
toes:** Melt the butter in a
saucepan over medium heat
for 4 minutes, or until dark
brown with a nutty aroma.
Add the vanilla pulp, stir,
and remove from the heat.
Beat the sweet potatoes with

CONTINUED ON PAGE 100

an electric mixer for 2 minutes, or until smooth. Add the brown butter and mix for 2 minutes, or until smooth. Keep warm until ready to serve.

To prepare the apple:
Peel and core the apple and cut into 12 slices. Melt the remaining 2 tablespoons unsalted butter in a small saucepan and add the cinnamon and nutmeg. Add the apple slices and cook for 5 to 6 minutes, or until soft.

Place a quenelle of sweet potato purée on one side of each plate. Spoon some of the cabbage next to the potatoes. Place a chop on each plate with the bones between the cabbage and potatoes. Spoon the sauce over the meat and on the plate. Arrange 3 apple slices around one side of each pork chop and place 2 rosemary sprigs alongside the chops.

Cider-Pepper Glaze

2 cups unsweetened apple cider

$1/2$ large Granny Smith apple, peeled and cut into $1/2$-inch pieces

2 tablespoons cider vinegar

2 tablespoons honey

1 teaspoon minced garlic

1 sprig fresh thyme

1 teaspoon mustard seeds

3 juniper berries, crushed

1 teaspoon freshly ground pepper

Combine the apple cider, apple, vinegar, honey, garlic, thyme, mustard seeds, and juniper berries in a non-reactive medium saucepan and bring to a boil over high heat. Lower the heat to medium and simmer for 20 minutes, or until the apples are tender. Strain the mixture into another non-reactive saucepan, add the pepper, and cook over high heat for 15 to 20 minutes, or until reduced to $1/2$ cup.

Braised Red Cabbage

YIELD: ABOUT 1¼ CUPS

2 tablespoons butter

2 cups shredded red cabbage

1 cup red wine

1 tablespoon rice wine vinegar

2 tablespoons sugar

Salt and freshly ground black pepper

Place the butter in a hot sauté pan over medium heat. Add the cabbage and cook for 5 minutes. Add the wine, vinegar, and sugar and cook for 10 to 12 minutes, or until tender. Season to taste with salt and pepper and keep warm until ready to serve.

Serves 4

1/2 cup olive oil

1 teaspoon minced garlic

1 teaspoon minced
fresh rosemary

1 teaspoon minced
fresh thyme

1 teaspoon minced
fresh sage

1 teaspoon minced
fresh savory

1 loin-end rack of pork,
with 8 ribs, frenched

Salt

1 onion, coarsely chopped

1 shallot, coarsely chopped

2 cups Chicken Stock
(page 33)

1 tablespoon unsalted butter,
at room temperature

1 tablespoon
all-purpose flour

Freshly ground black pepper

Pork Roast Stuffing
(recipe follows)

To prepare the roast:

Combine the olive oil, garlic, rosemary, thyme, sage, and savory in a large glass pan. Add the pork and turn to thoroughly coat. Cover and refrigerate overnight.

Remove the pork from the refrigerator and let stand at room temperature for 1 hour. Heat a skillet over high heat. Remove the pork from the marinade, pat dry with paper towels, and season with salt. Place the roast in the skillet, fat side down first, and cook for 5 minutes on each side, or until browned. Remove the roast and place in a roasting pan. Drain and discard the fat from the skillet and set the skillet aside.

Preheat the oven to 350°. Sprinkle the onion and shallot in the roasting pan. Cook for 60 to 80 minutes, or until the meat registers 140°. Transfer to a carving board, cover with aluminum foil, and let rest for 30 minutes.

To prepare the sauce:

Add the stock to the skillet used for the pork and cook over high heat for 20 minutes, or until reduced by half. Skim off and discard any fat. Strain the drippings from the roasting pan and return them to the pan. Add the reduced stock and bring to a boil, scraping up any browned bits. Strain the gravy into a saucepan and bring to a boil. Combine the butter and flour to make a smooth paste. Whisk the paste into the gravy and boil, whisking constantly, for 3 minutes, or until thickened. Season to taste with salt and pepper.

Place the roast in the center of a serving platter. Spoon the stuffing around the roast and serve with gravy in a tureen on the side.

Sausage Stuffing

YIELD: 2 QUARTS

1 cup dried apricots

1 pound pork sausage,
flavored with sage

2 onions, diced

3 stalks celery, diced

3 cloves garlic, chopped

7 cups sourdough croutons

2 tablespoons chopped
fresh sage

1 tablespoon chopped
fresh thyme

1 tablespoon chopped fresh
marjoram

2 cups Chicken Stock
(page 33)

Salt and freshly
ground black pepper

Soak the apricots in 2 cups of water for at least 1 hour.

Crumble the sausage into a skillet and sauté for 5 to 7 minutes, or until cooked through. Drain, and return the fat to the pan, reserving the sausage. Add the onions to the pan and cook for 5 minutes, or until translucent. Add the celery and cook for 5 minutes. Add the garlic and cook for 2 minutes.

Preheat the oven to 350°. Pour the croutons into a large mixing bowl and add the onion mixture. Drain and coarsely chop the apricots. Stir the apricots, sausage, sage, thyme, and marjoram into the crouton mixture. Add the stock and toss until thoroughly moistened. Season to taste with salt and pepper. Place the stuffing in a casserole dish and bake for 30 to 45 minutes, or until warm.

Frenched Pork Loin Roast

with Sausage Stuffing

If you can't find sage-flavored sausage, just add a little chopped fresh sage to the sausage while it cooks.

101

Serves 4

1/2 cup sliced red onion

1 tablespoon olive oil

Kosher salt and freshly
ground black pepper

4 pieces soft lavash bread (or
pita bread or flour tortillas)

1/2 cup Roasted Garlic Aioli
(recipe follows)

1/4 cup julienned romaine

1/4 cup diced roasted
Idaho potatoes

4 Oven-Roasted Tomato
Halves (recipe follows)

1/2 pound smoked roasted
pork loin, thinly sliced

1 cucumber, peeled, seeded,
and cut in medium dice

1 beefsteak tomato, seeded
and cut in medium dice

5 fresh basil
leaves, julienned

1 tablespoon
red wine vinegar

3 tablespoons olive oil

4 small sprigs globe basil

To prepare the onions:
Preheat the oven to 350°.
Spread the onions on a sheet
pan and drizzle with the olive
oil. Sprinkle with kosher salt
and pepper to taste and roast
for 3 to 5 minutes, or until
tender and transparent.

To prepare the sandwich:
Lay out the lavash bread on
a work surface and spread
each piece with some of the
aioli, leaving a 1/2-inch border
across the top. Layer some of
the lettuce, potatoes, and
onions on the aioli. Place
some of the tomatoes in a line
across the center of the bread
and top with the pork slices.
Tightly roll the sandwiches
from the bottom to the top
and firmly press the border to
seal the roll. Wrap tightly in
plastic wrap and refrigerate
for at least 30 minutes, or
until the rolls are firm.

**To prepare the cucumber
salad:** In a bowl, toss together
the cucumber, tomato, and
basil. Add the vinegar and
olive oil and salt and pepper
to taste and toss to coat.

Cut the ends off the rolls
and discard. Cut each roll in
half on the diagonal. Place
2 pieces of the roll upright
in the center of each plate.
Spoon some of the cucumber
salad in front of the sandwiches and top with a sprig
of globe basil.

Roasted Garlic Aioli

YIELD: ABOUT 1 CUP

1 egg yolk

4 Roasted Garlic Cloves
(page 96)

1/2 teaspoon Dijon mustard

1 tablespoon freshly
squeezed lemon juice

Salt and freshly
ground black pepper

3/4 cup olive oil

1 teaspoon chopped
fresh rosemary

Purée the egg yolk and
garlic for 1 minute, or until
it forms a paste. Add the
mustard, lemon juice, and
salt and pepper to taste.
Slowly blend in a steady
stream of olive oil and
continue blending until
the mixture develops a
mayonnaise consistency.
Stir in the rosemary.

**Oven-Roasted
Tomato Halves**

YIELD: 4 TOMATO HALVES

2 plum tomatoes, halved

1 tablespoon olive oil

1/4 teaspoon sugar

1 teaspoon chopped
fresh thyme

Salt and freshly
ground black pepper

Preheat the oven to 450°.
Place the tomatoes on a wire
rack–lined sheet pan. Drizzle
the tomatoes with the olive
oil and sprinkle with the
sugar, thyme, and salt and
pepper to taste. Roast for 5
to 7 minutes, or until the
tomatoes are tender but still
holding their shape.

Roast Pork Sandwich

with Cucumber, Tomato,
and Basil Salad

*This sandwich
can be made
several hours in
advance and
assembled at the
last minute.*

103

Serves 6

20 cloves garlic, sliced

1½ cups olive oil

2 tablespoons freshly ground black peppercorns

2 dried red chiles, crushed

3 teaspoons soy sauce

½ cup fresh rosemary leaves

Zest and juice of 1 lemon

3 lamb racks, trimmed (6 ribs each)

Salt and pepper

1 cup canola oil

¾ cup dried cannelini beans, soaked overnight in water, and drained

4 cups Chicken Stock (page 33)

1 bay leaf

4 sprigs thyme

1 small onion, peeled and studded with cloves

12 cloves garlic, peeled

Freshly squeezed lemon juice

18 wonton skins

1 egg, beaten

4 tablespoons butter

18 stalks Swiss chard, blanched

4 shallots, sliced

1 tablespoon sugar

2 tablespoons freshly grated Parmesan cheese

2 cups lamb jus

24 baby carrots

6 sprigs savory

2 tablespoons extra virgin olive oil

To prepare the lamb:
Combine the sliced garlic, ¾ cup of olive oil, the peppercorns, chiles, soy sauce, rosemary, lemon zest, and juice in a glass baking dish. Coat the lamb racks with the mixture, cover with plastic wrap, and refrigerate overnight.

Preheat the oven to 375°. Dry the racks with paper towels and season with salt and pepper. Heat the canola oil in a large sauté pan over high heat until the oil begins to smoke. Lower the heat to medium and place the racks in the pan meat side down. Sear the racks for 2 to 3 minutes on each side, or until dark brown. Place the lamb on wire rack–lined sheet pans meat side up. Roast for 20 minutes, or until the meat registers 135°. Remove the lamb from the oven, let it rest for 10 minutes, and carve.

To prepare the ravioli:
Combine the beans, stock, bay leaf, thyme, onion, and the whole garlic cloves in a pan and simmer over medium-low heat for 1 to 1½ hours, or until tender. (Additional stock may be added during cooking if necessary.) Strain the beans, reserve the liquid, remove and discard the garlic, bay leaf, onion, and thyme. Purée the beans in a food processor with ½ cup of the olive oil, the lemon juice, and salt and pepper to taste. Add some of the cooking liquid if necessary to create a thick paste.

Lay the wonton skins on a work surface. Spoon some of the purée onto the center of each wrapper. Brush the edges of the wrappers with the egg. Fold the wrappers in half and press firmly to seal the edges. Cook the ravioli in boiling salted water for 3 minutes and drain. Heat 2 tablespoons of the butter in a sauté pan over medium heat. Add the ravioli and cook for 2 to 3 minutes on each side, or until golden brown. Remove the ravioli from the pan and drain on paper towels.

To prepare the Swiss chard:
Cut the white stalk from the center of the chard leaves. Heat the remaining ¼ cup olive oil in a sauté pan, add the shallots, and cook for 2 minutes. Add the sugar, chard, and salt and pepper and cook for 2 to 3 minutes, or until hot. Remove from the heat, add the Parmesan cheese, and mix well. Drain the liquid and set aside.

To prepare the lamb sauce:
Simmer the lamb jus for 30 minutes, or until reduced to 1 cup. Whisk in the remaining 2 tablespoons butter and season with salt and pepper.

To prepare the carrots:
Blanch the carrots in boiling salted water for 5 to 7 minutes, or until tender.

Spread some of the chard on one side of each plate. Place 3 ravioli next to the chard and arrange some of the carrots in front of the ravioli. Place 3 lamb chops on the chard and spoon the sauce around the plates. Place a sprig of savory between 2 of the chops and drizzle the extra virgin olive oil around the plates.

Rack of Lamb
with Crispy White Bean Ravioli

The crispy ravioli are a perfect textural foil to the luscious lamb in this dish.

105

Rabbit Loin

with Leeks and
Wild Mushrooms

You can also make this dish with chicken breasts.

Serves 4

4 boneless rabbit loins

4 rabbit livers

1 small carrot, chopped

1 small onion, chopped

2 shallots, chopped

2 cloves garlic, crushed

1 small bay leaf

4 sprigs thyme

3 tablespoons olive oil

3 tablespoons clarified butter

3/4 cup white wine

2 cups Chicken Stock
(page 33)

2 cups water

1/2 cup heavy
whipping cream

Salt and freshly
ground black pepper

Dash of lemon juice

1/2 cup butter

4 leeks, julienned
(white part only)

12 ounces mixed wild
mushrooms, quartered

16 small sprigs globe basil

To prepare the rabbit:
Toss together the rabbit and livers in a glass bowl with the carrot, onion, shallots, garlic, bay leaf, 2 sprigs of the thyme, and the olive oil and refrigerate overnight.

Remove the rabbit, livers, and vegetables from the pan and discard the marinade.

To prepare the sauce:
Heat 1 tablespoon of the clarified butter in a saucepan. Add the vegetables and cook for 3 minutes. Add the wine and cook for 10 minutes, or until reduced to 1/4 cup. Add the stock, water, and the remaining 2 thyme sprigs and bring to a boil. Simmer for 30 minutes, or until reduced to 2 cups and strain through a fine-mesh sieve. Bring the sauce to a boil and add the cream. Cook over medium heat for 5 minutes, or until it coats the back of a spoon. Season to taste with salt and pepper and add the lemon juice. Whisk in 5 tablespoons of the butter, a little at a time, and keep warm.

To prepare the leeks:
Melt 1 tablespoon of the butter in sauté pan over medium-high heat. Add the leeks and season to taste with salt and pepper. Cover and cook for 8 minutes, or until tender.

To prepare the mushrooms:
Sauté the mushrooms in the remaining 2 tablespoons butter for 5 minutes, or until slightly golden brown. Combine the mushrooms and leeks and season to taste with salt and pepper.

To cook the rabbit loins:
Heat 1 tablespoon of the clarified butter in a small sauté pan. Season the rabbit to taste with salt and pepper and cook over medium-high heat for 2 minutes on each side, or until browned on the outside and slightly pink in the center. Remove the rabbit from the pan and keep the meat warm.

To prepare the livers:
Sauté the livers in the remaining 1 tablespoon clarified butter for 3 minutes, or until firm but pink inside. Season to taste with salt and pepper and slice each liver in 3 pieces.

Slice the loins into long, thin slices. Arrange some of the mushroom mixture in the center of each plate and overlap the rabbit slices on the mushrooms. Spoon the sauce around the rabbit. Place of the liver pieces next to rabbit, and top with freshly ground black pepper. Arrange the basil sprigs around the rabbit.

Grilled Lamb Chops

with Tomato and Black Olive Couscous and Braised Fennel

This marinade is also great for rack of lamb.

Serves 6

1¼ cups olive oil

2 sprigs rosemary

3 shallots, sliced

4 cloves garlic, sliced

12 lamb loin chops

Salt and freshly ground black pepper

¼ cup plus 2 tablespoons extra virgin olive oil

1 onion, finely diced

2 cloves garlic, finely chopped

1 cup tomato juice

1 cup couscous

6 tablespoons sherry wine vinegar

24 kalamata olives, pitted

2 tablespoons chopped fresh oregano leaves

3 large bulbs fennel

2 cups Vegetable Stock (page 67)

Roasted Tomato Sauce (recipe follows)

12 sprigs oregano

To prepare the lamb:
Combine 1 cup of the olive oil, the rosemary, shallots, and garlic in a glass baking dish. Add the lamb to the pan and toss to completely coat the chops. Cover with plastic wrap and refrigerate overnight.

Preheat a grill until hot. Remove the lamb from the pan and pat dry with paper towels. Season to taste with salt and pepper. Cook the lamb on a medium-high grill for 4 to 5 minutes on each side, or until medium-rare.

To prepare the couscous:
Heat ¼ cup of the extra virgin olive oil in a saucepan. Add the onion and season with salt and pepper. Cook for 5 minutes, or until the onions are translucent. Stir in the garlic, add the tomato juice, and bring to a boil. Stir in the couscous and remove from the heat. Cover and let stand for 7 minutes. Pour the couscous into a bowl and fluff with a fork. Whisk together the vinegar and the remaining 2 tablespoons extra virgin olive oil and pour over the couscous. Coarsely chop 12 of the olives. Stir the olives and oregano into the couscous and season to taste with salt and pepper.

To prepare the fennel:
Cut each fennel bulb into 6 wedges. Heat a large sauté pan over high heat until almost smoking. Lower the heat to medium and add the remaining ¼ cup olive oil and the fennel wedges. Sear the wedges on each side for 1 to 2 minutes, or until golden brown. Add 1 cup of the stock and simmer for 15 minutes. Turn the fennel over and add the remaining 1 cup stock. Cook for 10 to 15 minutes, or until the fennel is

tender but not falling apart. Remove from the pan and keep warm.

Fill four 4-ounce molds with the couscous and firmly pack it down. Invert a mold on one side of each plate. Spoon the tomato sauce in the center of each plate, place 3 fennel wedges next to the couscous, and overlap 2 lamb chops against the fennel. Place an oregano sprig in the center of the remaining 12 olives and arrange 2 on top of the lamb chops on each plate.

Roasted Tomato Sauce

YIELD: ABOUT 1½ CUPS

1 tablespoon olive oil

10 Oven-Roasted Tomato Halves (page 103)

3 shallots, quartered

3 cloves garlic, quartered

1 jalapeño pepper, seeded and quartered

2 sprigs thyme

2½ cups Chicken Stock (page 33)

½ cup plus 3 tablespoons butter, at room temperature

1 teaspoon freshly squeezed lemon juice

Salt and freshly ground black pepper

Heat the olive oil in a hot sauté pan. Add the tomatoes, shallots, garlic, jalapeño, and thyme and cook for 5 to 7 minutes, or until tender. Add the stock and cook for 10 minutes, or until reduced by half. Purée for 1 minute, or until smooth. Strain through a fine-mesh sieve and return to the pan. Whisk in the butter, lemon juice, and salt and pepper to taste and keep warm until ready to use.

109

Merlot-Braised Short Ribs

with Horseradish Mashed Potatoes

These ribs are so tender they almost fall off the bone.

Serves 4

2¹/₂ pounds beef short ribs, cut in 5-inch lengths

Salt and freshly ground black pepper

¹/₄ cup canola oil

¹/₄ cup diced onion

¹/₄ cup diced carrot

¹/₄ cup diced celery

3 cloves garlic, peeled

4 sprigs thyme

¹/₂ bay leaf

1 bottle Merlot (750 ml)

3 cups Chicken Stock (page 33)

1 cup tomato sauce

5 russet potatoes, peeled and boiled

¹/₂ cup butter

1 cup heavy whipping cream

¹/₄ cup freshly grated horseradish

4 sprigs rosemary

To prepare the ribs:
Season the ribs to taste with salt and pepper. Sauté the ribs in the oil in a stockpot over high heat for 3 to 4 minutes, or until browned. Add the onion and carrot and cook for 5 minutes, or until the carrots are soft. Stir in the celery, garlic, thyme, and bay leaf. Add the Merlot and simmer for 15 to 20 minutes, or until reduced by half. Add 2 cups of the stock and the tomato sauce and bring to a boil. Reduce the heat to low and cover with a tight-fitting lid. Cook for 2 hours, or until the ribs are tender. (Additional stock may be added if the liquid becomes too thick.)

Remove the ribs from the pan. Skim the fat from the top of the cooking liquid and strain the remaining liquid. Bring the liquid to a boil and cook for 10 minutes, or until the sauce coats the back of a spoon. Season to taste with salt and pepper.

To prepare the potatoes:
Beat the potatoes with an electric mixer for 2 minutes, or until smooth. Add the butter and mix for 1 minute, or until smooth. Add the cream until the desired consistency is reached. Add the horseradish and mix well. Season to taste with salt and pepper.

Place a mound of potatoes in the center of each plate and top with some of the ribs. Spoon a little of the sauce over the meat. Place a rosemary sprig between the ribs.

Venison Loin

with Butternut Squash Purée and Huckleberry Sauce

If you have trouble finding huckleberries, blackberries will also work well.

Serves 4

2 pounds venison loin

3 pounds venison bones

1 carrot, chopped

1 onion, chopped

1 leek, chopped

6 cloves garlic

1 stalk celery, chopped

1 bottle red wine (750 ml)

10 juniper berries

2 bay leaves

10 black peppercorns

10 sprigs thyme

1 tablespoon tomato paste

1 quart Chicken Stock (page 33)

3 cups fresh huckleberries

Salt and freshly ground black pepper

1 large butternut squash, halved lengthwise

1/4 cup butter

2 tablespoons olive oil

2 tablespoons chopped chives

To prepare the sauce:
Place the venison loin and bones in a deep container with the carrot, onion, leek, garlic, celery, wine, juniper berries, bay leaves, peppercorns, and thyme. Cover and refrigerate overnight.

Preheat the oven to 350°. Remove the saddle from the marinade, reserving the marinade. Wrap the meat in plastic wrap and return it to the refrigerator. Place the bones in a roasting pan and bake for 30 minutes, or until golden brown. Strain the remaining marinade, reserving the vegetables and the liquid. Place the vegetables in a stockpot and sauté over medium heat for 10 minutes, or until golden brown. Add the marinade liquid, bring to a boil, and then simmer for 10 minutes. Add the tomato paste, stock, and bones, bring to a boil, and then simmer for 45 minutes to 1 hour, or until reduced to about 3 cups. Strain through a fine-mesh sieve and return the sauce to the heat. Add 2 cups of the huckleberries and cook for 30 minutes, or until reduced to about 1 1/2 cups. Strain through a fine-mesh sieve and season to taste with salt and pepper.

To prepare the squash:
Preheat the oven to 350°. Place the squash on a baking sheet, cut side down, and bake at 350° for 45 minutes, or until tender. Remove the skin and purée the squash in a food processor with the butter, and salt and pepper to taste.

To prepare the venison:
Cut the venison saddle into 12 medallions and season to taste with salt and pepper. Heat the olive oil in a large sauté pan over high heat. Add the medallions and sear for 2 minutes on each side, or until just rare.

Bring the sauce to a boil, remove from the heat, and add the remaining 1 cup huckleberries.

Place 3 quenelles of the squash purée across the center of each plate. Fan out a medallion against each quenelle and spoon the sauce over the medallions. Sprinkle the medallions with the chives.

Seared Foie Gras

with Sweet-and-Sour Quince

The crunchy nuts add a great textural contrast to the melt-in-your-mouth foie gras.

Serves 4

1 bay leaf

1 sprig thyme

5 peppercorns

2 quince, peeled and halved

1 cup water

1 cup cider vinegar

2 cups sugar

1 cup freshly squeezed beet juice

1/3 cup olive oil

4 2-ounce pieces foie gras

Salt and freshly ground black pepper

1/2 cup coarsely chopped walnuts

Chive Oil (page 62)

1 tablespoon diagonal-cut chives

To prepare the quince:
Place the bay leaf, thyme, and peppercorns in a piece of cheesecloth and tie to secure. Place the spice bag in a medium saucepan with the quince, water, vinegar, and sugar and bring to a boil. Reduce the heat and simmer for 15 minutes, or until the quince are tender. Remove from the heat and allow the quince to cool in the liquid.

To prepare the beet oil:
Simmer the beet juice over medium heat for 30 minutes, or until reduced to about 1/3 cup. Remove from the heat and whisk in the olive oil.

To prepare the foie gras:
Season the foie gras to taste with salt and pepper and press the walnuts into both sides of each piece. Heat a sauté pan over medium-high heat, add the foie gras, and cook for 1 minute on each side, or until golden brown.

Thinly slice the quince and fan some of it on one side of each plate. Place a piece of foie gras on each plate, slightly overlapping the quince. Drizzle the beet and chive oils around the plates and sprinkle with the chives.

Patrick gave me many wonderful

memories that will unite us always and forever.

But his most precious gifts to me

are our five children—

Preston, Aleia, Ashley, Brooke, and Cameron;

they are always and forever a testament to Patrick's

and my passion and love for life

and for each other.

LYNETTE CLARK

Comet Rice Pudding

with Fresh Fruit Gratin

Try infusing the rice with different herbs, such as tarragon or thyme, as it cooks.

Serves 8

3 cups half-and-half

3 cups heavy
whipping cream

1 1/4 cups granulated sugar

1 1/4 cups comet rice
(or long-grain rice)

3 tablespoons rum

3 sticks cinnamon

Pulp and pod of
1 vanilla bean

1 tablespoon finely chopped
orange zest

2 tablespoons butter

2 egg yolks

2 cups fresh raspberries

3 tablespoons Chambord

3 tablespoons Grand Marnier

1/2 cup firmly packed light
brown sugar plus additional
for caramelizing

40 small sprigs mint

To prepare the pudding:
Combine the half-and-half, cream, 1 cup of the granulated sugar, the rice, rum, cinnamon sticks, vanilla pulp and pod, and orange zest in a heavy-bottomed saucepan. Cook over medium-low heat, stirring continuously, for 40 minutes, or until the rice is tender. Remove and discard the cinnamon sticks and vanilla bean. Stir in the butter and the egg yolks and set aside.

To prepare the fruit:
Toss together the raspberries, Chambord, Grand Marnier, the remaining 1/4 cup of granulated sugar and the brown sugar and let stand for 15 minutes.

Wrap the bottom and sides of eight 2 1/2-inch diameter ring molds with aluminum foil and place on a baking sheet. Place the fruit and some of the liquid in each ring mold and spoon in the pudding. Refrigerate for at least 30 minutes.

Sprinkle the tops of the puddings with light brown sugar. Place a spatula over the top of 1 of the puddings and invert it onto the spatula. Remove the foil from the ring mold and place a dessert plate over the mold. Invert the pudding onto the plate and remove the ring mold. Repeat this process with the remaining molds. Caramelize the sugar with a blowtorch for 20 seconds, or until golden brown. Arrange the mint sprigs around the base of the pudding.

Homemade Applesauce in Baked Apples

This is a great, healthy dessert that kids love.

Serves 4

8 Granny Smith apples

1 tablespoon brown sugar

$^{1}/_{2}$ teaspoon
ground cinnamon

4 teaspoons butter

$^{1}/_{4}$ cup water

1 tablespoon honey

12 sprigs mint

To prepare the apples:
Preheat the oven to 375°.
Core 4 of the apples and peel
some of the skin from around
the top. Mix the brown sugar
and cinnamon together and
sprinkle over the apples.
Add 1 teaspoon of butter on
top of each apple and place in
a baking dish. Add $^{1}/_{2}$ inch of
water to pan, cover, and bake
for 40 minutes, or until just
cooked. Remove from the
oven and let cool before
handling. Scoop most of the
flesh from the inside of the
apples and set aside, leaving
the skin intact.

To prepare the applesauce:
Peel, core, and chop the
4 remaining apples. Cook the
apple, water, and honey for
7 to 9 minutes, or until tender. Purée the apples for
1 minute, or until smooth.
Add the reserved apple and
mix well.

Place an apple shell in the
center of each plate and
spoon in the applesauce.
Arrange the mint sprigs
around the base of the apples.

*This recipe
will work well
with any type
of dried fruits.*

Serves 12

1 cup dried apricots

1/3 cup apricot brandy

14 ounces semisweet chocolate, coarsely chopped

1/2 cup brewed espresso

11/4 cups plus 1 tablespoon butter

6 egg yolks

8 egg whites

1 cup heavy whipping cream

1/4 cup confectioners' sugar

3 cups fresh or canned apricot slices

Soak the apricots in the brandy for 1 hour.

To make the fondant: Heat the chocolate and espresso in the top of a double boiler over barely simmering water, stirring until smooth. Add the butter a little at a time, stirring until melted. Remove from the heat.

Beat the egg yolks until pale yellow and fluffy and fold in the apricots and brandy. Slowly pour the chocolate mixture into apricot mixture and gently fold until combined. Let cool for 30 minutes.

Beat the egg whites until stiff peaks form. Gently fold the egg whites into the chocolate mixture. Pour into a plastic wrap–lined loaf pan and freeze for 6 hours.

Beat the cream with an electric mixer until soft peaks form. Add the confectioners' sugar and beat until stiff peaks form.

Cut the fondant into 3/4-inch-thick slices. Place 1 slice in the center of each plate and top with some of the whipped cream. Arrange the apricot slices around the plates.

To prepare the tarts:
Preheat the oven to 325°. Bring the cream and Kahlúa to a boil and remove from the heat. Add the chocolate, stirring continuously, until smooth. Add the egg yolks one at a time. Strain through a fine-mesh sieve and pour into the Tart Shells. Bake for 5 to 7 minutes, or until the tarts are barely set and shiny. Cool slightly, and refrigerate until ready to serve.

Place a tart in the center of each plate and drizzle the chocolate sauce around the tart. Place a quenelle of Honey Ice Cream on the center of each tart and garnish with a mint sprig.

Tart Shells

YIELD: 4 TART SHELLS

1/2 cup butter

1 cup sifted confectioners' sugar

1 egg

1 teaspoon lemon zest

1/4 teaspoon pure vanilla extract

2 1/2 cups sifted cake flour

1/2 teaspoon salt

Cream the butter and sugar. Add the egg, lemon zest, and vanilla and mix well. Add the flour and salt and mix until just combined. Form into a thick disk, cover in plastic wrap, and let rest for 2 hours.

Roll out the dough to 1/8 inch thick and cut four 6-inch circles. Line four 5-inch-wide tart shells with the dough and freeze for 20 minutes. Preheat the oven to 325°. Remove the shells from the freezer and bake for 8 to 10 minutes, or until lightly browned.

Bittersweet Chocolate Sauce

YIELD: ABOUT 1 CUP

2 1/2 ounces bittersweet chocolate

3/4 cup water

1/3 cup sugar

2 tablespoons light corn syrup

1/3 cup unsweetened cocoa powder, sifted

Melt the chocolate in a double boiler over barely simmering water. Bring the water, sugar, and corn syrup to a boil in a small saucepan. Add the melted chocolate and stir until combined. Stir in the cocoa powder, strain through a fine-mesh sieve, and hold at room temperature until ready to use.

Honey Ice Cream

YIELD: ABOUT 1 QUART

2 3/4 cups milk

3/4 cup plus 2 tablespoons honey

4 egg yolks

1/2 cup plus 1 tablespoon heavy whipping cream

Bring the milk to a boil. Whisk the honey and egg yolks to the ribbon stage and slowly pour in some of the hot milk to temper the eggs. Pour the egg mixture into the milk and cook for 3 minutes, or until the mixture coats the back of a spoon. Add the cream and chill over an ice bath. Freeze in an ice cream machine and keep frozen until ready to use.

Serves 4

3/4 cup heavy whipping cream

1 teaspoon Kahlúa

5 ounces bittersweet chocolate

3 egg yolks

4 Tart Shells (recipe follows)

Bittersweet Chocolate Sauce (recipe follows)

Honey Ice Cream (recipe follows)

4 sprigs mint

Warm Chocolate Tarts

with Bittersweet Chocolate Sauce and Honey Ice Cream

This creamy chocolate tart is perfect for a dinner party. It can be made in advance and assembled at the last moment.

121

Pecan-Banana Tart

This is a great variation on the traditional banana cream pie.

Serves 6

1/2 cup butter, cold

1 1/2 cups ground pecans

1 cup plus 3 tablespoons granulated sugar

1 1/4 cups plus 1 tablespoon all-purpose flour

Pinch of salt

5 egg yolks

2 cups plus 1 tablespoon milk

1/4 cup butter, at room temperature

1 egg

1/2 cup heavy whipping cream

1/2 teaspoon pure vanilla extract

2 tablespoons cornstarch

2 ripe bananas

36 toasted pecan halves

Confectioners' sugar for dusting

To prepare the tart: Combine the cold butter, 1/2 cup of the pecans, 1/3 cup of the granulated sugar, 1 cup plus 3 tablespoons of the flour, and the salt in a food processor until crumbly. Add 1 of the egg yolks and 1 tablespoon of the milk and process until the dough forms a ball. Roll out the dough to 1/8 inch thick and cut into a 9-inch circle. Line an 8-inch tart pan with the dough, place on a sheet pan, and refrigerate for 1 hour. Preheat the oven to 375°. Bake for 10 to 12 minutes, or until golden brown.

To prepare the pecan cream: Combine the softened butter, the whole egg, the remaining 1 cup ground pecans, 1/2 cup of the granulated sugar, the cream, and 1/4 teaspoon of the vanilla in a mixing bowl. Spread a 1/4-inch layer of the mixture in the bottom of the tart. Bake at 350° for 10 minutes, or until the pecan cream is set. Remove from the oven and set aside.

To prepare the pastry cream: Bring the remaining 2 cups milk and 1/3 cup granulated sugar to a boil. Whisk together the remaining 4 egg yolks and 1/3 cup granulated sugar in a bowl. Sift the remaining 2 tablespoons flour and the cornstarch together over the egg yolk mixture and whisk until smooth. Add the remaining 1/4 teaspoon vanilla and one-third of the milk mixture and whisk until combined. Return the remaining milk mixture to a boil. Pour the yolk mixture into the milk, stirring continuously, until thickened and remove from the heat.

To prepare the tart: Cut the bananas into 1/4-inch-thick slices and arrange in a single layer over the pecan cream in the tart shell. Spoon the pastry cream over the bananas and smooth with spatula. Lower the oven heat to 350° and bake for 10 minutes. Remove from the oven and cool slightly, then refrigerate for at least 1 hour.

Cut the tart into 6 slices and place a slice in the center of each plate. Arrange the toasted pecans on each slice and dust with confectioners' sugar.

Double "Dipt" Crème Brûlée

Shaved chocolate on top of the mousse adds an elegant touch to this dish.

Serves 6

2 cups heavy whipping cream

Pulp of 2 vanilla beans

8 egg yolks

$1/2$ cup plus $1 1/2$ tablespoons sugar

$5 1/2$ ounces bittersweet chocolate

$1/4$ cup plus 1 tablespoon butter

4 egg whites

$1/2$ cup firmly packed light brown sugar

1 cup raspberries

To prepare the crème brûlée: Preheat the oven to 300°. Bring the cream and vanilla pulp to a boil. Cover and let steep for 20 minutes. Stir together 5 of the egg yolks and $1/2$ cup of the sugar. Stir the cream into the eggs and strain through a fine-mesh sieve. Spoon the mixture into six 8-ounce brûlée dishes and set on a sheet pan filled with $1/2$ inch water. Bake for 30 to 40 minutes, or until just set. (The center should jiggle when the dishes are shaken.) Remove from the oven, let cool, and refrigerate the brûlées until very cold.

To prepare the chocolate mousse: Melt the chocolate and butter in the top of a double boiler over barely simmering water. Remove the pan from the heat and whisk in the remaining 3 egg yolks, one at a time. Beat the egg whites until soft peaks form, add the remaining $1 1/2$ tablespoons sugar, and beat until stiff peaks form. Fold the egg whites into the chocolate mixture. Spread the chocolate mousse over the brûlées and refrigerate for 1 hour, or until very cold.

Place a brûlée dish in the center of each plate. Sprinkle the tops with the brown sugar and caramelize with a blowtorch for 30 seconds, or until golden brown. Arrange the raspberries on top of the brûlées and place a mint sprig in the center of each dish.

Chocolate Truffles

Yield: about 8 dozen truffles

3/4 cup heavy whipping cream

1 1/4 cups butter

1/4 cup liqueur (such as Grand Marnier, Kahlúa, or bourbon)

1 pound bittersweet chocolate, chopped

1/2 cup unsweetened cocoa

To prepare the truffles: Bring the cream, butter, and liqueur to a boil. Pour over the chocolate and stir until smooth. Refrigerate for 2 hours, or until hard.

Scoop the chocolate mixture into balls and roll in the cocoa. Refrigerate for up to 3 days.

For a sweeter truffle, roll them in a mixture of equal parts cocoa and confectioners' sugar.

125

Banana Upside-Down Cake

For a taste variation try using maple syrup instead of brown sugar.

Serves 8

2 tablespoons freshly squeezed lime juice

1/4 cup freshly squeezed lemon juice

1 teaspoon minced lemon zest

1 tablespoon melted butter

1 cup firmly packed light brown sugar

2 cups sliced ripe banana

1/2 cup butter

2/3 cup superfine granulated sugar

2 eggs, beaten

1 1/2 cups all-purpose flour

1 1/2 teaspoons baking powder

Pinch of salt

1/2 cup milk

1 banana, cut in small wedges

To prepare the bananas:
Combine the lime juice, 3 tablespoons of the lemon juice, the lemon zest, melted butter and 1/2 cup of the brown sugar in a small bowl. Wrap the bottoms of eight 2 1/2-inch-diameter by 1 1/2-inch-high ring molds with aluminum foil. Sprinkle the brown sugar mixture in the bottom of each ring mold and arrange the banana slices in a pinwheel over the sugar.

To prepare the cake:
Preheat the oven to 350°. Cream 1/4 cup of the butter and the granulated sugar until smooth. Add the eggs and mix until well blended. Mix in the flour, baking powder, and salt, and stir in the milk. Pour over the bananas and bake for 20 to 25 minutes, or until a toothpick inserted in the center comes out clean.

To prepare the sauce:
Melt the remaining 1/4 cup butter in a pan. Add 1/2 cup brown sugar and 1 tablespoon lemon juice and cook for 3 minutes, or until the sugar is melted. Add the banana wedges and cook for 2 minutes.

Invert a cake in the center of each plate. Remove the ring mold and spoon the sauce over and around the cake. Arrange the banana wedges around the cake.

Lemon Pudding Cake

with Raspberry Sauce

You can use Meyer lemons in this cake for a lighter, more floral flavor.

Serves 8

4 eggs, separated

1³⁄₄ cups sugar

¹⁄₄ cup all-purpose flour

1 cup freshly squeezed lemon juice

¹⁄₄ teaspoon salt

1¹⁄₄ cups milk

4 cups raspberries

8 sprigs mint

To prepare the cake:
Preheat the oven to 325°. Whip the egg yolks and 1 cup of the sugar until it reaches the ribbon stage. Add the flour and mix well. Whisk in the lemon juice, salt, and milk until completely combined. In a separate bowl, whip the egg whites until soft peaks form. Add ¹⁄₂ cup of the sugar, and whip until stiff peaks form. Gently fold the egg whites into the lemon mixture. Pour the batter into a plastic wrap-lined 9 by 13-inch pan and bake for 30 minutes, or until lightly browned. Remove the cake from the oven and let cool slightly, then refrigerate for at least 1 hour.

Place a piece of plastic wrap over the pudding cake and flip it onto a flat surface. Cut eight 3-inch circles with a ring cutter.

To prepare the sauce:
Reserve 16 raspberries for the garnish. Purée the remaining raspberries with the remaining ¹⁄₄ cup sugar for 2 minutes, or until smooth. Strain through a fine-mesh sieve.

Spoon some of the raspberry sauce in the center of each plate and top with a circle of pudding cake. Place 2 raspberries and a mint sprig in the center of each cake.

Persimmon Crème Caramel

Small bits of persimmon can be added to the crème caramel for even more fruit flavor.

Serves 8

1 cup sugar

1/2 cup water

4 eggs

3 egg yolks

1/2 cup heavy whipping cream

3/4 cup plus 2 tablespoons milk

2 cups persimmon purée

To prepare the crème caramel: Cook 1/2 cup of the sugar and the water in a small sauté pan over medium-high heat for 5 minutes, or until caramelized. Spoon the caramelized sugar into the bottom of 8 custard dishes, swirling to coat the entire bottom.

Preheat the oven to 325°. Combine 1/4 cup of the sugar, the eggs, egg yolks, cream, milk, and 1 cup of the persimmon purée in a large bowl. Ladle the mixture into the custard dishes and place in a baking dish with 1/2 inch of water. Bake for 35 to 45 minutes, or until the custard is set. Remove from the oven and cool slightly.

To prepare the sauce: Combine the remaining 1 cup persimmon purée and 1/4 cup sugar in a small saucepan. Cook for 5 minutes, or until the sugar is completely dissolved. Strain through a fine-mesh sieve.

Invert a crème caramel onto the center of each plate and drizzle the persimmon sauce around the plates.

129

At age, 42, Patrick was taken from

us much too soon. However, while he was here, the

fullness of his life and his relationships both

personal and professional, was enough to cover two

lifetimes! Patrick's circle of culinary colleagues

in particular, was so wide that it has been difficult to

acknowledge them all. Different circumstances

evoke different memories—certain foods conjure up

images of those who inspired him—various recipes

remind me of those who worked on them with him,

and it goes on like that, like snapshots

in a family album.

GUEST CHEFS

Regrettably, it was not possible to mention each life that touched ours in these few pages. Please know that the imprint you have left on our lives and what you meant to Patrick will be forever in our hearts and memories.
It is what comforts my family and I as we struggle to adjust in a world without Patrick.
Lynette Clark

JODY ADAMS

JEFFREY BUBEN

TRACI DES JARDINS

STEPHEN MOISE

KENNETH ORINGER

GIOVANNI PINATO

MICHEL RICHARD

MICHAEL ROMANO

ALLEN SUSSER

ALICE WATERS

ROBERTO DONNA

GEOFF FELSENTHAL

THOMAS KELLER

MICHAEL LOMONACO

CHARLIE PALMER

ALAIN SAILHAC

JIMMY SNEED

CHARLIE TROTTER

NORMAN VAN AKEN

BRIAN WHITMER

ALAIN DUCASSE

MARK FILIPPO

BOB KINKEAD

EMERIL LAGASSE

DONNIE MASTERTON

NOBUYUKI MATSUHISA

FEDELE PANZARINO

MARCUS SAMUELSSON

JOACHIM SPLICHAL

REGINALD WATKINS

HERB WILSON

OCTAVIO BECERRA

JODY DENTON

TODD ENGLISH

DEAN FEARING

MARK MILLER

DREW NIEPERONT

DANIELLE REED

CAL STAMENOV

ROY YAMAGUCHI

DANIEL BOULUD

MELISSA DE MAYO

MASON IRVING

GRAY KUNZ

GEORGE MORRONE

BRADLEY OGDEN

FRANCOIS PAYARD

JACQUES PEPIN

JUDY SCHMITT

NANCY SILVERTON

BILL YOSSES

Jody Adams

Jody Adams emulated her mother's love of cooking, but it wasn't until she was in college that her interest in food took a professional turn when she took a part-time job with Nancy Verde Barr, a professional food writer and teacher. Jody's culinary career began in Boston in 1983 at Seasons Restaurant under chef Lydia Shire. Three years later she became Gordon Hamersley's sous chef at Hamersley's Bistro. She moved to Michela's in 1990 and was executive chef there until early 1994. In the spring of 1994 Jody formed a partnership to open Rialto. Four months after the restaurant opened, the *Boston Globe* gave Rialto a four-star rating.

I became acquainted with Patrick at fundraisers, James Beard Awards events, and at various guest chef events. It may be something of a cliché to describe someone as an inspiration, but in a profession filled with hype, Patrick was the genuine article—a great manager and a super cook. He was the calm at the center of the storm that is often the atmosphere of an off-site event. The orchestrator of many such events, he expected his participants to deliver their best.

Patrick set his own culinary standard. While not disdainful of dramatic presentation, he practiced a more modest style. *He was an advocate of nuance. His food lay low on the plate, as though inviting diners to draw close, within whispering distance, to where a dish's virtues might be intimately appreciated.*

Finally, it is as a chef with a family, as I am, that I remember Patrick. At the 1994 James Beard Awards he was sitting in front of me, with several vacant seats on either side of him. We both had been nominated, and I was churning with nerves, squeezing my husband's hand as the moment neared when the winner in my division would be announced. I wondered about his family. Some time later, when he visited Boston, he came to eat in my restaurant, and we had our first leisurely conversation. After he ordered, he produced photographs of his family. We shared our thoughts on how hard restaurant life is on family life. I imagined his wife and five children sitting together at home, waiting to hear whether he had won that night at the Beard Awards. And of course, he had won. When his name was announced, the room exploded with applause, as I'm sure it did in his home. We all had been holding hands for him.

Toasted Chive Spaetzle

with Peas and Smoked Salmon Cream

These spaetzle also make a wonderful side dish.

133

Serves 4

SPAETZLE

1½ cups flour

2 eggs

½ cup water

2 tablespoons finely minced chives

¾ teaspoon kosher salt

½ teaspoon freshly ground black pepper

1 tablespoon vegetable oil

SAUCE

1 tablespoon butter

1 tablespoon minced shallots

1½ cups heavy whipping cream

¼ cup fresh or frozen peas, blanched

¼ cup blanched fava beans (if fava beans are unavailable, increase the amount of peas to ½ cup)

2 ounces smoked salmon, cut into ¼-inch strips

Kosher salt and freshly ground black pepper

1 tablespoon chopped fresh chervil

———

1 tablespoon butter

To prepare the spaetzle:
Beat the flour, eggs, and water together to form a smooth, thick batter with an elastic consistency. Stir in the chives and season with the salt and pepper.

Bring a stockpot of salted water to a boil. (Add 1½ teaspoons salt per quart of water.) Holding a large-holed colander over the stockpot, push the spaetzle batter through the colander with the back of a spoon, forming small, irregular dumplings that drop into the boiling water. Cook until the spaetzle floats to the surface, then transfer to a bowl of ice water to cool. Drain well and toss with the vegetable oil. Cover and refrigerate until ready to use. (The recipe can be prepared up to one day ahead to this point.)

To prepare the sauce:
Heat the butter in a small saucepan over medium heat. Add the shallots and cook for 4 to 5 minutes, or until tender. Add the cream and reduce by one-quarter. Decrease the heat to low, add the peas, fava beans, and salmon, and simmer for 1 minute. Season to taste with salt and pepper and add the chervil.

Heat the butter over medium-high heat in a large frying pan. When the foam subsides, add the spaetzle and cook until toasted and golden brown on one side, about 5 minutes.

Divide the sauce evenly into 4 warm bowls and top with the warm spaetzle.

134

Jeffrey Buben

Jeffrey Buben and his wife, Sallie, are partners in the Fully-Baked Restaurant Group, which has owned and managed Vidalia in Washington, D.C., since 1993. Fall of 1998 heralded the opening of their second restaurant, Bistro Bis, located at the new Hotel George on Capitol Hill.

Jeffrey, a graduate of the Culinary Institute of America, has worked in such notable New York restaurants as the Sign of the Dove, Le Cygne, and Le Chantilly, and several hotels, including the Four Seasons, the Mayflower, and Hotel Pierre. Buben has been voted Chef of the Year by the Restaurant Association of Metropolitan Washington and nominated four consecutive times by the James Beard Foundation for Best Chef: Mid-Atlantic.

When Patrick worked in Washington, D.C., his son, Preston, attended school with my daughter, Sarah. As part of Career Development Day at the school, I volunteered to talk about my career as a chef. Believing that sixth-grade students would only possess a passing interest in cuisine, I proceeded to give an overview of a chef's job and shared some ideas about possibilities in the business. When it was time for questions from the class, I received a few general questions, as I'd expected would happen. **Then came the ringer. A boy in the group asked how I prepare venison,** *how I like to prepare certain types of fish, how I prepare different sauces, and on from there. The class finally ended and I escaped, I believe, with some credibility left intact. Later, Sarah informed me of the identity of the potential future chef.*

The sweetness of the onions perfectly offsets the tanginess of the blue cheese in these tartlets.

135

Serves 4

TARTLETS

¼ cup olive oil

4 cups julienned Vidalia onions

4 teaspoons chopped fresh basil

2 eggs

2 cups crumbled Maytag blue cheese

½ cup freshly grated Parmesan cheese plus Parmesan cheese for dusting

1 tablespoon Worcestershire sauce

¼ teaspoon Tabasco sauce

⅛ teaspoon ground nutmeg

⅛ teaspoon cayenne pepper

Salt and freshly ground black pepper

4 3-inch diameter prebaked tartlet shells

SWISS CHARD

1 cup chiffonade-cut red Swiss chard

½ cup julienned thick-slab bacon, browned, and drained

2 teaspoons minced shallots

3 tablespoons balsamic vinegar

3 tablespoons warm bacon fat

To prepare the filling: Preheat the oven to 350°. Heat the olive oil in a heavy 1-quart sauté pan over medium heat. Add the onions and sauté for about 12 minutes, or until well-browned. Do not allow the onions to burn. Transfer the onions to a large mixing bowl and set aside to cool completely. Add the basil, eggs, blue cheese, Parmesan cheese, Worcestershire sauce, Tabasco, nutmeg, cayenne pepper, and salt and pepper to taste, and fold together gently. Divide the mixture evenly between the tartlet shells and sprinkle with some of the remaining Parmesan cheese. Bake for approximately 12 minutes, or until golden brown and bubbly.

To prepare the Swiss chard: In a large bowl, toss the Swiss chard with the bacon, shallots, balsamic vinegar, and bacon fat.

Place a tartlet in the center of each plate. Twist together some of the Swiss chard mixture and place in the center of the tartlets.

Traci Des Jardins

Traci Des Jardins's passion for food is evident at her restaurant, Jardiniere, which opened in 1997. Traci started her career working for Joachim Splichal in Los Angeles. She then served four apprenticeships in France, working with Michel and Pierre Troisgros, Alain Senderens, Alain Ducasse, and Alain Passard. After relocating to Manhattan, Traci worked as sous chef at Montrachet. In 1989 she became chef de cuisine, opening Splichal's Patina, and then went on to San Francisco to help open Aqua and then Elka.

Traci became chef at Rubicon, in San Francisco, in 1993. There, she gathered many awards, including the James Beard Foundation's Rising Star Chef of the Year. She has received a nomination for the James Beard Foundation's Best New Restaurant award, and was named one of *Food & Wine* magazine's Best New Chefs for 1995.

I had heard of Patrick Clark during my New York cooking days and from a series of talented cooks who worked for me after having spent their formative years under his watchful eye. My first encounter with Patrick was at the Masters of Food and Wine at the Highlands Inn in Carmel, California. This event—working side by side with the culinary talents of the world—is always an extraordinary experience. Along with all of the talented stars and innovative foods comes a great deal of pressure, anxiety, and sometimes, butting egos. Patrick was the appointed chef of chefs at the event for a number of years. He handled everything with an ease, graciousness, firmness, and precision that facilitated the smooth execution both for the diners and also for everyone fortunate enough to work in the kitchen with him. **He executed his own food with a deft hand and admirable style.** *We will always miss him—his booming voice, sparkling eyes, kind smile, and great palate.*

Ahi Tuna Carpaccio à la Niçoise

You can order sushi-grade tuna from most seafood markets.

Serves 6

1¼ pounds sushi-grade Ahi tuna, center loin cut

BASIL OIL

1 bunch basil, stemmed

¼ cup extra virgin olive oil

TOMATOES

1 pound plum tomatoes, blanched and peeled

1 tablespoon extra virgin olive oil

2 tablespoons chopped fresh thyme

Salt and freshly ground black pepper

VINAIGRETTE

2 tablespoons balsamic vinegar

¼ cup extra virgin olive oil

Salt and freshly ground black pepper

―――

1 bulb fennel, thinly sliced

1 bunch upland cress or watercress, stemmed

1 bunch scallions, thinly sliced

¼ cup pitted niçoise olives

To prepare the tuna:
Trim any sinew from the tuna loin and cut into 6 thin pieces. Place each piece between 2 sheets of plastic wrap and pound until about ⅙ inch thick. Refrigerate until ready to use.

To prepare the basil oil:
Blanch the basil in well-salted boiling water and shock in ice water to cool quickly. Place in a blender, add the olive oil, and blend until smooth. Strain through cheesecloth into a small bowl to extract the green oil. Set aside.

To prepare the tomatoes:
Preheat the oven to 225°. Cut the tomatoes into quarters lengthwise. Remove and discard the seeds and inner membranes. Coat a baking sheet with the olive oil, thyme, and salt and pepper. Place the tomato pieces on the baking sheet and season the top side with salt and pepper. Place the pan in the oven and cook for about 3 hours, or until the tomatoes are dehydrated. Remove the tomatoes from the pan and set aside to cool.

To prepare the vinaigrette:
Whisk together the balsamic vinegar and olive oil and season to taste with salt and pepper.

Divide the thinly pounded tuna evenly among 6 chilled plates and season to taste with salt and pepper. Drizzle the balsamic vinaigrette over the tuna. Scatter the fennel, upland cress, scallions, olives, and tomatoes over the tuna and drizzle the basil oil around the plates.

138

Stephen Moise

Stephen Moise's family has been in the hotel and restaurant business for three generations. He grew up being taught the correct way to prepare foods. He initially worked in the front of the house, but quickly realized he loved cooking and wanted to devote his life to learning the art. Stephen worked at several local restaurants before working for Brian Whitmer at the Highlands Inn in Carmel, California. It was there that Stephen met Patrick Clark and was offered a garde-manger position with him. He soon went on to become Patrick's executive sous chef at Tavern on the Green, a position he held until after Patrick's death. He is currently executive chef at the City Athletic Club, one of the oldest private clubs in New York City.

The first time I saw Patrick at the Masters, he greeted me with his famous smile and big handshake, and then put me to work. His presence in the kitchen was so powerful and the respect everyone had for him was so contagious that I wanted to be a part of that. Thanks to Patrick, I got that chance at Tavern on the Green.

Patrick had quite an impact on me as a young chef. I will never see, smell, taste, or listen to food in the same way again. *And I wish I could thank him for sharing his knowledge, skill, and love of food and life with me. I know now what it is to have a passion for cooking. He demonstrated that every day, sometimes to an extreme, but that's how I learned. In those magic years, we sweated, laughed, cried, and dreamed together. There were times I woke from a deep sleep yelling, "Yes, Chef!" I'll cherish those times forever.*

Corn Cakes

with Smoked Salmon, Caviar, and Lemon Crème Fraîche

These could also be served as canapés by simply topping each corn cake with a small amount of salmon, caviar, and crème fraîche.

Serves 8

CORN CAKES

1½ cups fresh sweet corn kernels

Pinch of salt

⅓ cup yellow cornmeal

⅓ cup flour

½ teaspoon baking powder

⅛ teaspoon ground white pepper

2 eggs

⅔ cup heavy whipping cream

½ cup melted butter

LEMON CRÈME FRAÎCHE

1 cup crème fraîche

1 tablespoon freshly squeezed lemon juice

Salt and freshly ground black pepper

8 ounces smoked salmon, julienned

1 ounce beluga caviar

½ cup minced chives

To prepare the corn cakes: Put the corn kernels and a pinch of salt in a food processor and pulse until partially liquid; some whole kernels should remain. Combine the cornmeal, flour, baking powder, and white pepper in a medium bowl. In a separate bowl, whisk together the eggs, cream, and 2 tablespoons of the butter. Pour the egg mixture into the dry ingredients and stir until combined. Add the corn purée and mix well.

Heat a nonstick pan over medium heat and add 2 tablespoons of the melted butter. Drop the batter into the pan 1 tablespoon at a time to form individual cakes. Cook for 1 to 2 minutes on each side, or until golden brown. Transfer the cakes to a paper towel and continue the process with the remaining batter and melted butter.

To prepare the crème fraîche: Whisk together the crème fraîche and lemon juice and season to taste with salt and black pepper.

Arrange 3 corn cakes in the center of each plate and place a teaspoon of the julienned salmon on each cake. Drizzle the crème fraîche across the plates in a zigzag pattern and top the salmon with some of the caviar. Sprinkle the chives around the plates.

Kenneth Oringer

Ken Oringer's career has unfolded on both the East and West coasts. He was voted Most Likely to Succeed at the Culinary Institute of America in 1987. His first position was at the River Café in New York, and then he went on to Al Forno in Providence, Rhode Island. He worked briefly under Jean-Georges Vongerichten at Boston's Le Marquis de Lafayette, and after that opened a trattoria in Greenwich, Connecticut. Ken next moved to Silks, in the Mandarin Oriental Hotel, in San Francisco, where he began to attract attention from *Zagat, Gourmet,* and *Traveler Magazine.* Returning east again, Ken won raves for his work at Tosca in Hingham, Massachusetts. In June 1997 Ken opened Clio in Boston, Massachusetts, where he is at the helm as co-owner and chef. That same year Clio earned the distinction of being named Best Newcomer by *Gourmet.* In 1998 Ken was nominated for Best Chef: Northeast, by the James Beard Foundation.

Meeting Patrick at the annual Masters of Food and Wine event in Carmel, California was like meeting a legend. He quietly yet confidently oversaw the entire event with such good humor and kindness toward everyone that even newcomers like me felt comfortable. **His level of professionalism made a strong impression on me, as did his obvious love of people and food in general.**

Serves 6

VEGETABLES

¾ cup vegetable stock

½ cup butter

8 baby gold beets, roasted and sliced

8 baby candy cane beets, roasted and sliced

½ cup diced rutabaga, blanched

½ cup sliced baby turnips, blanched

½ cup sliced purple kohlrabi, blanched

12 white pearl onions, peeled and blanched

12 red pearl onions, peeled and blanched

¼ cup kabocha squash, blanched and diced into cubes

¼ cup finely shredded green cabbage, blanched

¼ cup red bell pepper diamonds

¼ cup yellow bell pepper diamonds

1 tablespoon chopped fresh thyme leaves

3 tablespoons chopped chives

3 tablespoons oxalis leaves

3 tablespoons cilantro leaves

1 teaspoon peeled and chopped fresh ginger

1 tablespoon chopped shallots

Salt and freshly ground black pepper

PUFF PASTRY

6 4-inch-diameter rounds puff pastry

1 egg, beaten

Sea salt and freshly ground black pepper

2 tablespoons sesame seeds

Sweet Pepper Broth (recipe follows)

2 tablespoons fresh chervil leaves

2 tablespoons chive batons

To prepare the vegetables: Simmer the stock in a large saucepan for 2 to 3 minutes, or until reduced by half. Whisk in the butter. Add all of the vegetables and cook, stirring continuously, until the vegetables are warm and completely coated with the glaze. Add the herbs, ginger, and shallots, and season to taste with salt and pepper. Keep warm until ready to use.

To prepare the pastry: Preheat the oven to 350°. Brush the puff pastry with the egg and season with sea salt and pepper. Sprinkle with the sesame seeds and bake for 15 to 20 minutes, or until golden brown and dry. Cut the top off the pastry with a sharp knife and reserve.

Place a puff pastry in the center of each plate. Fill each pastry with some of the vegetable mixture. Pour some of the broth over the vegetables, sprinkle with the chives and chervil, and cover with the pastry tops.

Sweet Pepper Broth

YIELD: ABOUT ¾ CUP

2 tablespoons olive oil

3 red bell peppers, seeded and chopped

3 shallots, sliced

½ onion, sliced

1 teaspoon coriander seeds

2 stalks lemongrass, chopped

½ teaspoon fennel seeds

3 slices peeled fresh ginger

2 sprigs thyme

1 sprig cilantro

Heat the olive oil in a saucepan over medium heat and add the remaining ingredients. Cook, stirring continuously, until the onion and shallots are translucent but not browned. Add enough water to cover the bottom of the pan and simmer for 5 minutes to marry the flavors. Purée to a coarse consistency with a handheld blender and strain through a fine-mesh sieve, discarding the solids.

Cassoulet of Autumn Vegetables en Bouche

with Wild Herbs and Sweet Pepper Broth

This dish can be served as an entrée by increasing the portion size.

141

Giovanni Pinato

142

Giovanni Pinato was raised in the northeastern region of Padova and weaned on rustic Italian fare. After perfecting his culinary skills at Taverna del Colleoni and the Excelsior Hotel in Venice, Pinato came to New York in 1988 to assume the helm of alo alo. One year later, he opened Cafe Roma, also in New York. In 1990 Pinato moved to Los Angeles to team up with Patrick Clark at Bicé. He has returned to New York, where he opened Giovanni, Manhattan's newest Italian eatery, showcasing the cuisine of his homeland.

With deepest respect and admiration, I dedicate this recipe to Patrick Clark, **a man who has inspired all of his peers,** *for his culinary vision, charisma, generosity, and sincere appreciation for excellence in cooking.*

Sardines in Sauce, Venetian Style

Using an aged balsamic vinegar will give the sauce a smoother flavor.

Serves 4 to 6

SARDINES

16 fresh sardines

1 cup flour

2 cups vegetable oil

SAUCE

¼ cup salt

3 red onions, sliced

1 cup balsamic vinegar

½ cup extra virgin olive oil

Salt and freshly ground black pepper

———

½ cup pine nuts

½ cup golden raisins

To prepare the sardines:
Wash and dry the sardines and dust them with the flour. Heat the oil in a large sauté pan over medium-high heat. Fry the sardines in the hot oil for 2 to 3 minutes, or until golden brown. Drain on paper towels.

To prepare the sauce:
Bring 5 cups of water to a boil in a medium saucepan. Add the salt and onions, cook for 3 minutes, and then drain. In a large bowl, mix the vinegar and olive oil, add the cooked onions, and set aside to marinate for 1 hour. Season to taste with salt and pepper.

Place the sardines on a serving platter and garnish with the cooked onions. Spoon the remaining liquid from the onions around the sardines, and sprinkle the pine nuts and raisins around the plate.

Michel Richard

Michel Richard is an internationally acclaimed chef and restaurateur. He has been a recipient of the most prestigious culinary honors and appears frequently on nationally televised cooking shows, including award-winning productions with Julia Child. He is the author of *Michel Richard's Home Cooking with a French Accent*. A native of Brittany, France, Michel came to the United States in 1974 to open Gaston Lenotre's New York City Pastry Shop. He went on to open his own pastry shop in Santa Fe, and continued on to Los Angeles, where he opened a second pastry shop, the Broadway Deli, and his renowned restaurant, Citrus. In 1991 Michel created a partnership with CapStar Hotel Company and opened Citronelle in Santa Barbara, followed by Citronelle, in Washington, D.C.

I was impressed by Patrick's enthusiasm to give of himself. *It was always a pleasure to work with him and his big smile. We've lost a great man.*

Mashed Potato Dip

with Wasabe Vinaigrette

This dip could also be served hot and used as a side dish for a piece of fish.

145

Serves 4

VINAIGRETTE

1 teaspoon wasabe

2 tablespoons olive oil

1 tablespoon rice vinegar

1 tablespoon flying fish roe

POTATOES

1 pound yellow potatoes, peeled and quartered

¼ cup heavy whipping cream

½ cup butter, at room temperature

Salt

To prepare the vinaigrette: Whisk together the wasabe, olive oil, and rice vinegar in a small bowl. Gently stir in the flying fish roe.

To prepare the potatoes: Steam the potatoes until thoroughly cooked and then pass them through a sieve into a large bowl. Add the cream and butter and season to taste with salt. Stir in the wasabe vinaigrette.

Serve the dip lukewarm with crackers, chips, or raw vegetables.

Michael Romano

While cooking at Serendipity, Michael Romano was introduced to James Beard, who advised him in charting his culinary career. Beard recommended New York City Technical College, where Michael subsequently studied and blossomed as a cook.

Michael's first "stage" at the illustrious Hotel Bristol in Paris was followed by several others, including Regine's in Paris, Regine's in New York, and Eugénie-Les-Bains. He became chef de cuisine at Chez Max in Zurich before crossing the Atlantic again, in 1984, to become chef de cuisine at La Caravelle in New York City.

Union Square Cafe became Michael's home in 1988; a year later the restaurant was elevated to three-star status by the *New York Times*. In 1997 the restaurant received the James Beard Outstanding Restaurant Award.

I knew Patrick as a fellow alumni of New York City Technical and was impressed with his dedication to the field and capacity for hard work. I recall working alongside him in the kitchens of Regine's in New York in the mid-1970s. Michel Guerard was the consulting chef, and we all were very excited about cooking his food. This was during Patrick's bodybuilding period; **he would amaze us by deadlifting enormously heavy stockpots** *filled to the brim with bones and broth.*

One afternoon, Patrick was on duty to prepare family meal for the staff. I decided to cook up some french fries, a real treat for the staff. We did not have a fryer, so Patrick placed a large pot filled with fat on the stovetop. When it came time to fry the potatoes, a few things happened that nearly spelled disaster for us all. First, there was too much fat in the pot. Second, the fat was too hot. Third, Patrick inadvertently added too many potatoes at once. The next thing we knew, the hot oil was cascading over the stovetop and behind the stoves, and it burst into flames. Everyone except Patrick and me cleared out of the kitchen. I grabbed a fire extinguisher and attacked the flames while Patrick bravely attempted to remove the still overflowing pot from the heat. Some of the oil splashed on Patrick's wrist, causing him to drop the pot to the floor. Now we both stood in hot oil, faced with the blistering heat of the fire. We finally realized we needed to get down low and spray the flames from underneath the stoves. And that is how we were able to put out the fire. Patrick recovered from his burn, but we never forgot that incident in all of our years of friendship.

Orrechiette with Broccoli Rabe and Tomatoes

Serves 4 to 6

2 tomatoes (about 1 pound)

2 bunches broccoli rabe (about 1½ pounds), cleaned and stemmed

¼ cup olive oil

1 teaspoon minced garlic

⅛ teaspoon red pepper flakes

1 tablespoon plus ½ teaspoon kosher salt

3 cups tomato sauce

½ cup water

½ pound orrechiette

½ cup finely grated pecorino Romano (about 2 ounces)

⅛ teaspoon freshly ground black pepper

To prepare the tomatoes:
Cut the tomatoes in half and squeeze out and discard the seeds. Chop the tomato into ¾-inch pieces and set aside.

To prepare the broccoli rabe:
Separate the leaves and florets and tear the largest leaves into 2 to 3-inch pieces. Combine the olive oil, garlic, and red pepper flakes in a 3-quart saucepan or a skillet large enough to hold all of the broccoli rabe. Cook over medium-high heat for 45 seconds to flavor the oil; do not allow the garlic to brown. Add the broccoli rabe and cook for 2 to 3 minutes to wilt, turning constantly with tongs or a kitchen fork. Season with ½ teaspoon of the salt. Add the chopped tomatoes, tomato sauce, and water. Return to a simmer and cook for 3 to 5 minutes, or until it reaches a brothy consistency. Keep warm until ready to serve.

To prepare the pasta:
Bring 1 gallon of water to a boil in a large pot. Add the remaining 1 tablespoon salt and cook the pasta until al dente. Drain the pasta, and while it is still in the colander, sprinkle it with half the pecorino. Transfer the pasta to a large bowl and toss with the broccoli rabe until combined.

Spoon the pasta onto the center of each plate, sprinkle with the remaining cheese, and top with the black pepper.

Be sure to choose broccoli rabe that has a vibrant green color, absolutely no yellowing in the florets, and tender, not woody stalks.

Allen Susser

Allen Susser was born in Brooklyn, New York, into a family heritage rich with celebrating life through food. He graduated in 1976 from New York City Technical College at the top of his class and received his bachelor's degree in hospitality from Florida International University. Widely accepted as the creator of New World Cuisine, chef Allen has forged an innovative signature with his dramatic translation of the bounty of South Florida's foodstuffs. Chef Allen's, opened in 1986, has won accolades from local and national food writers: *Food & Wine* named Allen Susser Best New Chef in America in 1991; *Time* magazine called Allen's cuisine "a New World marvel"; and, in 1994, the James Beard Foundation awarded him Best Chef: Southeast.

Patrick and I shared many stoves, cuts, and tests. It was in Professor Panzarino's class—Culinary 101—at New York City Technical that we met and began to learn our way around the stove. I remember Patrick with a copy of Escoffier *under his arm, a sharp knife, and a big smile, ready to cook. He was always focused on the details of his work. On graduation, when the possibility of working in France became a reality, we crammed together through dozens of French lessons to earn our place in a great French kitchen.* **We were young, wide-eyed, and open to all that life had to offer**. *Patrick, I'll miss you.*

Pan-Roasted Shrimp

with Orange, Tarragon, and Arugula

Make sure to thoroughly clean the arugula to remove all the sand and grit.

Serves 4

SHRIMP

16 jumbo shrimp, cleaned

1 tablespoon fresh
tarragon leaves

2 tablespoons olive oil

½ teaspoon minced garlic

1 teaspoon kosher salt

½ teaspoon freshly
ground black pepper

½ cup freshly squeezed
orange juice

2 large Valencia oranges,
1 zested, both peeled and
sliced crosswise

ARUGULA

2 tablespoons olive oil

¼ cup champagne vinegar

2 bunches arugula, washed
and dried

1 small red onion, peeled
and sliced thinly crosswise

1 tablespoon fresh tarragon
leaves

To roast the shrimp:
Preheat the oven to 425°.
In a large bowl, season the
shrimp with the tarragon,
olive oil, garlic, salt, and pepper. Warm a large ovenproof
pan, add the shrimp, and
sauté over medium heat for
1 minute. Arrange the shrimp
in a circular shape in the
pan and put the pan in the
oven for 2 minutes. Turn the
shrimp over, add the orange
juice and zest, and return the
pan to the oven for 1 to 2
minutes, or until the shrimp
are rosy pink.

To prepare the arugula:
In a small bowl, whisk
together the olive oil, vinegar,
and shrimp pan juices, and
toss with the arugula.

Arrange the sliced oranges
and onions on each plate.
Arrange the arugula on the
plates along with the warm
shrimp. Sprinkle the tarragon
leaves over the shrimp and
around the plates.

150

Alice Waters

Alice Waters, internationally known chef, author, and proprietor of Chez Panisse, in Berkeley, California, pioneered the culinary philosophy of using only the freshest ingredients, picked in season. In order to supply the restaurant, Chez Panisse has cultivated a network of local farmers who are committed to sustainable agriculture. Alice Waters has introduced her ideas into the schools, conceiving and launching the Edible Schoolyard program at Berkeley's Martin Luther King Jr. Middle School. This highly acclaimed curriculum directly involves students in planting, harvesting, and cooking their school lunches. It teaches them about the vital role food plays in their lives while instilling in them respect for others and the earth.

One of the most sublime parties I have ever been to in my life was the memorial tribute to Patrick at Tavern on the Green in New York. **The beauty of the food and the huge number of celebrated chefs preparing it was a true reflection of Patrick's spirit and his enormous contribution to food in this country.**

Fava Bean Purée

Be sure to remove the white germ from the bean. It can cause the purée to be bitter.

Serves 8 to 10

3 pounds midseason fava beans

½ to ¾ cup extra virgin olive oil

Salt and freshly ground black pepper

2 cloves garlic, finely chopped

¼ bay leaf

1 small sprig sage

1 small sprig rosemary

½ lemon

48 small slices grilled bread (sourdough, whole grain, or French)

To prepare the purée:
Bring a large pot of water to a boil. Shell the fava beans, discarding the pods. Parboil the shelled beans for 1 minute. Drain and immediately plunge them in ice water for a few minutes to cool and then drain them again. Remove their pale green skins, piercing the outer skin of each bean with a thumbnail and popping out the bright green bean inside with a pinch of the thumbnail and forefinger.

Warm about ½ cup of the olive oil in a shallow, nonreactive sauté pan. Add the beans and salt lightly. Add the garlic, bay leaf, sage, and rosemary, and a splash of water. Cook at a slow simmer, stirring and tasting frequently, for about 30 minutes, or until the beans are completely soft and pale green and easily mashed into a purée. Add another splash of water periodically to prevent the beans from drying out and sticking to the pan.

When the beans are done, remove them from the pan and discard the herbs. Mash the beans into a paste using a wooden spoon, and pass them through a sieve or food mill or purée in a food processor. Season to taste with salt and pepper and add more olive oil and a few drops of lemon juice to taste. If the purée is at all dry and tight, add more olive oil. Don't be stingy with the oil; good olive oil is as important to the flavor of the purée as the beans.

Place the warm bean purée in a bowl in the center of a serving platter and arrange the bread slices around the platter.

152

Roberto Donna

A native of Italy's Piedmont region, James Beard Award–winning chef and restaurateur Roberto Donna is an ambassador of Italian cuisine. In 1997 he published his first cookbook, *Cooking in Piedmont with Roberto Donna*. In his twelve unique restaurants, located in Washington, D.C., Roberto puts into practice his belief in pure, simple cuisine using only the freshest ingredients.

After expanding his culinary horizons early in his career by working in kitchens across England, France, and Switzerland, Roberto arrived in Washington, D.C., in 1980, at the age of nineteen. Four years later he opened his first restaurant. With restaurants ranging in style from his formal, four-star flagship, Galileo, to the Il Radicchio "all you can eat" spaghetteria concept, Roberto caters to a range of palates.

When Patrick Clark walked into a room, his smile made everyone light up. The short time that he was part of the Washington, D.C., restaurant community was special; his presence added so much. **I feel fortunate to have shared his friendship and laughter**

Serves 8

SOUP

1 capon, breasts removed and reserved

1 onion, chopped

2 carrots, chopped

4 celery stalks, chopped

2 bay leaves

2 bunches parsley stems

1 clove garlic

1 tomato, chopped

Salt and black pepper

12 egg whites, lightly whisked

30 blanched almonds, peeled

1/2 teaspoon sugar

1/2 cup heavy cream

1 potato, peeled and boiled

3 leeks, blanched and chopped

Pinch of ground nutmeg

Pinch of ground cinnamon

1 1/2 cups freshly grated Parmesan cheese

1/4 cup plus 2 tablespoons butter

BREAD PUDDING

4 ounces day-old Italian bread, crusts removed

2 cups heavy cream

4 bay leaves

1/2 teaspoon chopped fresh rosemary

1/2 teaspoon chopped fresh sage

1/2 teaspoon saffron threads

6 ounces grated Swiss cheese

3 eggs, beaten

Salt and black pepper

LEEKS

2 leeks, julienned

1/2 cup flour

2 cups olive oil

———

1/4 cup butter

Salt and black pepper

To prepare the consommé: Place the capon in a stockpot, cover with cold water, and bring to a boil. As soon as the water starts to boil, drain and discard the liquid. Add the onion, carrots, celery, bay leaves, parsley, garlic, tomato, salt and pepper to taste, and 4 gallons of cold water to the stockpot. Simmer for 3 hours, or until reduced to 1 gallon, skimming the surface periodically. Strain through a fine-mesh sieve into a small stockpot.

Whisk the egg whites into the stock and bring to a slow simmer, stirring continuously in one direction. Stir for 15 minutes, or until the egg whites begin to form a raft. Break a small hole in the raft and simmer over medium-low heat for 45 minutes, or until the liquid is crystal-clear. Strain through a cheesecloth-lined fine-mesh sieve, being careful not to break the raft. Discard the raft and season the consommé with salt and pepper.

Purée the almonds, sugar, and cream until smooth and add to the consommé. Purée the potato and leeks until smooth. Add the potato purée to the consommé and stir well. Add the nutmeg, cinnamon, Parmesan cheese, and butter and bring to a slow simmer.

To prepare the bread pudding: Preheat the oven to 300°. Soak the bread in 1 cup of the consommé. Bring the cream and bay leaves to a boil in a large saucepan. Remove from the heat and discard the bay leaves. Add the rosemary, sage, and saffron. Drain the bread and add it to the cream. Add the Swiss cheese and eggs and season with salt and pepper. Divide the bread mixture into 8 small buttered timbale molds, cover with parchment paper, and bake in a water bath for 15 minutes.

To prepare the leeks: Toss the leeks in the flour and shake off any excess. Heat the olive oil in a small saucepan until hot. Add some of the leeks and cook for 1 to 2 minutes, or until lightly browned and crispy. Remove the leeks and drain on paper towels. Repeat with the remaining leeks.

To prepare the capon: Cut the breast in thin strips and sauté in the butter over medium heat for 3 to 4 minutes, or until just done. Season with salt and pepper.

Place a timbale in the center of each bowl, remove the mold, and top with the fried leeks. Pour the soup in the bowls and arrange the capon strips around the puddings.

Capon-Almond-Potato Soup

with Swiss Cheese-Herbed Bread Pudding and Fried Leeks

If capons are unavailable, rock Cornish game hens will also work well.

Geoff Felsenthal

Geoff Felsenthal graduated from the Culinary Academy of California in 1983. He spent the next several years fine-tuning his craft in various restaurants in California with such notable chefs as Bradley Ogden, Jeremiah Tower, and Mark Stech-Novak. In 1987 Geoff returned to his hometown, Chicago, to become the opening sous chef of Charlie Trotter's. After five years with Trotter, Geoff went on to become the executive chef of Bella Vista restaurant. In 1996 Geoff joined Lettuce Entertain You as the chef of Avanzaré where he remained until fall of 1998, when he became the opening executive chef of Lettuce Entertain You's newest venture, Vong, in Chicago.

I knew Patrick for about eight years. When I first met him in California at the Masters of Food and Wine I knew immediately that there was something special about him—his warm, friendly smile, his desire to teach others, his great care, and his true love of cuisine. **I will always remember that warm smile.** *I hope that one day I will be able to give to others in the way that Patrick has done.*

5 cups chicken stock

12 pitted, marinated green olives, cut into strips

———

3 tablespoons white peppercorns

1½ tablespoons coriander seeds

1½ tablespoons fennel seeds

Salt

1 pound Ahi tuna loin

2 tablespoons canola oil

Serves 4

POLENTA

1 cup polenta

4 cups water

¼ cup freshly grated Parmesan cheese

Salt and freshly ground black pepper

Flour for dredging

¼ cup canola oil

WILTED GREENS

½ ounce fresh basil leaves, finely chopped

½ ounce flat-leaf parsley leaves, finely chopped

Juice of 2 lemons

Salt and freshly ground black pepper

1 cup olive oil

4 ounces arugula, large stems removed

4 ounces watercress, large stems removed

4 ounces frisée

ONIONS

16 to 20 pearl onions

¼ cup olive oil

2 tablespoons butter

To prepare the polenta:
Put the polenta in a small pitcher so it can be poured in a steady stream. Bring the water to a boil in a large saucepan. Slowly add the polenta, whisking gently until completely blended. Cook until the polenta comes to a rolling boil and then decrease the heat to the lowest setting and cook for 40 to 45 minutes, stirring occasionally with a wooden spoon to prevent a skin from forming. The polenta is cooked when there is no grit remaining. Remove the polenta from the heat and stir in the Parmesan cheese, salt, and pepper. Pour the mixture into a buttered baking sheet and set aside to cool.

Cut the cooled polenta into 1-inch squares. Dredge the squares in flour, shaking off any excess, and sauté in the canola oil until golden brown and crispy. Remove from the pan and drain on paper towels.

To prepare the wilted greens: In a small bowl, combine the basil, parsley, lemon juice, and salt and pepper to taste. Slowly drizzle in the olive oil, whisking vigorously. Set aside.

Remove the dark green leaves from the frisée. Wash the arugula, watercress, and frisée in a large bowl of cold water, allowing the greens to soak briefly. Lift the greens out of the water and spin them dry with a small salad spinner or pat dry with kitchen towels. In a small sauté pan, wilt the greens over medium heat with 2 tablespoons of the lemon dressing, and season to taste with salt and pepper.

To prepare the onions:
Remove the outer skin from the onions. Sauté the onions in a pan with the olive oil and butter over medium-high heat for 5 to 7 minutes, or until caramelized. Add the chicken stock and slowly cook for 15 to 20 minutes, or until tender. Remove the onions from the pan and let them cool. Halve the onions and combine them with the greens, polenta, and olives.

To prepare the tuna:
Grind the white pepper and coriander and fennel seeds in a spice grinder. (If no spice grinder is available, place the spices between 2 sheets of paper and slowly crack with a heavy-bottomed pot.) Salt the tuna and roll it in the spice mixture, making sure it is completely covered. In a sauté pan, heat the oil over medium-high heat, add the tuna, and sear for 2 to 3 minutes on each side, or to the desired doneness. Remove the tuna from the heat, let it rest for 5 minutes, and then slice it thinly.

Place some of the polenta mixture in the center of each plate and arrange the tuna slices across the top. Drizzle the remaining dressing over the tuna.

Spiced Tuna Salad

with Crispy Polenta, Wilted Greens, and Tiny Onions

The polenta can be prepared a day ahead and sautéed just prior to serving.

Thomas Keller

Thomas Keller, chef and owner of The French Laundry in Yountville, California, is renowned for his innovation and dedication. He has received numerous accolades throughout his career, including the James Beard Foundation's 1997 Outstanding Chef: America and 1996 Best American Chef: California awards. Thomas Keller also received *Restaurants & Institutions'* 1996 Ivy Award and was named 1997 Best Bay Area Chef by *SF Focus* magazine.

Thomas first gained national recognition as chef at La Réserve and Restaurant Raphael in New York. He then moved abroad and served an *estagiere* apprenticeship in the kitchens of Guy Savoy, Michael Pasquet, Gerard Besson, Taillevant, Le Toit de Passey, Chiberta, and Le Pré Catélan. After returning to New York, Thomas opened Rakel. Four years later, he moved to California to become executive chef of Checkers Hotel in Los Angeles.

I first became acquainted with Patrick through various charity events in New York. He had just opened Metro, and I had just opened Rakel. Unfortunately, both restaurants also closed about the same time, and both Patrick and I landed in Los Angeles. Patrick was executive chef at Bicé, and I was executive chef at Checkers. Soon after arriving in Los Angeles we both participated in a charity event with several other chefs. On the day of the event Patrick and I arrived with our mise-en-place all ready to go. We chatted a little as we watched several of the other chefs scramble to get prepared. Patrick turned to me, smiled, shook his head, and said, "They'd never make it in New York." From that point on we shared a kinship as two chefs "banished" from New York.

I miss the cuisine, and I miss the smile, but most of all I miss the humor—"Patrick-style."

Serves 4

4 vine-ripened tomatoes

1 cup canola oil

MARMALADE

10 large navel oranges

¼ cup honey

½ cup sherry vinegar

¾ cup diced sweet onion

———

2 shallots, minced

Freshly ground black pepper

Pinch of gray salt
(or sea salt)

Basil-Infused Extra Virgin
Olive Oil (recipe follows)

To prepare the tomatoes:
Remove the core and lightly
score the bottom of the
tomatoes. Immerse the tomatoes in boiling water for 15
to 20 seconds, remove them
immediately, and plunge
them into ice water. Peel
the tomatoes; the skin
should be easy to remove.
Reserve the skin for the fried
garnish. Using a meat slicer
or sharp knife, slice the
tomatoes as thinly as possible. Reassemble the tomatoes
in their original shapes and
refrigerate for 1 hour, or
until thoroughly chilled.

**To prepare the tomato
skins:** Heat the canola oil in
a small saucepan until very
hot. Add the tomato skins
and fry for 1 to 2 minutes,
or until crispy.

To prepare the marmalade:
Zest the oranges and reserve.
Peel the oranges, separate
the segments, and remove
the membranes. In a heavy-
bottomed pot, cook the
honey and sherry vinegar
over medium heat until they
begin to caramelize. Add the
orange zest, onion, and
orange segments, lower the
heat, and continue cooking
for 30 to 40 minutes, or
until the mixture reaches a
marmalade consistency.
Remove from the heat
and transfer to a plastic
container. Set aside to cool
slightly, then refrigerate
until chilled.

Place a tomato in the center
of each plate and alternate
seasoning to taste between
each slice with the shallots,
pepper, and gray salt. Top
each tomato with a spoonful
of the marmalade and gar-
nish with the fried tomato
skins. Drizzle the Basil-
Infused Extra Virgin Olive
Oil around the plate.

**Basil-Infused Extra Virgin
Olive Oil**

2 tablespoons kosher salt

3 cups tightly packed
basil leaves

2 cups extra virgin olive oil

Bring 4 to 5 quarts of water to
a full boil in a large saucepan,
add the kosher salt and basil
and blanch for 45 seconds.
Drain the basil in a strainer
and cool under running
water. Squeeze the excess
water from the basil and place
it in a blender with the olive
oil. Blend at low speed just to
break up the leaves. Once the
basil begins to blend freely,
increase the speed to high
and continue blending for
3 to 4 minutes. Transfer the
mixture to a glass container
with a tight-fitting lid and
refrigerate overnight; the
refrigeration ensures an
intensely flavored and richly
colored oil.

Secure a piece of cheesecloth
around the rim of a shallow,
wide-mouthed container.
Slowly pour the oil over
the cheesecloth to strain it;
this will take up to 1 hour,
depending on the temperature
of the oil. After the oil has
completely strained through,
gently wring the cheesecloth
over the mouth of the container for maximum extrac-
tion. The remaining basil
pulp may be used in pesto,
as a marinade for chicken,
in sauces, or on pasta.

The infused extra virgin
olive oil may be stored in the
refrigerator for 3 to 4 weeks.

Vine-Ripened Tomato Salad

with a Navel Orange
and Onion Marmalade

*The success of this
dish rests solely
on the quality of
the tomatoes.
Make sure you
choose firm,
ripe tomatoes.*

157

Michael Lomonaco

Michael Lomonaco, the chef and director of Windows on the World, graduated from New York City Technical College in 1984. He spent the next three years working in some of New York's more prestigious restaurants, including Le Cirque and Maxwell's Plum. In 1989 he accepted the position of executive chef at the "21" Club. It was in this position that the accolades began pouring in: Highly favorable reviews in magazines and newspapers, including *New York Magazine*, *Gourmet*, *Food & Wine*, the *New York Times*, and *Newsday*, credited Michael with scaling heights never before attained at the 75-year-old former speakeasy.

Michael is the host of *Michael's Place* on the Television Food Network and author of the best-selling *"21" Cookbook*.

When I think of Patrick I think of a generous and kind person. His humanity, his great love for his family, his humility regarding his achievements, his gentle and easy smile—all of these images rush to mind. I wish there had been time to have known him better, to have known his favorite little restaurant or movie or book. But time is fleeting and we must be content to have had any time at all together.

I met Patrick in 1982. He was then the much-acclaimed chef at New York's Odeon, and I was an actor between jobs. To pay my rent, I was driving a taxi. I was a devoted foodie and a serious amateur cook and knew all of the hot restaurants and important chefs in town. When the call came in at 12:45 A.M. to pick up the chef at the Odeon and take him home, I knew Patrick Clark would be my passenger. I really wanted to meet this celebrated chef and have an opportunity to ask a few key questions.

I got more than I dreamed possible. Patrick not only answered my questions, he freely offered advice. He encouraged me to seek out a life in the kitchen. *It was hard work, yes, but well worth the effort. He described for me his culinary training at New York City Technical College, his time abroad, and his experiences in New York. He even offered information about his upbringing as the son of a chef. His passion was right there on his sleeve, and he was proud. He inspired me, and changed my life forever, in a thirty-five–minute ride out to Brooklyn. I entered the restaurant program at New York City Technical just a few months later and graduated from Patrick's alma mater.*

I will always be indebted to Patrick Clark for his generous insight, encouragement, and support—support that continued throughout the fifteen years of our friendship. On behalf of the many other young people you've mentored as well as for all you've given me, I want to thank you, Patrick.

Better and Hotter Tijuana Caesar

This refreshing salad is a spicy twist on a traditional caesar.

Serves 4 to 6

½ ripe avocado, peeled, pitted, and sliced

Juice of 1 lime (about 2 tablespoons)

2 large cloves garlic, peeled and finely chopped

2 tablespoons Dijon mustard

2 tablespoons white wine vinegar

1 fresh jalapeño pepper, seeded, and chopped

¼ teaspoon salt

½ cup extra virgin olive oil

1 head romaine lettuce, coarse outer leaves discarded, washed and dried, and torn into bite-size pieces

1 can anchovy fillets (2-ounce), drained and finely chopped

Freshly ground black pepper

¼ cup freshly grated Monterey Jack cheese

4 flour tortillas, grilled and sliced

To prepare the salad:
Combine the sliced avocado and lime juice in a wooden bowl, mashing the avocado with the back of a spoon. Add the garlic, mustard, vinegar, jalapeño, and salt and stir until the mixture is creamy. Add ¼ cup of the olive oil and stir to incorporate. Add the romaine and stir to coat completely. Stir in the remaining ¼ cup olive oil in a slow, steady stream and add the anchovies, evenly distributing the chopped bits. Season with pepper to taste. Add the Jack cheese and grilled tortillas and toss the salad again to coat the greens evenly.

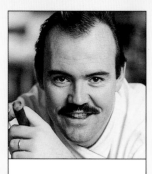

Charlie Palmer

Charlie Palmer is one of the most highly regarded chefs in the United States. He is best known as the chef and owner of New York's Aureole, which he opened in 1988. Raised in upstate New York, Charlie received his formal training at the Culinary Institute of America. His first job after graduating was at New York's La Côte Basque. After three years working there alongside chef Jean-Jacques Rachou, Charlie left to become head chef at the Waccabuc Country Club in Westchester County, New York. In 1983 Charlie became executive chef at the River Café.

Charlie has received numerous awards, including the James Beard Foundation's 1997 Best Chef: New York, the 1996 *Restaurants & Institutions* Ivy Award, and member status in Relais & Chateaux in 1997.

There are many great chefs in this country who possess a variety of talents, but very **few have the combination of qualities that Patrick offered** *as a professional and, more important, as a friend.*

Chilled Snap Pea Soup

This soup makes an elegant starter for a dinner party, and it's simple to prepare.

Serves 6

⅛ teaspoon saffron threads

3 carrots, peeled and cut into 18 ½-inch-thick discs

———

¾ pound snap peas, ends trimmed

4 cups low-sodium vegetable stock

¼ cup chopped scallions

¼ cup diced celery

1 tablespoon minced fresh oregano

1 teaspoon coarse salt

¾ teaspoon freshly ground white pepper

½ cup plain nonfat yogurt

6 sprigs oregano

To prepare the carrots:
Place 3 cups of water and the saffron in a small saucepan over medium-high heat and bring to a boil. Add the carrots, return to a boil, and then remove from the heat and allow the carrots to cool in the saffron water. The carrots should be just tender and well flavored with saffron. When cool, drain the carrots and pat dry. Cover and refrigerate until ready to serve.

To prepare the soup:
Bring 4 cups of water to a boil in a saucepan. Add the peas and cook over high heat for 30 seconds, or until crisp-tender and bright green. Immediately remove the peas from the heat and drain in a sieve. Rinse the peas under cold running water until well chilled, then drain and dry them well. Refrigerate 18 of the snap peas in a covered container until ready to serve.

Bring the vegetable stock to a boil in a large saucepan over medium-high heat. Add the remaining snap peas, the scallions, celery, minced oregano, salt, and pepper, and return to a boil. Immediately lower the heat and simmer for 3 minutes. Pour the soup into a blender or a food processor fitted with the metal blade and process until smooth. Pour into a glass or metal bowl and place in an ice bath to cool quickly. Cover and refrigerate for 4 hours, or until well chilled.

Just prior to serving, whisk the yogurt into the soup and adjust seasonings to taste.

Divide the soup evenly among 6 chilled shallow soup plates. Float 3 carrot discs and 3 of the reserved snap peas in each bowl. Garnish with a sprig of oregano and serve immediately.

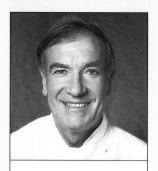

162

Alain Sailhac

Alain began his culinary career at the age of fourteen, working as an apprentice at the Capion in Millau, France. From 1954 to 1956, he refined his cooking skills in Paris, working in restaurants at the Hotel Claridge and Normandie Hotel and later at Club Med and Relais Gastronomique. He next honed his talents at the Grand Hotel in Guadeloupe and in Rhodes, and at Le Perroquet, in Chicago. In the 1970s Alain moved to New York City, where he was awarded the coveted four stars from the *New York Times* at Le Cygne restaurant before moving on to Le Cirque, the "21" Club, and the Plaza Hotel.

Alain Sailhac joined the French Culinary Institute as dean of culinary studies in 1991, where he oversees both the faculty and students.

I remember the first time I saw Patrick Clark. I dined at the restaurant— Metro, in New York City—where he was chef. At the end of the meal I decided to visit the kitchen. **When I opened the door, I was absolutely stunned and forever impressed**—*you could not see the kitchen for this commanding, remarkable chef.*

Salad of Artichoke, Cucumber, and Tomato

The artichokes can be prepared earlier in the day. Just layer them on waxed paper, wrap them in plastic wrap, and refrigerate until ready to use.

Serves 4

VINAIGRETTE

2 tablespoons balsamic vinegar

6 tablespoons olive oil

½ teaspoon peeled and grated fresh ginger

Salt and pepper

SALAD

2 seedless cucumbers, peeled

4 artichokes

1 lemon, halved

1 tablespoon flour

2 tablespoons plus ¼ teaspoon olive oil

2 teaspoons salt plus additional to taste

4¼ cups water

Freshly ground black pepper

4 plum tomatoes

4 cups mesclun greens

To prepare the vinaigrette: Whisk together the balsamic vinegar, olive oil, ginger, and salt and pepper to taste.

To prepare the salad: Using a vegetable peeler, shave the cucumbers into paper-thin strips. Store the strips in ice water until ready to use.

To prepare the artichokes: Cut off the tops and, using a paring knife, trim the stem and remove the outer layer of leaves. Rub the artichokes with a lemon half to prevent discoloration and discard the lemon half. In a saucepan, combine the flour, olive oil, the 2 teaspoons salt, and the juice of the remaining lemon half. Slowly add the water and mix well. Add the artichokes to the pan, bring to a boil, and simmer for 7 minutes. Drain the artichoke and let cool. When cool, thinly slice the artichokes. Season the slices to taste with salt and pepper and moisten with some of the vinaigrette.

To assemble the salad: Peel and seed the tomatoes, then julienne.

Drain the cucumber strips and dry with a clean kitchen towel. In a bowl, combine one half of the cucumber strips with the tomato strips and toss with some of the vinaigrette. In a separate bowl, toss the mesclun greens with the remaining vinaigrette. Fan the artichoke slices around the edge of each plate and mound some of the mesclun greens in the center. Place some of the tomato mixture on top of the mesclun and mound the remaining cucumber on the top of the tomato mixture.

Jimmy Sneed

Jimmy Sneed's culinary initia-
tion came while translating
for American students at Le
Cordon Bleu. It was there
that he was exposed to the
philosophy of the grand cuisine. After a year in Paris,
Jimmy returned to the United
States to pursue a culinary
career and spent the next
seven years under the tute-
lage of Jean-Louis Palladin
and Guenter Seeger.

Jimmy and his partner, Adam
Steely, opened The Frog and
the Redneck in Richmond,
Virginia, in April 1993. Six
months after opening, the
restaurant was named One
of the Best New Restaurants
in America by *Esquire
Magazine*. It has since been
written about in *Gourmet,
Bon Appetit, USA Today,*
the *New York Times*, and
numerous other publications.

*I first met Patrick when he arrived in Washington, D.C., as chef of the Hay
Adams Hotel. I must confess to some feelings of propriety on behalf of my
friends in the D.C. restaurant community, when Patrick won the James
Beard Award for the region over such talented local chefs as Roberto Donna,
Bob Kinkead, Jeff Buben, and others.*

**But as I came to know him and his cooking, those feelings were
quickly replaced by a sense of camaraderie and a shared vision of
food. It was easy to become friends with Patrick.**

*In the spring of '96 I invited Patrick to be a featured guest chef at my
restaurant in Richmond. He arrived with an appetite. "Where can we get
a real Southern breakfast?" he asked. My kind of chef. His event was sold
out and a huge hit with the Richmond dining crowd.*

*Patrick once again offered his services for an event in May 1998, in
Richmond, to help raise funds for spinal muscular atrophy, a disease that
mostly affects kids. He did this despite the fact that he was waiting for a
heart transplant. Always generous, always willing—I'll miss him.*

Cream of Ramp Soup

with Surrey Ham

If you can't find ramps, baby leeks also work well.

Serves 6

1 pound ramps, cleaned and washed

¼ cup olive oil

2½ cups (approximately) chicken stock

6 shallots, sliced

1 onion, sliced

1 cup white wine

¾ cup plus 2 tablespoons heavy cream

Sea salt and freshly ground black pepper

½ pound Surrey ham, diced

2 tablespoons chopped chives

To prepare the ramps:
Sauté the ramps in 2 tablespoons of the olive oil in a hot pan, until tender. Add enough of the chicken stock to stop the cooking process. Purée the mixture in a blender or a food processor fitted with a metal blade, adding additional stock as needed to facilitate puréeing. Set aside.

To prepare the cream base:
Heat a heavy saucepan and add the remaining 2 tablespoons olive oil. Add the shallots and onion and cook, stirring continuously, until the onion is translucent. Add the white wine and reduce over high heat until almost completely dry. Add 1 cup of the chicken stock and reduce until nearly dry. Add the heavy cream and simmer until reduced by one-fifth. Strain through a fine-mesh sieve.

To prepare the soup:
Mix the cream base with the ramp purée. Adjust the consistency with the remaining stock and season to taste with salt and pepper.

To serve, pour the soup into hot soup bowls and sprinkle with the ham and chives.

Charlie Trotter

Charlie Trotter is chef and owner of Charlie Trotter's, in Chicago. Charlie Trotter's has been recognized by many prestigious institutions, garnering Relais & Chateaux: Relais Gourmand, Mobil Five Stars, AAA Five Diamonds, and the James Beard Foundation's Best Chef: Midwest. In 1998 Charlie Trotter's was named Best Restaurant in the World for Food and Wine by *Wine Spectator.*

Charlie began cooking in 1982, embarking on an intense four-year period of work, study, and travel that included stints with chefs Norman Van Aken, Bradley Ogden, and Gordon Sinclair. Through this experience he began to shape the concept of his dream restaurant, which became a reality in 1987.

Charlie Trotter is the author of six cookbooks, including *Charlie Trotter's, Gourmet Cooking for Dummies*, and the companion book to his cooking show *The Kitchen Sessions with Charlie Trotter.*

*I remember the year we hosted a James Beard fundraising dinner at the restaurant and Patrick was one of our featured chefs. Two highlights of his visit remain vivid in my memory. One highlight was watching his incredible facial expressions while he worked on and stirred the polenta for his rabbit preparation—***it was a mixture of joy, intensity, passion, and love. Few people work with that range of emotion.** *The second highlight took place that evening. After I had entertained Patrick and the other visiting chefs with an elaborate food and wine dinner, Patrick had a question for me: "Where can I get the best ribs in Chicago?" My wife, Lynn, promptly went to four rib places and rounded up an assortment. When they were presented to Patrick, he decided that the Château d'Yquem he was sipping went ideally with the ribs. What an amazing human being!*

Israeli Couscous Salad

with Preserved Shiitake Mushrooms, Asparagus, and Four Herb–Parmesan Cheese Vinaigrette

The asparagus and mushrooms in this dish would go well with a delicate, earthy wine with racy acidity, like a Weissenkirchner "Steinriegl" Federspiel Riesling, from Franz Prager. Richer Loire Valley wines will also work well.

Serves 4 to 6

1½ cups Israeli couscous

3 tablespoons olive oil

___

2 cups shiitake mushrooms, stemmed, and julienned

2 cups pickling juice, (recipe follows)

VINAIGRETTE

1 large shallot, minced

⅓ cup freshly squeezed lemon juice

1 cup extra virgin olive oil

2 tablespoons chopped chives

2 tablespoons chopped fresh basil

2 tablespoons chopped chervil

2 tablespoons chopped fresh thyme

⅓ cup freshly grated Parmesan cheese

Salt and freshly ground black pepper

___

12 spears asparagus, cleaned, blanched, and cut into 1-inch pieces on the diagonal

2 cups red or yellow teardrop tomatoes, halved

1 small red onion, finely julienned

1 English cucumber, diced

Salt and freshly ground black pepper

___

2 tablespoons shaved Parmesan cheese

4 teaspoons chives, cut into 1-inch long pieces on the diagonal

To prepare the Israeli couscous: Rinse the couscous under cold water until the water runs clear. Put the couscous in a large saucepan and cover with 3 cups of water. Bring the mixture to a simmer and cook for 15 to 20 minutes, or until the couscous is cooked al dente. Transfer the couscous to a colander and immediately rinse with cold water to remove any excess starch. Toss with of the olive oil and refrigerate until needed.

To prepare the mushrooms: Place the mushrooms in the pickling juice and refrigerate for 1 hour. Remove the preserved shiitakes from the pickling juice. (The pickling juice may be stored in the refrigerator for up to 1 month for another use.)

To prepare the vinaigrette: Put the shallot and lemon juice in a medium bowl and slowly whisk in the olive oil. Add the chopped herbs and grated Parmesan cheese and season to taste with salt and pepper.

To prepare the salad: Put the Israeli couscous in a large bowl and add the shiitake mushrooms, asparagus, tomatoes, red onion, and cucumber. Toss together and fold in three quarters of the vinaigrette. Season to taste with salt and pepper.

To serve, place a mound of the salad in the center of each plate and spoon some of the remaining vinaigrette around the salad. Sprinkle the salad with the shaved Parmesan cheese and the chives, and top with freshly ground black pepper.

Pickling Juice

YIELD: 2 CUPS

1 cup water

½ cup rice vinegar

⅓ cup plus 2 tablespoons sugar

2 tablespoons kosher salt

1 whole clove

1 teaspoon mustard seed

1 teaspoon black peppercorns

1 teaspoon peeled and chopped fresh ginger

½ fresh jalapeño, seeded and chopped

Combine all of the ingredients in a small saucepan and bring to a simmer, allowing the salt and sugar to completely dissolve. Let cool and use as needed.

Norman Van Aken

Norman Van Aken is the chef and owner of the award-winning NORMAN'S, in the historic Coral Gables section of Miami. He is widely credited as the father of New World Cuisine, and he coined the term "Fusion Cuisine." Chef Van Aken has cooked, consulted, written, and lectured internationally on New World Cuisine. He has appeared on CNN, *Good Morning America*, *CBS This Morning*, *TV Food Network*, *Emeril Live*, and many other television programs. Chef Van Aken is celebrity consulting chef for United Airlines for flights to and from all of Latin America and the Caribbean.

Charlie Trotter had asked me to join him and nine other chefs from all around the country to cook a James Beard Foundation dinner. I remember his excitement when he told me that I would have a chance to meet Patrick Clark. "You are gonna love this guy!"

I arrived at the kitchen early in the morning because I knew that work space was going to be at a premium. Patrick was already there and rocking through a mountain of mise-en-place that would go into his rabbit dish. I surveyed the scene around him. A case of seedless grapes was being meticulously peeled; tiny rabbit tenderloins were being carefully cleaned; a small pile of herbs was being plucked. But what really captured my attention was when I looked on the floor and saw an entire case of red wine that had been opened, with the corks yanked straight through the capsules. The bottles looked like he had willed them to explode, shooting the wine in a perfect arc into a pot. The wine was now vigorously reducing on the stove behind him. How much sauce could he need, I wondered, for a dinner that would include twelve courses for only 100 guests?

After warm hellos and handshakes, I had to ask. "Patrick, just how much do you take the wine down for this sauce?" He smiled that dazzling, big Patrick Clark smile, and said, simply, "To about a cup or so."

Charlie was right. I loved him. **Just for that singular illustration of intensity and all of the commitment it bespoke of his cuisine.**

That is only one of the incidents I remember fondly when I think about Patrick.

Shanghai Noodle Salad

This dish would work well with the addition of flank steak or smoked meat such as chicken or ham.

Serves 4 to 6

VINAIGRETTE

1½ teaspoons garlic, finely minced

1½ teaspoons peeled and finely minced fresh ginger

2 tablespoons chopped cilantro

½ teaspoon salt

½ teaspoon freshly ground black pepper

⅓ cup red wine vinegar

⅓ cup soy sauce

1 tablespoon hot chile oil

⅓ cup sesame oil

NOODLE SALAD

3 cups cooked Shanghai noodles (about 7½ ounces)

1 tablespoon sesame oil

1½ cups finely julienned mixed vegetables (such as napa or purple cabbage, carrot, cucumber, daikon, blanched snow peas or asparagus, or bell peppers)

1 cup diced avocado

1 cup diced tofu

To prepare the vinaigrette: Whisk together all of the ingredients in a bowl and refrigerate until ready to use. (This can be made a day ahead.)

To prepare the salad: In a large bowl, toss the Shanghai noodles with the sesame oil, cover, and refrigerate until chilled. Add the remaining ingredients to the bowl with the noodles and toss with enough of the vinaigrette to coat lightly.

Place some of the noodle salad in each bowl and serve with a pair of chopsticks.

B. Whitmer

170

Brian Whitmer

Brian Whitmer is executive chef and managing partner of Moose's in San Francisco. He started his career at the American Restaurant in Kansas City. At age twenty-one he moved to New York as banquet chef at Tavern on the Green, and with Daniel Boulud at the Polo in the Westbury Hotel. In 1984 he became opening sous chef of Campton Place in San Francisco. Brian left there to head his first restaurant, Manhattan's Montrachet, which won three stars in *The New York Times Guide to Restaurants*. In 1988 he became executive chef of the Highlands Inn in Carmel, California, where he gained national acclaim. In 1995 Brian opened Montrio, in Monterey. *Esquire's* John Mariani ranked Montrio the Restaurant of the Year, and called Brian one of America's finest chefs.

One of my fondest memories with Pat was in the early 1990s, when he was chef at Bicé in Beverly Hills. I picked him up after work, and we went downtown to the Checkers Hotel to hang out in the kitchen with our good friend chef Thomas Keller. We watched plates go out of the kitchen and talked food, as chefs are always so happy to do. From there we went to the counter at Chinois on Main Street in Santa Monica. The image that remains in my memory is this: Pat and I, sitting at that bustling counter just feet away from the cooks who were preparing food at a dizzying pace while we ate, and ate, and ate, ordering plate after plate, **loving the food, loving the act of eating, loving the action, and, most of all, savoring each other's precious company.**

Dungeness Crab Salad

with Watsonville Artichokes, Blue Lake Beans and Meyer Lemon Vinaigrette

If you're really adventurous you can purchase a whole crab, cook it, and clean the crabmeat yourself.

Serves 4

ARTICHOKES

½ small yellow onion, cut into large dice

2 cloves garlic, peeled and smashed

1 carrot, peeled and cut into large dice

2 tablespoons extra virgin olive oil

½ cup white wine

1½ cups chicken stock

2 sprigs thyme

2 artichokes, peeled of hard outer layer and tops removed

VINAIGRETTE

3 tablespoons freshly squeezed Meyer lemon juice

1 teaspoon sugar

3 tablespoons extra virgin olive oil

Salt and freshly ground black pepper

———

4 bunches watercress, stemmed

1 head radicchio or treviso, julienned

2 spears endive, cut thinly lengthwise

1 cup mixed Blue Lake and yellow wax string beans, snipped, blanched, and halved lengthwise

6 ounces cleaned Dungeness or Maine crabmeat

1 bunch chives, finely chopped (optional)

To prepare the artichokes: Sauté the onion, garlic, and carrot in the olive oil until translucent. Add the white wine, chicken stock, thyme, and artichokes and cook, covered, for 20 minutes, or until tender. Remove from the heat and cool the artichokes in the liquid, then strain out and discard the other vegetables, reserving the liquid and the artichokes.

To prepare the vinaigrette: In a bowl, whisk together the lemon juice, sugar, ½ cup of the artichoke cooking liquid, and the olive oil, and season to taste with salt and pepper.

To prepare the salad: Put the watercress, radicchio, endive, and beans in a large bowl and toss with the vinaigrette.

Place a mound of the salad in the center of each plate, top with some of the crabmeat, and sprinkle with chives.

Alain Ducasse

Alain Ducasse started his
apprenticeship at the age of
sixteen at the restaurant the
Pavillon Landals in Soustons.
After attending the Bordeaux
School of Hotel and Catering
Management, he entered
Michel Guerard's establish-
ment in Eugénie-Les-Bains. In
1977 Alain moved to Le
Moulin de Mougins, and then
on to Mionnay. Three years
later he became the chef at
L'Amandier in Mougins, and
the next year he took over La
Terrasse, where he obtained
two Michelin stars. In 1987
Alain became the chef at Le
Louis XV, in the Hotel de
Paris, in Monaco. In 1995 he
opened La Bastide de
Moustiers, a country inn, in
Provence. In 1996 he opened
the restaurant Alain Ducasse,
in the Le Parc Westin
Demeure Hôtel, in Paris.

*I remember Patrick as a loyal colleague. He was one of my first commis
of Michel Guerard's restaurant, and he followed me for the opening of Regine's
in New York.* **He was a talented young chef with a tremendous will to
succeed.** *Thanks to his character and culinary skills, he was able to run one
of the best restaurants of its kind, the Tavern on the Green.*

Tuna Loin

with Green Peppers
and Piment d'Espelette

It is best to use sushi-grade tuna for this dish.

Serves 6

6 green bell peppers, halved
lengthwise, seeded, and
deribbed

1 onion, minced

¼ cup plus 1 tablespoon
extra virgin olive oil

1 clove garlic, peeled

1 slice prosciutto, diced

Fleur de sel (French sea salt)

1 teaspoon piment
d'espelette or freshly
ground black pepper

18 ounces tuna loin

1 tablespoon sherry vinegar

1 tablespoon chopped
flat-leaf parsley

To prepare the green pepper:
Cut the pepper halves into
2-inch-long strips. Sauté the
strips and onion in 2 tablespoons of the olive oil over
high heat for 2 minutes and
then lower the heat. Crush
the garlic with the flat side
of a chef's knife. In a small
bowl, combine the garlic,
prosciutto, fleur de sel, and
piment d'espelette. Add the
mixture to the green peppers
and cook for 3 minutes.

To prepare the tuna:
In a hot sauté pan coated
with 2 tablespoons of the
olive oil, cook the tuna loin
for 1 minute on each side.
Remove the tuna from the
pan and set it aside to rest
for 3 minutes. The interior
should be cooked to medium.
Cut the tuna into thin slices.

Add the sherry vinegar to
the pan and stir to deglaze.

To serve, spoon the green
pepper mixture into the
center of each chilled plate
and top with the tuna slices.
Coat the tuna with some of
the vinegar from the pan and
the remaining 1 tablespoon
olive oil. Sprinkle the parsley
around the plates.

Mark Filippo

After attending the New York City Technical College, Mark worked at Le Chantilly in New York City. He worked with some of Westchester County's finest chefs, including Maxime Ribera, and then went on to the Quilted Giraffe in New York City. In 1981 Mark opened his dream restaurant, Jillyflowers; it became an overnight success. Seven years later, Mark went into consulting so that he could work with other chefs but maintain a reasonable home life.

In 1989 Patrick Clark offered Mark a job at Metro, in New York, which he accepted and where he worked until 1990, when he left to work briefly with Gray Kunz. Later that year he became the sous chef at La Panetière, where he remained until 1995, when he became the chef at Cafe Mezé.

Patrick and I met in 1976 at the New York City College Hotel & Restaurant School. Professor Thomas Ahrens introduced us, and I attended many classes with Patrick's wife, Lynette. We developed a rare and special friendship that grew stronger over the years as we shared personal and career highs and lows. We often exchanged culinary ideas while cooking together at school, and later, at Patrick's New York restaurant, Metro. Patrick was a true inspiration.

Throughout our friendship we shared many experiences, participating in various fundraisers and events all over the United States and in Japan. Eating with Patrick in the world's great restaurants was always exciting, and God help me if I told him not to eat so much!

What I admired most about my great friend was his commitment to his family. *He was a truly wonderful father and husband, as well as a great chef. Patrick Clark will always be my dear friend.*

Sautéed Shrimp, Asparagus, and Oyster Mushrooms
with Thyme-Lemon Sauce

The silky texture of the oyster mushrooms in this dish is balanced by the crispy asparagus and the tender shrimp.

Serves 4

THYME-LEMON SAUCE

10 pounds chicken bones

2 cups red wine

1 onion, sliced

3 celery stalks, coarsely chopped

1 leek, washed thoroughly and chopped

1 head of garlic, divided in half

2 cups white wine

1 tablespoon whole white peppercorns

5 quarts chicken stock

1/4 cup unsalted butter

1 ounce fresh thyme

2 tablespoons chopped fresh parsley

1/4 cup freshly squeezed lemon juice

1 tablespoon chopped garlic

Salt and freshly ground black pepper

24 asparagus spears, peeled and cut into 3-inch lengths

1 pound small oyster mushrooms

2 tablespoons olive oil

1 tablespoon chopped fresh parsley

1 1/2 teaspoons chopped garlic

Salt and freshly ground black pepper

1 tablespoon unsalted butter

32 shrimp, peeled, deveined, and seasoned with salt and pepper

4 sprigs thyme

To prepare the sauce: Preheat the oven to 400°. Place the chicken bones in a heavy roasting pan and roast in the oven for 1 hour, or until lightly browned. Carefully remove the bones from the roasting pan and place them in a heavy-bottomed, 2 1/2-gallon pot. Add the red wine and reduce over medium heat to 1/2 cup.

Drain the grease from the roasting pan and place the pan over medium heat. Add the onion, celery, leek, and garlic halves and sauté for 10 minutes, or until lightly browned. Drain the vegetables and place them in a 4-quart saucepan. Add the white wine and reduce over medium heat to 1/2 cup. Add the vegetable mixture, white peppercorns, and chicken stock to the pot with the roasted chicken bones and bring to a boil over high heat. Reduce the heat and simmer slowly, uncovered, for 4 hours.

Strain the chicken stock through a fine-mesh sieve into a 4-quart saucepan and discard the vegetables and bones. Cook over medium heat until the liquid is reduced by half. Set aside 1 1/4 cups of the stock and freeze the remainder for later use.

Heat the butter over medium heat in a heavy-bottomed 2-quart saucepan until it is medium brown in color. Working quickly, whisk in the thyme, parsley, lemon juice, and the chopped garlic. Add the reserved chicken stock and simmer over medium heat for 5 minutes. Season to taste with salt and pepper. Strain through a fine-mesh sieve into a saucepan and keep warm over low heat.

To prepare the asparagus: Blanch the asparagus in boiling, salted water for 1 minute. Remove the asparagus to an ice bath for 2 minutes, and then drain.

To prepare the mushrooms: Sauté the mushrooms in 1 tablespoon of the olive oil in a heavy-bottomed sauté pan over medium heat for 5 minutes. Add the parsley, garlic, and salt and pepper to taste, and stir to combine. Set aside.

To prepare the shrimp: Add the remaining 1 tablespoon olive oil, the butter, and the shrimp to a 12-inch, heavy-bottomed sauté pan and cook over high heat for 2 minutes, stirring twice. Add the asparagus and oyster mushrooms and cook for 1 minute. Add the Thyme-Lemon sauce, stir, and remove from the heat.

Divide the shrimp and vegetables evenly among 4 warmed, shallow soup bowls. Pour 1/4 cup of sauce in each bowl and place a thyme sprig in the center of each bowl.

Bob Kinkead

Bob Kinkead is a self-trained chef who began his career as a teenager working summers in restaurants on Cape Cod. Bob's experience includes Joseph's in Boston; the Sheraton Commander Hotel and the Harvest Restaurant in Cambridge, Massachusetts; and Chillingsworth, in Brewster, Massachusetts. In 1985 Bob signed on as consulting chef of Twenty-One Federal in Nantucket, Massachusetts, later becoming executive chef and partner. In 1987 he moved to Washington, D.C., to supervise the planning, design and construction of Twenty-One Federal. In 1993 Bob opened his newest restaurant in Washington, D.C., Kinkead's, an American brasserie-style restaurant featuring fresh seafood.

Bob has received numerous local and national awards, including four James Beard Award nominations for Best Chef: Mid-Atlantic. He was selected as a 1992 James Beard Foundation Great Regional Chef.

Patrick and I were often paired at charity events and fundraisers. We worked well together and enjoyed seeing one another. He was always quick to laugh, and I highly value a great sense of humor. He was a great cook, too. Patrick continually came up with creative and delicious dishes for every event. **He was one of the very few chefs in America who could continually put an original twist on his cooking.** *But most of all, Patrick was a very nice man, and I was proud to call him my friend.*

Serves 8

CAULIFLOWER FLAN

½ small head cauliflower, cut into florets (2 cups)

1 cup heavy whipping cream

1 cup milk

2 cloves garlic, peeled

Salt and freshly ground white pepper

2 eggs

1 egg yolk

¼ cup freshly grated Parmesan cheese

Vegetable oil cooking spray

SHERRY BEET SAUCE

⅓ cup sherry

⅓ cup sherry vinegar

½ cup white wine

3 shiitake mushrooms, sliced

1 clove garlic, minced

½ teaspoon fresh thyme leaves

1 shallot, minced

½ teaspoon whole black peppercorns

1 cup reduced chicken stock

2 cups fresh beet juice (about 6 to 8 large beets)

½ cup butter

Salt and freshly ground black pepper

——

¼ cup butter

6 ounces walnuts, toasted

2 cups bread crumbs

Salt and freshly ground black pepper

8 4-ounce rockfish fillets or other firm white fish, skinned

⅓ cup buttermilk

Peanut or vegetable oil for cooking

——

2 red beets, peeled, cooked and julienned

2 tablespoons butter

To prepare the flans:
Bring the cauliflower, cream, milk, garlic, and salt and pepper to taste to a boil in a nonreactive saucepan and cook until the cauliflower is tender. Remove from the heat and let cool, then purée in a blender with the eggs, egg yolk, and Parmesan cheese. (The flan may be prepared to this point up to 1 day ahead.)

Preheat the oven to 300°. Spray eight 2-ounce molds or plastic cups, with vegetable oil cooking spray and pour in the cauliflower mixture. Place the molds in a water bath and bake for 2½ to 3 hours, or until the flans are set. (A toothpick inserted in the center should come out clean.) Keep in a warm place until ready to serve.

Note: It is impractical to make this recipe in less quantity. You will have more than you need, but the cauliflower mixture will keep for a few days in the refrigerator.

To prepare the beet sauce:
Simmer the sherry, sherry vinegar, white wine, shiitakes, garlic, thyme leaves, shallot, and peppercorns in a non-reactive saucepan until reduced by half. Strain through a fine-mesh chinois, add the reduced chicken stock, and cook until reduced by two-thirds. Add the beet juice, increase the heat, and bring to a boil for 5 minutes. Whisk in the butter and season to taste with salt and pepper. The sauce should have the consistency of light cream; if it does not, add more butter. Remove the sauce from the heat, and keep warm.

To prepare the rockfish:
Melt the butter in a saucepan and keep warm. In a food processor combine the walnuts, bread crumbs, salt and pepper to taste, and melted butter and pulse 3 to 4 times, or just until chopped and mixed well. Dredge one side of the rockfish fillets in the buttermilk and then in the walnut-crumb mixture.

Preheat the oven to 400°. Sauté the fish in the peanut oil over medium-high heat, breaded side down, until crispy. Turn the fillets over, place the pan in the oven, and cook for 5 to 7 minutes, or until cooked through.

To prepare the beets:
Sauté the beets in the butter and keep warm.

To serve, ladle ¼ cup of the sauce on each warmed plate. Place some of the julienned beets in the center of each plate and top with a rockfish fillet. Unmold the flans and place one alongside the fish.

Walnut-Crusted Chesapeake Rockfish

with Sherry Beet Sauce and Cauliflower Flan

A small spoonful of horseradish crème fraîche on the fish makes a great addition to this dish.

Emeril Lagasse

Emeril is the chef and proprietor of five restaurants. Three—Emeril's Restaurant, Nola Restaurant, and Delmonico's Restaurant and Bar—are located in New Orleans. Emeril's New Orleans Fish House is in Las Vegas, and Emeril's Orlando is located in Universal Studios Citiwalk.

After receiving his doctorate from Johnson and Wales University, Emeril Lagasse practiced his art in several fine restaurants in New York, Boston, and Philadelphia before heading south to New Orleans. He was lured to "the Big Easy" by Dick and Ella Brennan of Commander's Palace, where he was executive chef for almost eight years.

Chef Lagasse is the host of the Food Network's *The Essence of Emeril* and *Emeril Live* and is the author of *Emeril's New New Orleans Cooking, Louisiana Real & Rustic, Emeril's Creole Christmas*, and *Emeril's TV Dinners*.

I have so many memories of Patrick, but there is one that stands out above the rest. Several years ago I hosted a fundraising dinner in New Orleans for the James Beard Foundation. Patrick was one of the chefs invited to prepare a course for the dinner. As he was preparing this amazing scallop dish, he took the time to really talk with many different members of my staff. I could see the awe in their faces as they spoke with him. **It seemed as if their visions for their own futures became clearer and seemed more obtainable to them. He was a true inspiration** *for them. Patrick touched an astounding number of young cooks not only because of what he accomplished as a chef, but as a family man and a human being.*

Serves 8

MASHED VEGETABLES

1½ pounds fresh celery root, peeled

2 Idaho potatoes (8 ounces), peeled and diced

Salt

¼ cup heavy whipping cream

1 tablespoon butter

Dash of white truffle oil

Freshly ground white pepper

WILD MUSHROOM STEW

2 tablespoons olive oil

½ cup minced yellow onion

Salt and freshly ground black pepper

4 cups sliced assorted wild mushrooms (such as shiitakes, chanterelles, black trumpets)

1 tablespoon chopped garlic

1 tablespoon finely chopped fresh parsley leaves

2 cups veal stock reduction

2 tablespoons butter

CELERY ROOT FRENCH FRIES

1 pound whole celery root, peeled and cut into 2 by 1-inch batons

1 cup flour

1 cup bread crumbs

Salt and freshly ground black pepper

1 egg, beaten

Oil for frying

———

8 diver scallops, shucked and cleaned

Salt and freshly ground black pepper

1 tablespoon olive oil

———

2 tablespoons white truffle oil

2 ounces shaved Parmigiano-Reggiano cheese

1 tablespoon finely chopped chives

1 small black truffle, shaved

To prepare the mashed vegetables: Cut two thirds of the celery root into 2 by 1-inch batons and set aside. Dice the remaining celery root and add it to a saucepan with the potatoes, cover with water, and season to taste with salt. Bring the liquid to a boil, and then lower the heat to a simmer. Cook for 10 to 12 minutes, or until the potatoes are fork-tender.

Drain the vegetables and return them to the saucepan. Using a handheld potato masher, mash the vegetables and season to taste with salt and white pepper. Add the cream and butter and mix well. Season with the truffle oil and salt and white pepper to taste. Keep warm until ready to use.

To prepare the mushrooms: Heat the olive oil in a large sauté pan. Add the onion, season to taste with salt and pepper, and cook over medium-high heat for 2 minutes. Add the mushrooms and garlic, season to taste with salt and pepper, and cook for 3 to 4 minutes, or until the mushrooms are softened. Add the parsley and veal stock reduction and bring to a boil. Lower the heat and simmer for 2 minutes. Remove from the heat, stir in the butter, and keep warm.

To prepare the celery root french fries: Season the celery root batons, flour, and bread crumbs with salt and pepper. Lightly toss the celery root in the flour and dip into the egg, letting the excess egg drip off. Dredge the celery root in the bread crumbs, coating each side completely. Fry the batons in 375° oil, stirring occasionally, for 3 to 4 minutes, or until golden brown. Remove from the oil and drain on paper towels. Season to taste with salt and pepper and keep warm.

To prepare the scallops: Season the scallops to taste with salt and pepper. Heat the olive oil in a large sauté pan over medium heat. Add the scallops and cook for 2 minutes on each side.

To serve, spoon some of the mushrooms and the reduction in the center of each plate and top with a spoonful of the mashed vegetables. Place a scallop on top of the vegetables and arrange some of the french fries around the scallops. Drizzle with white truffle oil, and sprinkle some of the cheese, chives, and shaved truffle over the scallops and around the plates.

Patrick's Seared Diver Scallops

with Wild Mushroom Stew and Celery Root French Fries

Patrick prepared this wonderful scallop dish at a charity dinner in New Orleans. It was a huge hit.

Donnie Masterton

When he was fifteen years old Donnie Masterton announced that he was going to be a chef. At the time the Los Angelean was living in New York and participating in a school program that included business externships. Choosing a restaurant for its convenient location, Donnie found himself with David Bouley at Montrachet. One year later, Donnie went to work at Metro for Patrick Clark. It was the beginning of a ten-year relationship which influenced him profoundly on both the personal and professional levels. He worked with Patrick at Bicé, the Hay Adams Hotel, and finally, at Tavern on the Green, as chef de cuisine. In February 1998, after having worked with some of the finest chefs on the East and West coasts, Donnie Masterton returned to California as chef de cuisine at Zibibbo.

Its difficult to put into words what Patrick meant to me after working together for ten years. **As my mentor, he not only guided my career, but was often a father figure to me.**

When we were at the Hay Adams Hotel in Washington, D.C., Patrick was asked to prepare the presidential dinner for Nelson Mandela at the White House. Patrick was honored to accept the offer. The White House later informed Patrick that he was to attend the dinner with his wife, Lynette. Patrick was as passionate as he was protective of his food, so he told the White House he would feel more confident if his own chef were to execute his entrée. I felt unbelievably honored and proud to be representing not only the White House but also Patrick Clark. This was definitely one of the highlights of my career and a turning point in my relationship with Patrick. I was Patrick's chef, but he was always within arm's reach of his food. On that night, he had to let go. I prepared a sesame and wasabe-crusted halibut. The meal was flawless. The next day, Patrick told me I had done justice to his dish and had made him proud.

Patrick is still an inspiration to me. He is the foundation of all my cooking. His knowledge and creativity were endless. He was a tireless perfectionist and everything I aspire to become. I dedicate my career to Patrick Clark.

Sesame and Wasabe-Crusted Halibut

with Carrot Broth

This dish was served at a dinner in honor of Nelson Mandela at the White House.

Serves 4

½ cup black sesame seeds

½ cup white sesame seeds

4 7-ounce halibut fillets

Salt and freshly ground black pepper

Flour for dusting

2 tablespoons wasabe paste

¼ cup plus 2 tablespoons olive oil

———

6 carrots, peeled

1½ teaspoons cornstarch

2 tablespoons butter

Salt and freshly ground black pepper

Ground nutmeg

———

Extra virgin olive oil

12 sprigs chervil

To prepare the halibut:
Mix together the black and white sesame seeds on a plate. Season the halibut with salt and pepper and dust the flat side of the halibut with flour. With a spatula or small knife, spread the wasabe paste on the dusted side of the halibut, avoiding the sides of the fillet. Lay the fillets paste side down in the sesame seeds, pressing the fish into the seeds to ensure complete coverage. Place on a plate, cover, and refrigerate until ready to cook.

Preheat the oven to 350°. Heat the olive oil in a large, non-stick, ovenproof sauté pan over medium heat. Place the halibut in the pan crust side down and sear the crust until golden. Turn the halibut over and place the pan in the oven for 4 to 5 minutes, or until cooked medium rare.

To prepare the carrots:
Scoop the carrots with a Parisian baller, reserving the scraps. Blanch the carrot balls in salted water for 3 minutes, strain, and shock in ice water. Remove from the water and set aside.

To prepare the carrot broth:
Juice the carrot scraps and strain through a fine-mesh sieve. In a small bowl, mix 4 tablespoons of the carrot juice with the cornstarch to create a slurry. Put the remaining carrot juice in a saucepan and bring to a boil, then lower the heat to a simmer, and whisk in the slurry and butter. Transfer the broth to a double boiler and add the carrot balls. Season to taste with salt, pepper, and nutmeg and keep warm.

To serve, place a halibut fillet in the center of each large, shallow bowl. Spoon the carrot balls and the sauce evenly around fish. Drizzle a few drops of the extra virgin olive oil into the broth and arrange the chervil sprigs around the bowls.

182

Nobuyuki Matsuhisa

Born and raised in Japan, Matsuhisa apprenticed in the sushi bars of Tokyo before venturing overseas to Lima, Peru. Classically trained, he was challenged by the culture and regional ingredients that kindled his inventive style. He continued on to Buenos Aires, then went back to Japan, on to Alaska, and finally, settled in Los Angeles, where he opened his restaurant, Matsuhisa, in 1987. In 1988 *Los Angeles Times Magazine* included him among Southern California's rising stars, while in 1993 the *New York Times* chose Matsuhisa as one of the top ten restaurant destinations of the world. In 1994 New York City saw the opening of his restaurant, Nobu, which was named the Best New Restaurant by the James Beard Foundation. In 1997 he opened Nobu in London and Matsuhisa in Aspen, Colorado.

I had several opportunities to work with Patrick for different charities and events. My first impression was that he was an excellent chef and a hard worker, but as I got to know him better **I could see he had a form of leadership that warmed the hearts of many people.** *He was a person who was dedicated to his work and helping others.*

Chilean Sea Bass Anticucho

You can adjust the spiciness of this dish to your taste by using more or less of the sauce.

Serves 4

ANTICUCHO SAUCE

3 ounces Aji Panka (Peruvian chile paste)

½ cup rice wine vinegar

1 tablespoon garlic purée

¾ teaspoon ground cumin

¾ teaspoon dried oregano

¼ tablespoon salt

3 tablespoons olive oil

———

16 to 20 ounces Chilean sea bass

2 tablespoons chopped chives

To prepare the anticucho:
Whisk together all of the ingredients in a medium bowl.

To prepare the bass:
Dice the bass into three-quarter-inch pieces and divide evenly among 8 wooden skewers. Dip the skewers in the hot and spicy anticucho sauce and grill over medium-high heat for 1 minute on each side, or until just done.

Place 2 of the skewers on each plate and top with chopped chives.

Fedele Panzarino

Fedele Panzarino spent many years working in various Restaurant Associates restaurants and eventually became supervising chef of the airport division. In 1971 he joined New York City Technical College as director of culinary education.

Patrick Clark was a student at the New York City Technical College who immediately after entering the program became a student leader, gaining the respect of both faculty and fellow students. He wanted more than what he was taught in classes, so he volunteered to be my technical assistant in a basic skills culinary arts class. **With his pleasant demeanor and love of food preparation, he excelled in all his culinary and pastry arts classes.** *He was chosen to participate in the study abroad program, and this turned out to be the beginning of his illustrious career.*

As Patrick's career progressed, he never forgot his alma mater. He became a role model for our students. He hired our students whenever he could. He gave career advice to students. He visited our school to demonstrate his signature dishes. He was once voted Alumnus of the Year. Students and faculty alike were proud of Patrick Clark.

Brook Trout Baked in Corn Husks

Cooking the trout in the corn husks gives the fish a subtle corn flavor.

185

Serves 4

4 tablespoons
unsalted butter

⅓ cup finely diced
red bell pepper

2 tablespoons chopped
fresh parsley

½ teaspoon chile powder

½ teaspoon salt

⅛ teaspoon freshly ground
black pepper

1 tablespoon freshly
squeezed lemon juice

———

4 ears sweet corn

4 brook trout, boned,
rinsed, and patted dry

1 cup apple cider

To prepare the seasoned butter: Combine the butter, red bell pepper, parsley, chile powder, salt, pepper, and lemon juice in a small bowl.

To prepare the trout: Remove the corn husks, being careful not to tear them. Discard the silk and set the corn aside. Lay 4 corn husks overlapping slightly on a flat surface. Place the brook trout on the corn husks, spread with the seasoned butter and cover with the remaining husks. Tie a length of kitchen twine around the center of the covered trout and tie the husks at the top and bottom of each trout closed.

Preheat the oven to 350°. Place the trout in a lightly buttered 18 by 13-inch baking pan and spoon the apple cider over the trout. Bake for 15 minutes, basting the trout twice during baking. Remove the trout from the oven and untie and discard the cord and the upper husks.

To prepare the corn: Steam the corn on the cobs for 10 minutes, or until cooked through.

Place a trout (with the bottom husk) on each warmed plate alongside a piece of corn.

Marcus Samuelsson

Marcus Samuelsson discovered his passion for cooking at an early age, spending hours with his adopted grandmother learning how to make traditional Swedish foods. At age sixteen he attended classes at the Culinary Institute in Göteborg and cooked in local restaurants at night.

Marcus worked in Switzerland and Austria before coming to Aquavit in New York for an eight-month apprenticeship. He returned to Europe to work with Georges Blanc in Lyons, France, and in 1994 returned to Aquavit. He was appointed executive chef in 1995 and three months later, at age twenty-four, he earned a three-star rating from the *New York Times*, making him the youngest three-star chef in New York City. Marcus was nominated by the James Beard Foundation as a Rising Star Chef of the Year in 1997.

As a young chef arriving in New York, I frequently looked to Patrick for guidance and inspiration. Being the most famous and respected black chef in the U.S. was a huge responsibility for him, and one he gladly accepted. As a role model and leader, **Patrick opened many doors for young, aspiring chefs** *who otherwise would not have chosen this industry.*

Serves 4

BOUILLABAISE

2 lobster shells

2 tablespoons olive oil

1 large shallot,
coarsely chopped

1 clove garlic, sliced

1-inch length fresh ginger,
peeled and coarsely chopped

½ cup coarsely
chopped fennel

3 whole canned plum
tomatoes, with juice

¼ cup plus 2 tablespoons
ice wine, Sauternes, or
white port

2 cups fish broth or bottled
clam juice

2 cups chicken broth

4 sprigs thyme

4 sprigs mint

1 bay leaf

½ teaspoon kosher salt
plus extra to taste

Freshly ground black pepper

12 mussels, scrubbed
and debearded

12 clams, scrubbed

4 6-ounce fillets arctic char,
skin on

1 tablespoon olive oil plus
extra for brushing

Salt and freshly ground
black pepper

2 fingerling potatoes, sliced
into paper thin circles

2 tablespoons butter

1 pound fresh spinach,
washed and thick stems
removed

To prepare the broth:
Sauté the lobster shells in
the olive oil in a large pot
over medium-high heat for
2 minutes, crushing the
shells with a wooden spoon
as they cook. Add the shallot, garlic, ginger, and fennel
and sauté for 3 minutes, or
until softened on the edges.
Add the tomatoes, crushing
them with the back of a
spoon. Lower the heat to
medium and cook for 2 minutes. Stir in ¼ cup of the
ice wine, the fish broth,
chicken broth, thyme, mint,
bay leaf, salt, and pepper to
taste. Reduce the heat to low
and simmer, uncovered, for
20 minutes.

Strain the broth into a
medium saucepan and place
over medium heat. Add
the mussels and clams and
cook for 7 to 10 minutes,
or until the shells are fully
opened. Remove the pan from
the heat, add the remaining
2 tablespoons ice wine, cover,
and keep warm.

To prepare the fish:
Brush the fillets with olive
oil and season to taste with
salt and pepper. Arrange
the potato slices on the skin
side of the fish so they are
overlapping to look like fish
scales. Brush the potato
slices with olive oil, and
season to taste with salt
and pepper.

Combine 1 tablespoon of
the butter and the remaining
1 tablespoon olive oil in a
large, nonstick skillet over
medium-high heat. Transfer
the char to the skillet by
placing a spatula over the
layer of potatoes and flipping
the fillet over, then slide the
fillet, potato side down, into
the skillet. Press the fillets
with the back of a spatula
to condense and flatten the
layers of potato. Sauté for
2 to 3 minutes, or until the
potatoes are well browned
and the fish has contracted
on the edges. Turn the fish,
add the remaining 1 tablespoon butter, and sauté until
the fish is almost cooked but
remains slightly pink inside.
Transfer the fish to a plate
and keep warm.

To prepare the spinach:
Return the skillet to medium
heat and add the spinach.
Toss the spinach to wilt it,
and season with salt and pepper to taste. Remove the pan
from the heat and keep warm.

To serve, place some of the
spinach in the center of
each bowl and top with a
piece of char, potato side up.
Ladle the bouillabaisse into
the bowls to surround the
spinach and char.

Potato-Crusted Arctic Char
with Ice Wine Bouillabaisse

If you can't find fingerling potatoes, tiny red potatoes would also work well.

187

Joachim Splichal

Joachim Splichal is a leading
figure in America's evolving
food and restaurant industry.
Joachim and his wife,
Christine, opened the famed
restaurant Patina in Los
Angeles in 1989. He has since
gone on to open five more
French bistro-style restau-
rants, a museum cafe, and a
catering division. In 1995 he
was inducted into the James
Beard Foundation's Who's
Who of Food & Beverage in
America. The foundation
named him Best Chef:
California in 1991, and he
was nominated for
Outstanding Chef in 1991
and 1994. In 1995 his book,
*Patina Cookbook: Spuds,
Truffles and Wild Gnocchi*,
with noted food historian and
Los Angeles Times staff writer
Charles Perry was published.
In 1997 he was voted
Restaurateur of the Year by
the California Restaurant
Writer's Association.

**Patrick's warmth and generosity of spirit were reflected in everything
he did.** *His heart was so big I could barely wrap my arms around him.
We are lucky that his legacy will live on in his children.*

Serves 6

SCALLOP ROLLS

¼ cup unsalted
butter, melted

Salt and freshly ground
white pepper

1 large or 2 medium Idaho
potatoes, peeled

1 cup loosely packed
spinach leaves, stemmed

12 large sea scallops
(about 1½ ounces each)

3 shallots, finely chopped

2 tablespoons clarified butter

SAUCE

⅔ cup unsalted butter, at
room temperature

2 tablespoons
balsamic vinegar

Salt and freshly ground
black pepper

———

3 plum tomatoes, peeled,
seeded, and diced

1 small bunch chives,
cut into 2-inch lengths

To prepare the potatoes:
Preheat the oven to 350°.
Line a baking sheet with
parchment paper. Brush
the paper with some of the
melted butter, and sprinkle it
with a little of the salt and
white pepper. Trim one long
edge of the potatoes to form
a beginning surface for slic-
ing. With a mandolin or a
sharp knife, cut the potatoes
lengthwise into ⅛-inch-thick
oval slices. Arrange them in
a single layer on the baking
sheet (you will need 18
slices). Brush the potatoes
well with the butter, sprinkle
with a little more salt and
pepper, and cover with another sheet of parchment paper.
Bake for 10 to 12 minutes, or
until just tender. Remove
from the oven and set aside
until cool enough to handle.

To prepare the scallop rolls:
Lay six 8-inch-long sheets of
plastic wrap on the work surface. Create a 4 by 6-inch
sheet with rounded edges by
slightly overlapping 3 slices
of the cooked potato parallel
in the center of each piece of
plastic. Place 3 or 4 spinach
leaves on the potatoes on
each sheet of plastic, covering
them completely. Place 2 scallops at the top of the short
end of each sheet, season to
taste with salt and pepper,
and sprinkle with one-third of
the shallots. Roll the scallops
tightly in the potato and
spinach, using the plastic
wrap to help roll. Seal the
plastic tightly and refrigerate
for 1 to 2 hours, or until the
rolls are firm.

Remove the plastic wrap from
the scallop rolls and place
them near the stove. Heat a
large, ovenproof, nonstick
skillet over medium heat. Add
the clarified butter, and, when
it is very hot, add the rolls to
the pan and sauté for about
2 minutes, or until they are
crisp and golden. Turn gently
with kitchen tongs during
cooking to brown all sides
evenly. Keep the rolls warm
in a low oven.

To prepare the sauce:
Melt ⅓ cup of the butter
in a small sauté pan over
medium-high heat. Watching
carefully, swirl the butter
until it turns golden brown
and then add the vinegar.
Stand back, as it will splatter.
Reduce the heat. Cut the
remaining ⅓ cup butter
into 3 pieces and add it to
the pan, stirring and swirling
until the sauce is just
thickened and emulsified.
Immediately remove the pan
from the heat and season to
taste with salt and pepper.

Place a scallop roll on
each warmed plate, and
spoon some of the sauce
over the top. Sprinkle the
edges of the plate with
the diced tomatoes, the remaining chopped shallots,
and the chives.

Scallop Roll

with Brown Butter
Vinaigrette
and Long Chives

*These scallop
"packages" are
guaranteed to
impress your
guests.*

189

Reginald Watkins

Reginald Watkins has worked for Charlie Trotter's restaurant since its opening in 1987. He started as a dishwasher while going to electronics school, but Charlie saw his potential and quickly promoted him. Soon Reginald realized that although it was not his chosen field, cooking was a passion for him. He gave up electronics and began his rotation through the different stations in the kitchen, eventually being promoted to sous chef. Chef Watkins plays an integral role in the restaurant and travels extensively with Charlie Trotter. He believes that one day, after years have passed and the many faces have come and gone, the restaurant will be run by two old men—Reginald Watkins and Charlie Trotter.

My memories of Patrick Clark stem from experiences working with him at special events through the years. I first met Patrick when he was in Chicago as a guest chef for the Meals on Wheels fundraiser taking place at Charlie Trotter's. I was not only Patrick's assistant for the day, but I was in charge of showing him Chicago. When we were driving past a housing project where I had grown up, I apologized to Patrick for driving him through a not-so-nice area of town. He immediately made me feel right at home by sharing with me that he too had grown up in the projects, in the Bronx. **I knew right then that this guy was all right.**

I was in charge of helping Patrick prepare his food for the event, and I was very nervous. I wanted everything to come out perfectly. Unfortunately for me, it did not. Just before service, when I thought I had everything ready, a few of the sauces got away from me and scorched on the bottom. Patrick smelled this from the other side of the kitchen and ran over shaking his head. He let me know this was unacceptable and said the sauces needed to be made again. I was a wreck. I could not believe I had ruined the sauces of such a respected chef, and I was willing to do anything to regain his respect.

Many years later I had the opportunity to work with Patrick at an event at the James Beard House, a benefit for the American Black Chef Scholarship Fund. I was once again paired with him. He looked at me while we were preparing the food at Tavern on the Green and said, "Reggie, please do not burn my food again." But he said it with a smile and a wink. Unfortunately, I didn't know that was the last time I would see and work with Patrick. I cherish my memories of him.

RISOTTO

1 tablespoon minced garlic

1 onion, cut in small dice

1/4 cup butter

1 1/2 cups arborio rice

1/3 cup freshly grated Parmesan cheese

4 tablespoons chopped flat-leaf parsley

Salt and freshly ground black pepper

——

4 tablespoons shaved Parmesan cheese

4 teaspoons chiffonade-cut flat-leaf parsley

To prepare the shrimp:
Place the rock shrimp, orange and lemon zest, thyme, and olive oil in a resealable plastic bag and refrigerate for 24 hours.

Remove the shrimp from the bag and place on a large sheet of heavy-duty aluminum foil. Fold up the edges of the foil, leaving a very large opening at the center for the smoke to get in. Prepare a grill with a few hot coals and place the dry hickory chips over the coals. Scatter one-third of the wet hickory chips over the dry chips and place the foil-wrapped shrimp on the grill. Cover with the grill lid and smoke for 30 to 45 minutes, or until cooked, adding additional wet chips to the coals during the smoking process to keep the temperature cool and steady and the smoke alive. Remove the smoked shrimp from the grill and set aside.

To prepare the mushrooms:
Sweat the shallot in 2 tablespoons of the butter in a hot sauté pan for 1 minute. Add the chanterelles and cook for 3 to 4 minutes, or until the mushrooms are tender. Season the mushrooms to taste with salt and pepper. Put one-third of the mushrooms in a blender and add enough of the vegetable stock to smoothly purée. Reserve the remainder of the stock and the mushrooms for the risotto. Place purée in a small saucepan and warm over medium heat. Whisk in the remaining 2 tablespoons butter and season to taste with additional salt and pepper

To prepare the risotto:
Sweat the garlic and onion in a saucepan with the butter for 2 minutes over medium heat, or until translucent. Add the arborio rice and stir with a wooden spoon, coating the rice with the onion mixture. Add the vegetable stock in 1/2-cup additions, stirring constantly, until all of the liquid has been absorbed by the rice. Continue adding the vegetable stock in 1/2-cup additions until the arborio rice is cooked al dente. Fold in the grated Parmesan cheese, chopped parsley, and the reserved chanterelle mushrooms, and season to taste with salt and pepper.

Place some of the risotto in the center of each plate and sprinkle with the shaved Parmesan cheese and parsley chiffonnade. Top with some of the shrimp and spoon the mushroom purée around the plates.

Smoked Rock Shrimp and Chanterelle Mushroom Risotto

When smoking the shrimp, you should be able to hold your hand over the wood chips on the grill and barely feel any heat.

Serves 4 to 6

SMOKED ROCK SHRIMP

1 pound rock shrimp, shelled and deveined

Zest of 1 orange

Zest of 1 lemon

4 sprigs thyme

1/2 cup olive oil

3 cups hickory chips, soaked overnight in water plus 2 cups dry hickory chips

MUSHROOM PURÉE

1 shallot, thinly sliced

1/4 cup butter

3 cups chanterelle mushrooms, cleaned and quartered

Salt and freshly ground black pepper

5 1/2 cups (approximately) vegetable stock

Herb Wilson

Herb Wilson has spent twenty years working in fine restaurants in France and New York. One of his mentors was Patrick Clark, with whom he worked early in his career. He also worked with Larry Forgione at The River Café for two years during the early days of his career. Herb went on to spend six months working in the prestigious French kitchens of Gerard Pangaud, and Le Freres Troisgros. Upon his return to the United States he worked briefly at Hubert's and Montrachet. He has also headed up the kitchens of Jack's, Le Refuge, and Zut! In 1996 Wilson opened Bambou, an upscale Caribbean concept and the first restaurant of its kind in New York City. The restaurant received two stars from the *New York Times.*

I met Patrick Clark about twenty years ago, when I was a young, skinny, impressionable kid who didn't know what he wanted to be when he grew up. Patrick gave me one of my first jobs in a professional restaurant environment. Patrick was a dedicated bodybuilder, with a 32-inch waistline, and he was an extreme perfectionist in the kitchen. Patrick's food was very complicated and I wasn't very skilled. I distinctly remember an apple tart I couldn't quite get the hang of. **Patrick pushed me and pushed me and would never let me give up!**

One day, Cupid's arrow struck. Patrick met Lynette and fell in love immediately. I thought to myself, Great! The chef is in love. Maybe he'll take it easy on me from now on. I had no such luck!

The most important gifts Patrick gave me were a total dedication to our craft, a respect for hard work and discipline, a wonderful exchange of ideas and recipes between chefs, and a thirst for knowledge. We read the latest nouvelle cuisine cookbooks and anything else we could get our hands on regarding food, and we ate out often to taste other chefs' cooking. But, most important, Patrick inspired me to be become a chef.

In 1995 I received a phone call from Lynette asking me if I would cook Patrick's fortieth birthday dinner. I told her I'd be honored. The moment I hung up the phone I felt nervous and wondered what in the world I was going to cook for him. He could have eaten anywhere for his fortieth. But it was an opportunity for the student to show the teacher he had learned his lesson well.

I don't want to dwell on losing a good friend. Instead, I want to celebrate his life. The hard part is that I'll miss the phone calls that always began, "Hey, chief. How ya doing?" But I do have one consolation. A week before Patrick passed away, I called him at the hospital in New Jersey. Before we hung up, I said to him, "I love you, Patrick. Thank you for everything."

Sautéed Soft-Shell Crabs

with a Ginger-Carrot Broth and Baby Bok Choy

This is a great treat to serve in the late spring when soft-shell crabs are in season.

Serves 4

SAUCE

4 carrots, peeled
and chopped

1 knob fresh ginger, peeled
and chopped

1½ quarts chicken stock

CRABS

2 cups Wondra flour
for dredging

1 tablespoon
Old Bay Seasoning

¼ cup cornmeal

8 soft-shell crabs, cleaned

½ cup milk

1 tablespoon canola oil

1 lemon

BOK CHOY

10 bunches baby
bok choy, cleaned

½ teaspoon chopped garlic

1 tablespoon butter

To prepare the sauce:
Cook the carrots, ginger, and chicken stock in a saucepan for 45 minutes, or until the carrots are very soft. Purée in a blender and strain through a fine-mesh sieve. Keep warm until ready to use.

To prepare the crabs:
Combine the flour, Old Bay Seasoning, and cornmeal in a shallow bowl. Dip the crabs in the milk and then dredge in the flour mixture. Heat a sauté pan with the canola oil until the pan is smoking, add the crabs, and sauté over medium-high heat for 2 minutes on each side, or until golden brown. Squeeze some lemon juice on each crab, remove the crab from the pan, and drain on a paper towel.

To prepare the bok choy:
Sauté the baby bok choy in a hot pan with the garlic and butter until wilted.

To serve, arrange the bok choy in the center of each plate, top with 2 soft-shell crabs, and spoon the sauce around the plates.

Octavio Becerra

Octavio was planning a
career as a commercial pho-
tographer when he happened
to observe guest chef
Joachim Splichal prepare two
special menus for the restaurant he was working for at
the time. Fourteen years later,
he was nominated for Rising
Chef Star of the Year by the
James Beard Foundation for
his culinary talents at Pinot
Bistro, and was made a partner of the restaurant on his
thirtieth birthday by his mentor, Joachim Splichal. Prior to
this accomplishment, Octavio
apprenticed at several two-
and three-star restaurants in
France and Spain. He was
sous-chef for Splichal at Max
au Triangle and chef du cuisine at Patina. Currently,
Octavio is a partner in The
Patina Group and he continues to serve as Executive
Chef at Pinot Bistro.

A man of wisdom,

patient and unassuming,

always noticed—not for his size or physical presence—

but for his spirit and strong gentleness.

He was always there, giving,

his kindness communicated through his smile and his eyes,

yet he was serious as hell when time came to cook.

In work and in play he brought out the best—

you could see it in his food, his cooks, his friends.

We lost a dear man, a friend, and a chef—

God bless you, Pat,

we miss you.

Serves 4

ONION

1 large red onion,
cut in thick slices

2 tablespoons balsamic vinegar

½ cup water

---

20 to 22 ounces venison loin,
cleaned and seasoned

BRAISED NAPA CABBAGE

¾ head napa cabbage, cut
lengthwise into 8 long wedges

1½ tablespoons
unsalted butter

3½ cups chicken stock, hot

Pinch of ground cardamom

CHIVE OIL

2 tablespoons garlic chives

1 cup grapeseed oil

---

1 cup oyster
mushrooms, sautéed

2 bunches baby leeks,
rinsed and blanched

SAUCE

Honey-Spice Glaze
(recipe follows)

Salt and pepper

1½ teaspoons unsalted butter

To prepare the onion:
Marinate the onion in the
balsamic vinegar for at least
24 hours. Sear the marinated
slices in a hot sauté pan.
Add the water and slowly cook
until the onion is tender.

To prepare the venison:
Preheat the oven to 375°.
Sear the venison loin on all
sides in a heavy-bottomed
sauté pan until deep brown.
Roast the loin in the oven
for 30 minutes, or until
medium-rare. Remove the
venison from the pan and
set aside to rest.

To prepare the cabbage:
Sauté the cabbage wedges in
a large sauté pan in 1 tablespoon of the butter until both
sides of each wedge are gold-
en brown. Cover the cabbage
with 1½ cups of the chicken
stock and season with the
cardamom. (Reserve the
remaining broth for the sauce.)
Cook over medium heat for
15 minutes, or until tender,
and then add the remaining
½ tablespoon butter.

To prepare the chive oil:
Blanch the garlic chives in
boiling salted water for 3 to 5
seconds and then immediately
shock in ice water and drain.
Purée the chives and the
grapeseed oil in a blender for
2 minutes, or until smooth
and bright green. Transfer to
a plastic squeeze bottle.

To prepare the mushrooms:
Gently reheat the oyster
mushrooms and leeks in a
medium sauté pan with a
dash of the chive oil. Keep
warm until ready to use.

To prepare the sauce:
Bring the remaining 2 cups
chicken stock to a boil and
add the glaze. Season to taste
with salt and pepper and stir
in the butter.

To serve, roll the cabbage
wedges into circles and place
in the center of a large serving
plate. Arrange the mushroom
mixture on top of the cabbage. Slice the venison loin
and shingle on top of the
mushrooms. Spoon the glaze
over and around the venison
and lightly bead the chive oil
into the glaze.

Honey-Spice Glaze

YIELD: ABOUT 1¼ CUPS

1 tablespoon coriander seed,
toasted and ground

1 teaspoon fennel seed,
toasted and ground

1 teaspoon caraway seed,
toasted and ground

½ teaspoon cumin seed,
toasted and ground

½ teaspoon ground
white pepper

½ teaspoon ground turmeric

½ teaspoon curry powder

½ teaspoon ground cinnamon

1 cup honey

10 saffron threads

½ cup balsamic vinegar

Heat the ground coriander,
fennel, caraway, cumin, white
pepper, turmeric, curry powder, and cinnamon in a heavy
saucepan. Toast lightly enough
over medium heat to bring
out the intense aromas of the
individual spices. Add the
honey and saffron, bring to a
boil, and then lower heat and
simmer very slowly for 5 minutes. Add the balsamic vinegar and simmer for 3 minutes.
Refrigerate in a glass jar for
up to 2 days. Reheat the glaze
when ready to use.

Roasted Venison Loin

with a Honey-Spice
Glaze and Braised
Napa Cabbage

*If you have
difficulty finding
venison, beef
tenderloin would
also work well.*

Jody Denton

Jody Denton believes traveling is one of the key ingredients to being a good chef because it gives him firsthand experience with cuisines from around the world. He demonstrates his appreciation of regional cuisines as executive chef and partner of San Francisco's Provençal-style Restaurant Lulu, and Palo Alto's Mediterranean restaurant, Zibibbo.

At age seventeen Denton enrolled in an apprenticeship program with the American Culinary Federation. After graduating in 1980, he further honed his culinary skills in fine dining establishments from Dallas to Switzerland, including The Mansion on Turtle Creek, Eureka Restaurant and Brewery, Red Sage, and The Eccentric. In 1995 Denton became executive chef at Restaurant Lulu. The next year, he took over the helm, inviting Marc Valiani to become his partner. Together, they opened Zibibbo in late 1997.

When Patrick was the chef at Bicé in Beverly Hills, I had dinner there, but he was off that night so I didn't get to meet him. A couple of years later, when I was living in Washington, D.C., I dined at the Hay Adams Hotel while Patrick was heading up that kitchen—again it was his day off and I did not have the opportunity to meet him. Nevertheless, both of those meals left an indelible impression on my senses, and **I was a fan of the beautifully simple yet elegant and technically perfect cuisine of Patrick Clark.**

In 1994, during my tenure as chef at the Eccentric restaurant in Chicago, I decided to start a guest chef program at the restaurant. Although Patrick and I had never spoken a word to each other, those meals remained in my mind and on my tongue, and he was the first person I called. He graciously accepted the offer to come to Chicago.

He arrived a few months later with his wife, Lynette, and his then–sous chef, Donnie Masterton (who, incidentally, works with me now as the chef at Zibibbo). While Lynette was busy enjoying Michigan Avenue, Patrick, Donnie, and I spent three days preparing for the opening night of Patrick Clark Week at the Eccentric.

We sliced, diced, poached, braised, boned, ground, pounded, and stuffed, and played with live lobsters. At night we wined and dined until we couldn't eat or drink any more. In the end, the event had gone smoothly, we'd all had an extremely good time, and I was left with incredible respect for Patrick. His food was fantastic, his professionalism was unequalled, his huge smile was contagious. I have never met a more all-around wonderful guy. The world of restaurants, kitchens, chefs, and people in general took a hard hit with his passing.

Serves 4

4 lamb shanks

Salt and black pepper

1 tablespoon olive or vegetable oil

1 white onion, coarsely chopped

1 carrot, coarsely chopped

2 stalks celery, coarsely chopped

1 bulb garlic, cloves peeled

2 sprigs thyme

1 sprig rosemary

2 teaspoons chopped anchovies or anchovy paste

¼ cup dried porcini mushrooms

1 tablespoon black peppercorns

1½ cups red wine

1½ cups red verjus

4 cups lamb broth (or beef or chicken broth)

2 tablespoons chopped flat-leaf parsley

2 tablespoons minced preserved lemon peel, or 1 tablespoon lemon zest

3 tablespoons chopped black olives (French or Italian)

Sweet Garlic Polenta (recipe follows)

To prepare the lamb:
Preheat the oven to 325°. Season the lamb shanks to taste with salt and pepper. Heat a braising pan over medium heat, add the oil, and sear the shanks on all sides until completely browned. Remove the shanks and set aside.

Add the onion, carrot, and celery to the pan and allow to brown lightly, stirring occasionally. Add the garlic, thyme, rosemary, anchovy, porcini, and peppercorns and cook for 5 minutes. Add the red wine, verjus, and lamb broth, and return the lamb shanks to the pan. Increase the heat and bring to a boil, cover, and cook in the oven for about 1½ hours, or until a toothpick can be easily inserted into the thickest part of the meat.

Remove the shanks from the pan and set aside. Strain all of the vegetables and herbs from the liquid. Discard the vegetables and return the liquid to the pan. Bring the liquid to a boil and then lower the heat and simmer until reduced to about 2 cups. Add the parsley, preserved lemon, and olives and cook until the liquid darkens and a light sauce texture develops. Remove from the heat and season to taste with salt and pepper.

To serve, spoon a mound of polenta onto each plate and top with a lamb shank. Spoon the sauce over the shank, allowing it to pool around the edge of the polenta.

Sweet Garlic Polenta

YIELD: ABOUT 2 CUPS

2 cups milk

2 cups water

½ cup polenta

½ cup garlic cloves, peeled

2 tablespoons butter, at room temperature

Salt and freshly ground black pepper

Bring the milk and water to a boil in a saucepan and whisk in the polenta. Lower the heat and cook slowly for 1 hour, stirring frequently.

Place the garlic in a small saucepan and add enough water to the pan to completely submerge the garlic. Boil for 5 minutes and then drain the water from the pan. Add more water to the pan and repeat the process twice. Place the garlic in a small bowl. Add the butter and mash the garlic and butter together with a fork until the mixture is smooth.

Add the garlic mixture to the polenta and season to taste with salt and pepper. Keep warm until ready to use.

Verjus-Braised Lamb Shanks
with Sweet Garlic Polenta

Try using roasted garlic in the polenta for an interesting taste variation.

Todd English

Todd English began his cooking career at the age of fifteen, when he first entered a professional kitchen. At twenty, he attended the Culinary Institute of America. He continued to hone his craft at New York's La Côte Basque and then in Italy, where he apprenticed at Dal Pescatore in Canto Sull O'lio and Paraccuchi in Locando D'Angello. It was in Italy that Todd developed his unique approach to food and cooking. He returned to the United States at twenty-five to open the award-winning restaurant Michela's.

Todd is now the chef and owner of Olives in Charlestown, Massachusetts, and Figs in Charlestown, Boston, Wellesley, and Chestnut Hill, Massachusetts. Olives, which Todd runs with his wife, Olivia, draws national and international attention for English's interpretive Mediterranean cuisine.

Patrick was not only a sincerely kind person and a gentleman, but he always seemed to carry himself with great confidence. **He possessed a wisdom well beyond his years.** *A brilliant chef, he was an inspiration to many aspiring chefs (me included). I greatly admired his aesthetics and the art of his cooking, which he so graciously shared with us over the all-too-short years. I also admired that, in addition to all of his professional accomplishments, he was a great father to five children. We will truly miss him.*

Olives's Family-Style Veal Roast

This dish is great served with a big bowl of Dijon mustard.

Serves 6

5 cloves garlic, minced

Zest of 1 lemon

2 tablespoons chopped fresh rosemary

1 tablespoon fresh thyme

1 teaspoon kosher salt

1 teaspoon freshly ground black pepper

3½ pounds veal shoulder roast, boned, rolled, and tied

2 tablespoons olive oil

2 ham hocks

4 12-ounce double-thick beef short ribs

2 Spanish onions, halved and thinly sliced

3 stems rosemary

2 stems thyme

3 carrots, peeled and chopped

2 cups white wine

6 cups chicken stock

3 bay leaves

1 teaspoon caraway seeds

2 kielbasa sausages

To prepare the meat:
Rub 3 of the garlic cloves, the lemon zest, rosemary, thyme, salt and pepper into the veal roast, getting as much inside as possible. Cover and refrigerate overnight.

Preheat the oven to 350°. Place a large skillet over medium-high heat. When it is hot, add the oil and the veal roast. Brown the roast on all sides and then transfer to a large roasting pan. Add the ham hocks and short ribs to the hot skillet, brown on all sides, and transfer to the roasting pan.

Reduce the heat to low and add the onions and the remaining 2 cloves garlic. Cook for 6 to 7 minutes, or until the garlic and onions are translucent. Add the remaining ingredients and cook for 10 minutes. Transfer the mixture to the roasting pan with the veal and cook in the oven for 3 hours.

Thinly slice the roast and return it to the roasting pan, or transfer the ingredients to a large serving dish with a lip.

Dean Fearing

Chef Dean Fearing was at the forefront of developing the New Southwest Cuisine genre when he became executive chef of Dallas's Mansion on Turtle Creek in 1985. Unrelentingly creative, the exuberant Chef Fearing, winner of the 1994 James Beard Best Chef: Southwest and the Mobil Five-Star award 1995 through 1997, creates new dishes each week.

Classically trained at the Culinary Institute of America, Dean began his career at Maisonette in Cincinnati, followed by the Pyramid Room at the Fairmont Hotel in Dallas. He was also chef and part owner of Agnew's restaurant, in Dallas. A decade and countless culinary awards later he continues to develop Southwest Cuisine using all varieties of Texas-grown products.

My most memorable experience with Patrick Clark was in 1994, when he and I both participated in a Masters of Food and Wine event at the Highland's Inn in Carmel, California. Upon entering the Highland's Inn kitchen, the sight that greeted me was Patrick's big, bright smile. In seconds, the smile disappeared and the intensity of the food was in his eyes. He turned, and I heard his voice of command yelling orders and witnessed his body in the action of a chef, hands waving through the air. As I am from Texas and never travel without good barbecue, I yelled to Patrick that lunch was on me. Within the hour I pulled some of Texas's best out of a convection oven. **I'll never forget the look in Patrick's eyes as I sliced the beef, slathered it with barbecue sauce, and placed it between a toasted baguette.** *Patrick was a true food lover, and for a brief moment, I had tamed the tiger of the Highlands Inn kitchen.*

Serves 4

1 small leg of wild boar (about 5 pounds), trimmed

Salt and black pepper

2 cups Mansion on Turtle Creek Barbecue Sauce

1 tablespoon canned chipotle chiles, puréed

4 8-inch flour tortillas, warmed

1 cup jalapeño jack cheese

1 quart vegetable oil

Mexican Potato Salad (recipe follows)

To prepare the boar:

Prepare a smoker for cold smoke. Place the wild boar leg on a smoker rack and season heavily with salt and pepper. Place in the smoker for 2 to 3 hours.

Preheat the oven to 350°. Place the boar leg in a heavy cast iron skillet and roast in the oven for 45 minutes. Remove from the oven and let rest for 20 minutes. Remove the bone from the leg with a sharp boning knife and thinly slice the meat with a sharp carving knife.

Place the meat in a medium saucepan over medium heat with the Mansion Barbecue Sauce and chipotle chiles. Bring the mixture to a boil, then lower the heat to a simmer and cook for 20 minutes, or until the meat is tender. Remove from the heat and set aside to cool.

To prepare the flautas:

Lay the warm tortillas out flat on a table. Spoon a small portion of the wild boar mixture in the center of each tortilla. Divide the jack cheese evenly and sprinkle it on top. Fold two sides of the tortilla into the middle and, starting from the bottom, roll into a cylinder shape. Secure the roll by "sewing" the edges closed with toothpicks to prevent the tortilla from opening during frying. Place the tortilla rolls in a 350° fryer and cook for 3 minutes, or until golden brown and crispy. Remove the flautas from the fryer and drain on paper towels. Carefully remove the toothpicks.

Using a serrated knife, cut each flauta in half on the diagonal. Place 1 half of the flauta upright on each plate and tuck the other piece next to the standing flauta. Spoon some of the warm Mexican Potato Salad next to the flautas and serve immediately.

Mexican Potato Salad

YIELD: ABOUT 6 CUPS

1 tablespoon olive oil

12 large red new potatoes, quartered, blanched, and shocked

1 large onion, cut into small dice

Salt

2 cloves garlic, minced

2 jalapeños, seeded and minced

2 teaspoons ground cumin

1/3 cup chorizo, cooked and drained

1/2 cup demiglace

1/2 cup salsa

Freshly squeezed lime juice

Heat the oil in a large sauté pan over medium heat. Add the potatoes, onion, and salt to taste and sauté for 5 minutes, or until light brown. Add the garlic, jalapeños, cumin, and chorizo and sauté for 2 minutes. Add the demiglace and salsa and cook for 2 minutes, or until the potatoes are well coated. Add the lime juice to taste. Keep warm until ready to use.

Wild Boar Flauta

with Ranchero Sauce and Warm Mexican Potato Salad

The Mansion on Turtle Creek Barbecue Sauce used in this recipe is available at most gourmet markets.

202

Mark Miller

Mark Miller started his culinary career at Chez Panisse with Alice Waters. He opened his first personal venture, the Fourth Street Grill, in Berkeley, in 1979. He opened the Santa Fe Bar & Grill, also in Berkeley, in 1981. In 1987 Mark opened the legendary Coyote Cafe in Santa Fe, and in 1992 he opened Red Sage in Washington, D.C. Mark next turned his expertise to Asian food, opening Raku: An Asian Diner, in two locations in Washington, D.C., and the Loongbar, in San Francisco.

Mark Miller has received numerous awards, including Best Southwestern Restaurant from the James Beard Foundation for Coyote Cafe, and *Esquire's* Restaurant of the Year, in 1992, for Red Sage. He is the author of nine cookbooks, including the best-selling *Coyote Cafe Cookbook* and *The Great Chile Book*.

Patrick was always open and willing to learn from new food experiences. He had a zest for great cooking from many cultures of the world.

When Patrick first moved to Washington, D.C., he was the executive chef of the Hay Adams Hotel. When he had to prepare a large banquet for an oil company from Texas, he called me at Red Sage. He said they wanted to have a meal with real Texas flavors. He told me he had ordered ten varieties of chiles to include in the dishes but he didn't know which chiles to use where. I invited him to come to the restaurant for a crash course on cooking with chiles. He ended up sweating his way through the quick orientation and saying that cooking with chiles was more difficult than making a demiglace! He returned to the Hay Adams and called me the following week to say that the meal had been a great success.

Patrick was always open and willing to learn from new food experiences. *He had a zest for great cooking from many parts and cultures of the world.*

Glazed Pork Back Ribs

with Black Coffee Guajillo Barbecue Sauce

If you like extra tender ribs, you can cook them longer in the foil.

Serves 4

MARINADE

4 tablespoons ground coriander

2 tablespoons chopped fresh thyme

6 tablespoons honey mustard

2 tablespoons freshly ground black pepper

1 tablespoon salt

2 tablespoons ground chile molido (pure chile powder)

1½ cups apple cider vinegar

1 cup balsamic vinegar

1 cup honey

¼ cup liquid smoke

2 slabs pork back ribs

SAUCE

1 cup chopped white onion

1½ teaspoons minced garlic

1 tablespoon butter

¼ cup sherry vinegar

1¼ cups tomato purée

½ teaspoon salt

1 teaspoon freshly ground black pepper

½ cup crushed guajillo chiles

1 cup strong, freshly brewed black coffee

⅓ cup molasses

To prepare marinade for the ribs: Mix together all the ingredients in a medium bowl. Place the ribs into a nonreactive pan, cover with the marinade, and refrigerate overnight. Remove the ribs from the marinade, strain the marinade, and reserve for glazing.

To prepare the ribs: Preheat the oven to 225°. Wrap the ribs in aluminum foil and place them on a baking sheet. Cook in the oven for 2 hours and then remove the ribs from the foil.

Heat the coals on a grill until hot. Place the ribs on the grill and cook for 3 to 5 minutes on each side, or until browned, brushing frequently with the glaze.

To prepare the sauce: In a medium sauté pan, sauté the onion and garlic in the butter over low heat for 10 minutes, being careful not to burn the garlic. Deglaze the pan with the sherry vinegar and add all of the remaining ingredients. Simmer over low heat for 20 to 30 minutes, or until the dried chiles are very soft. Purée until smooth and strain through a large sieve.

Place a half slab of ribs on each plate and serve the black coffee guajillo barbecue sauce on the side.

Drew Nieporent

Drew Nieporent is one of
the most respected and
celebrated restaurateurs in
the United States and is the
proud and energetic owner
of Montrachet, Tribeca Grill,
Rubicon, Nobu, Layla,
TriBakery, Nobu London, City
Wine & Cigar Co., and
FreeStyle—with more to
come. A 1977 graduate of
the Cornell University School
of Hotel Management, Drew
started his career in management at Maxwell's Plum,
Tavern on the Green, La
Réserve, Le Périgord, La
Grenouille, and Le Régence.
He is the recipient of many
honors, including being
named Man of the Year by
the Food & Beverage
Association, receiving the
Gates of Jerusalem Medal
from Israel Bonds, and the
Outstanding Service Award
from the James Beard
Foundation. In 1992 he was
inducted into Who's Who of
Cooking in America by the
James Beard Foundation.

*I've met and worked with many wonderful people in the restaurant business,
but no one was more special than my friend Patrick Clark. Patrick had a
big smile and a natural warmth that lit up an entire restaurant.* **He was
disarmingly friendly, and he loved to meet people.** *We shared a kinship
based on our weight. But he was big in so many ways. I always enjoyed
working with Patrick and being a part of his life. I'll miss that sweet guy.*

This dish looks impressive but it is very easy to prepare.

205

Serves 4

1 loaf white bread

4 Cornish hens, liver and gizzards reserved

1 cup chicken broth

2 tablespoons olive oil

3 tablespoons butter

1 stalk celery, diced

½ white onion, diced

1 tablespoon minced garlic

2 tablespoons minced fresh parsley

½ cup raisins

½ cup pine nuts

1 teaspoon salt

1 teaspoon freshly ground black pepper

To prepare the stuffing:
Preheat the oven to 350°. Remove the crusts from the bread and cut the bread into cubes. Place the cubes on a baking sheet and cook in the oven for 10 to 12 minutes, or until light golden brown. Stir the bread cubes occasionally to ensure even browning.

Drizzle the chicken broth over the toasted bread cubes. Heat the olive oil and 2 table-spoons of the butter in a large skillet. Sauté the celery, onion, garlic, parsley, and liver and gizzards, being careful not to overcook. Remove from the heat, add the remaining ingredients, and stir to mix thoroughly.

To prepare the hens:
Preheat the oven to 350°. Wash the hens in lightly salted water. Fill the cavity of each hen with the stuffing and dot the outsides of the hens with the remaining butter. Place the hens in a roasting pan, cover with aluminum foil, and roast in the oven for 30 minutes. Remove the foil and cook the hens for another 15 minutes, or until golden brown.

To serve, place a whole hen in the center of each plate.

Danielle Reed

Danielle Reed attended the California Culinary Academy. Upon graduation she worked for two years as banquet chef at the Mandarin Oriental Hotel before traveling for six months in Europe, completing a "stage" at the Connaught Hotel in London. Soon after her return, she met Patrick Clark at Bicé, in Beverly Hills, and her tenure with him—which included stints as sous chef at the Hay Adams Hotel and executive sous chef at Tavern on the Green—began. She then returned to France to work at Pain, Adour, et Fantasie, Patisserie Mandion, and with chef Lea Linster.

Following her return from France, Danielle became the chef at Aquamarine Restaurant in New York City and, after a brief period at Tribeca Grill, she returned to California as the chef of Ciudad Restaurant, owned by Mary Sue Millikin and Susan Feniger.

What did Patrick mean to me? First of all, it does not seem real that he is gone. In my years of working with him, Patrick proved to be such an immense force in the kitchen that even when he wasn't there physically, he was still there. His ways and ideas were in the air, and in every dish that went past the window.

Patrick is timeless. He was young, but he had the vision of a genius. *Patrick was a born chef. He never lacked confidence in anything he did, yet he encouraged my input and suggestions. He didn't give unwarranted compliments, and when he gave one, he meant it. One of his highest praises was, "You're a good cook." That meant you were solid and respectful of your craft. It also meant that you had his respect, and that meant everything to a cook. Patrick once told me, "The best things about California were the discovery of Chilean sea bass and you." More than a mentor, he was very protective of me while I was under his wing, and his wisdom was with me when I stepped out on my own. He was always there for me. I called on him often for recipe, menu, or management advice. That, I will sorely miss.*

Serves 6

SWEETBREADS

3 pounds veal sweetbreads

1 tablespoon salt,
plus more, to taste

1 lemon, halved

Freshly ground black pepper

2 cups Panko Japanese
bread crumbs

2 tablespoons olive oil

BARBECUE SAUCE

2 cups ketchup

1 cup rice wine vinegar

1 cup brown sugar

1 tablespoon Thai garlic
chile paste

1 tablespoon soy sauce

1 teaspoon
ground cardamom

5 star anise pods

⎯⎯⎯

5 large tomatoes

CONFIT

½ pound pancetta,
cut in ¼-inch dice

1 tablespoon olive oil

3 Spanish onions, julienned

¾ cup heavy
whipping cream

Salt and freshly ground
black pepper

1 bunch chives, chopped

CHIVE OIL

1 bunch chives, chopped

½ cup vegetable oil

To prepare the sweetbreads:
Place the sweetbreads in a
colander and run under cold
water for 30 minutes. Transfer
them to a saucepan, add cold
water to cover, and add the
salt. Squeeze the juice from
the lemon into the pan. Add
the 2 lemon halves and simmer over medium heat for 10
minutes. Drain the sweet-
breads and shock in ice water.
When cool, remove the thick
skin and some of the connec-
tive tissue, leaving enough
intact to keep the sweetbreads
from falling apart. Place them
in a colander and set a bowl
on top. Place 10 pounds of
weight in the bowl (bricks,
or heavy bowls or pans work
well). Put a larger bowl or
pan underneath the colander
to catch any liquid and
refrigerate overnight.

**To prepare the barbecue
sauce:** Combine all the
ingredients in a saucepan and
simmer over medium heat for
30 minutes, or until thick.

To prepare the tomatoes:
Preheat the oven to 325°.
Blanch the tomatoes and then
peel and quarter them and
remove the inside flesh. Brush
both sides of the petals with
some of the barbecue sauce,
place them on a baking
sheet, and dry in the oven
for 30 minutes. Remove from
the oven and set aside until
ready to use.

To prepare the confit:
Sauté the pancetta in the olive
oil until crispy. Remove the

pancetta from the pan and
pour off and discard any
excess fat. Add the onion to
the pan and slowly cook over
low heat to a light caramel
brown. Add the pancetta and
cream and cook over low heat
to a thick consistency. Season
to taste with salt and pepper.
Fold in the chives.

To prepare the chive oil:
Blanch the chives in heavily
salted water and shock in ice
water. Drain, but do not press
them too much. Place the
chives in a blender with ¼
cup of the vegetable oil and
purée until smooth. Slowly
add the remaining ¼ cup
vegetable oil. Strain the
emerald green oil through
a fine strainer into a
storage container.

To cook the sweetbreads:
Remove the weight from the
sweetbreads and pat dry.
Season both sides to taste
with salt and pepper. Brush
one side with the barbecue
sauce and press the sauced
side in the bread crumbs.
Sauté lightly in the olive oil
for 2 minutes on each side.

Spoon the confit in center of
each plate and top with some
of the sweetbreads. Arrange
3 tomato petals on each plate
and drizzle the chive oil
around plate.

Barbecued Sweetbreads

with Pancetta and
Sweet Onion Confit
and Chive Oil

*The chive oil in
this recipe can be
made up to two
days ahead
and kept in the
refrigerator.*

207

Cal Stamenov

As executive chef at Highlands Inn, Cal Stamenov directs an ambitious culinary program encompassing Pacific's Edge restaurant and the Masters of Food and Wine, an international event that each year brings together the world's premier chefs and wine makers.

Cal began his career in 1982 at New York's Four Seasons, after graduation from the California Culinary Academy. Thereafter he acquired experience in the European tradition by working for over seven years in the most demanding kitchens under some of the world's most prestigious chefs, including Alain Ducasse at Louis XV at the Hotel de Paris in Monaco, Pierre Gagnaire in St. Etienne, France; Masa Kobaiashi at Masa's Restaurant in San Francisco; Jean-Louis Palladin at Restaurant Jean-Louis in Washington, D.C.; and Michel Richard at Citrus Restaurant in Los Angeles.

I remember Pat at the seafood grill during the Masters of Food and Wine event, at his happiest moments—outside on the deck grilling shrimp with a big smile, making everyone there feel so comfortable and welcome. **He was the one chef I know who could make the best food with the least effort** *at large guest chef cooking events.*

Serves 4

SWEET POTATOES

3 sweet potatoes

¼ cup plus 2 tablespoons
butter softened

½ teaspoon ground nutmeg

Salt and freshly ground
black pepper

SAUCE

8 ounces venison scraps,
cut into 1-inch strips

2 carrots, peeled, diced,
and blanched

1 leek, thinly sliced

1 onion, thinly sliced

1 tablespoon olive oil

1 tablespoon sugar

1 cup blackberries

1 cup red wine

2 cups veal stock

MUSHROOMS

12 pearl onions

1 pound chanterelle
mushrooms

1 tablespoon butter

2 carrots, peeled, diced,
and blanched

———

8 ounces Hudson Valley
foie gras

———

1 pound venison loin,
cut into 4 portions

1 tablespoon olive oil

To prepare the sweet potatoes: Preheat the oven to 350°. Bake the sweet potatoes for 1 hour, or until tender. Remove and discard the skin. Put the flesh in a mixing bowl and, using an electric mixer, whip with the butter, nutmeg, and salt and pepper to taste. Keep warm until ready to use.

To prepare the sauce: Brown the meat scraps in a large, heavy-bottomed pan. Add the carrots, leek, and onion and sweat in the olive oil over medium heat for 20 minutes, or until tender. Add the sugar and blackberries and cook for 5 minutes. Add the red wine and cook until reduced to ¼ cup. Add the veal stock and simmer slowly for 1 hour. Strain through a fine-mesh sieve and set aside.

To prepare the mushrooms: Peel and blanch the pearl onions. Sauté the chanterelles in the butter in a medium sauté pan over medium-high heat for 5 minutes, or until tender. Add the pearl onions, the remaining carrots, and 2 tablespoons of the sauce and cook until warm. Keep warm until ready to use.

To prepare the foie gras: Season the foie gras with salt and pepper and cook in a medium sauté pan over medium heat for 3 minutes, or until browned. Turn the foie gras over and cook for 3 minutes, or until completely cooked, being careful not to burn it. Remove from the heat and keep warm until ready to use.

To prepare the venison: Season the venison with salt and pepper and cook with the olive oil in a large sauté pan over high heat until browned on both sides.

To serve, place some of the mushroom mixture in center of each warmed plate and top with some of the sweet potato purée. Lay a piece of the venison on top and place some of the foie gras over the venison. Drizzle the sauce over the foie gras and around the plates.

Roasted Cervena Venison

with Big Sur Chanterelles
and Foie Gras

If chanterelles are out of season, try using hedge hog mushrooms.

Roy Yamaguchi

After graduating from the Culinary Institute of America in 1976, Roy Yamaguchi began apprenticeships at L'Escoffier, and then at L'Ermitage under chef Jean Bertranou. In 1984, at his own restaurant, 385 North, Yamaguchi's cooking style—described as "California-French-Japanese eclectic"—first came into its own. After dissolving his L.A. partnership in 1988, he decided to renew his acquaintance with Hawaii.

Roy's Restaurant opened in December of 1988. In 1992 he opened Roy's Kahana Bar & Grill. Roy has numerous other Roy's restaurants, in locations as far and wide as Tokyo and Guam to Scottsdale and Pebble Beach. In 1993 he received the James Beard Foundation Best Chef: Pacific Northwest award.

Since 1994, Roy has hosted Hawaii Public Television's *Hawaii Cooks with Roy Yamaguchi*. His cookbook, *Roy's Feasts From Hawaii*, is enjoying both national and international acclaim.

Patrick and I first met at the 1992 Masters of Food and Wine in Carmel, California. I was just happy to be among some of the incredible talent gathered there, including Charlie Trotter, Daniel Boulud, Joachim Splichal, Roger Verge, and my old friend Jasper White, but it was especially gratifying to be welcomed with such easy warmth and respect by Patrick.

I can personally vouch for the fact that self-consciousness is pretty much a part of the life of a chef from a minority background, and you can bet that the class and work ethic with which I saw Patrick conduct himself has been an inspiration for me.

About a month after the Masters, Patrick rang me up in Hawaii to say hello and to ask about a sauce I had prepared at the event. I told him that one of the key ingredients I had used was shichimi, a Japanese "seven spice" that includes chile pepper, sesame and poppy seeds, seaweed, and orange peel. I was so flattered that I popped a five-pound bag of the stuff into the mail to him the next day, and I'm proud to say that he was hooked on it from then on.

I was very fortunate that in January of 1997 Patrick and Lynette were able to come over to Honolulu to help us celebrate the eighth anniversary of Roy's Restaurant. For the celebration dinner, Patrick crusted a Hawaiian swordfish with mustard seed and served it with shrimp in a coriander shrimp broth. **I'm always eager to show off real cooking "from the heart" to our families, friends, and staff, and, as usual, Patrick didn't let us down!**

Here's to you, Patrick. Someday I hope to touch half as many lives as you have!

New Chinatown Duck

Dried mushrooms and other exotic ingredients in this recipe are available at any Asian market.

Serves 4

MARINADE

1 tablespoon minced garlic

1 tablespoon peeled and minced fresh ginger

1 cup soy sauce

2 cups hoisin sauce

1 tablespoon Lanchi chile sauce (or any garlic chile paste)

2 cups sherry

1 cup honey

1 green onion, finely chopped

———

2 ducks

———

2 tablespoons olive oil

8 ounces dried shiitake mushrooms, soaked overnight in water and julienned

2 baby bok choy leaves or napa cabbage leaves

16 fresh water chestnuts, sliced

½ cup dried black fungus mushrooms, soaked overnight in water and julienned

½ cup green onion cut in 1-inch strips

1 teaspoon peeled and minced fresh ginger

Lanchi chile sauce (or any garlic chile paste)

To prepare the duck:
Combine the marinade ingredients in a large bowl. Add the ducks, cover with plastic wrap, and marinate in the refrigerator for 1 day.

Preheat the oven to 350°. Place the duck on a wire rack in a roasting pan and cook in the oven for 1 hour, or until done.

To prepare the vegetables:
Heat the oil in a large sauté pan over medium heat and cook the shiitake mushrooms, bok choy, water chestnuts, black fungus mushrooms, green onions, ginger, and chile sauce to taste for 30 seconds, or until the bok choy is slightly wilted.

To serve, remove the legs and breasts from the ducks and slice each breast into 3 pieces. Spoon the vegetables onto the center of each plate and arrange a duck leg and pieces of breast on top.

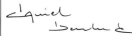

212

Daniel Boulud

Daniel Boulud was raised
on his family's farm near
Lyons, France, where he grew
up surrounded by produce
fresh from the fields and his
grandmother's inspiring
home cooking.

Following his apprenticeship,
Daniel went on to train in
some of France's and
Copenhagen's finest kitchens.
He made his way to the
United States as chef to the
European Commission in
Washington, D.C., and then
went on to open the Polo
Lounge at the Westbury
Hotel, Le Régence at the
Hotel Plaza Athénée, and
to the position of executive
chef at Le Cirque.

In 1993 he opened Res-
taurant Daniel, which has
been awarded four stars
by the *New York Times*. In
1998 he opened Cafe Boulud,
named for the gathering place
his great-grandparents tended
on their farm outside Lyons at
the turn of the century.

My fondest memories of Patrick date back to the early '80s when he was chef at Odeon. **I used to love to go there late at night after work for his really wonderful bistro food.**

Blueberry Brioche Bread Pudding

This lighter version of bread pudding has a minty flavor and is bursting with baked deep purple blueberries.

Serves 4

1 cup milk

1 cup heavy whipping cream

½ vanilla bean, split and pulp scraped out, or a few drops of pure vanilla extract

4 sprigs mint plus leaves only of 1 sprig, for garnish

Zest of 1 lemon, grated

½ cup sugar

4 sheets gelatin or 1 packet Knox gelatin

4 slices brioche or challah bread, cut ⅓ inch thick

8 ounces fresh blueberries

Preheat the oven to 325°. Combine the milk, cream, vanilla (bean and scrapings), 4 mint sprigs, and lemon zest in a small saucepan and bring to a boil over medium heat. Remove from the heat, stir in the sugar and gelatin, and let set for 3 minutes. Remove and discard the mint and vanilla bean.

Place a baking cup 3 inches in diameter and 1½ inches deep top side down on the center of a slice of bread to cut out a disk the size of the cup. Discard the bread trimmings and set the bread disk aside. Repeat with the remaining 3 bread slices.

Fill 4 baking cups halfway with blueberries. Pour the warm milk mixture over the blueberries to fill each cup three-fourths full. Place 1 bread disk in each cup over the blueberry mixture.

Transfer the cups to the oven and bake for 20 to 25 minutes (the custard should not be completely set). Turn on the broiler and broil until the bread is nicely toasted.

Remove from the oven and set aside to cool. Refrigerate for several hours before serving. The pudding can be prepared a day in advance. It is best when refrigerated for at least 6 hours before serving.

To unmold, run a small blade around the side of each cup and invert the blueberry bread pudding onto a dessert plate. Garnish with the reserved mint leaves.

213

Melissa DeMayo

214

Melissa DeMayo

Melissa DeMayo graduated
from New York University
with a degree in journalism,
but was inspired to become a
pastry chef after taking a
course with Nick Malgieri at
Peter Kump's Cooking School.
Since then she has worked at
Pâtisserie Lanciani, Rakel, Le
Cirque, the "21" Club, "44,"
and at the Royalton and the
Hay Adams Hotel in Wash-
ington, D.C. It was at the
Royalton that John Mariani
named DeMayo Best New
Pastry Chef of the Year in his
1992 roundup for *Esquire*.

Melissa DeMayo lives in
Bucks County, Pennsylvania,
and is a food stylist for such
publications as *New Woman*
magazine, *New York
Magazine*, and *Vogue*.

Patrick Clark was my first and also my final executive chef. When we met in 1987, he was consulting for a now-defunct restaurant in the theater district in New York City. I had very little experience, so Patrick supplied me with his recipes and taught me to make them. Six years later, when Patrick asked me to join him at the Hay Adams as his pastry chef, I came with my own recipes. **I believe this one was Patrick's favorite. He used to say, "It's the best-tasting dessert with the worst-sounding name!"**

Serves 8

10 sheets filo dough

½ cup unsalted
butter, melted

1 cup granulated sugar

———

3 tablespoons
unsalted butter

1 vanilla bean, split

6 ripe bananas, sliced
⅛ inch thick

½ cup firmly packed dark
brown sugar

1 cup heavy whipping cream

3 tablespoons
granulated sugar

1 cup sour cream

———

Caramel sauce
(recipe follows)

Confectioners' sugar
for dusting

To prepare the filo:
Preheat the oven to 350°.
Remove the filo dough from
the package and cover with
a damp cloth to keep the
sheets from drying out.
Arrange 2 sheets of the filo on
a waxed paper– or parchment-
lined baking sheet. Brush
with about 1½ tablespoons
of the butter and sprinkle
with 2 to 3 tablespoons of
sugar. Cover with 2 more filo
sheets, brush with 1½ tablespoons butter, and sprinkle
with 2 to 3 tablespoons sugar.
Cover with a final filo sheet.
Using a 3-inch circle (cup,
glass, or circular cookie cutter) and a knife, cut 12 circles
from the filo stack, discarding
the excess dough.

To make the tops:
Cut the 4 remaining filo
sheets in half and brush
each lightly with some of
the remaining butter. Crunch
each piece into a ball, but do
not squeeze or press. Sprinkle
with sugar and arrange on the
baking sheet with the circles.

Bake the filo for 8 to
10 minutes, or until the
sugar is melted and the filo is
browned. (Watch the circles
carefully and remove them
from the oven if the sugar
begins to burn.) Remove the
filo from the oven and allow
to cool before removing from
the baking sheet. (The recipe
may be made to this point
up to a day ahead and kept
in an airtight container at
room temperature.)

To prepare the filling:
Melt the butter in a saucepan.
Add the vanilla and stir until
the vanilla bean seeds begin
to appear in the butter.
Add the bananas and stir
for 1 minute. Add the brown
sugar and toss gently for
3 minutes, or until the
bananas are evenly coated

and the sugar is melted.
Remove and discard the
vanilla bean and allow the
mixture to cool. (The filling
can be made to this point up
to several hours ahead, but
do not refrigerate.)

Whip the cream with the
granulated sugar until stiff
peaks form. Beat in the sour
cream until just combined,
and let sit for 1 hour.
Combine the cream and
the banana mixture.

Spoon some of the caramel
sauce in the center of each
plate. Place a filo circle on
the sauce and spread each
one with a heaping table-
spoon of the banana filling.
Continue the layering until
there are 3 layers of filo
and banana filling on each
stack. Cover with one of the
tops and dust with confectioners' sugar.

Caramel Sauce

1 cup sugar

⅔ cup heavy whipping
cream, warmed

¼ to ⅓ cup freshly squeezed
lime juice

Cook the sugar in a heavy-
bottomed 2½-quart pot over
high heat for 3 minutes, or
until the sugar melts and is
light amber in color. Watch
carefully to make sure the
sugar does not burn. Stir the
cream in slowly until the
mixture is combined. (It will
bubble.) Remove from the
heat and stir in the lime
juice, adjusting the amount
to taste. If the sauce is not to
be used immediately, cover
and refrigerate. (The sauce
can be made up to 2 days
ahead and warmed just prior
to serving.)

Baklava of Banana

A few pomegranite seeds sprinkled around the baklava look great.

215

216

Mason Irving

While attending New York Tech's Hotel and Restaurant Management program, Mason became acquainted with Patrick Clark. He worked for him at La Boite while also apprenticing at Le Cirque. After graduation, he apprenticed at London's Dorchester Hotel. Upon his return to New York, Mason worked in several restaurants, including the Maurice and the Green Street Cafe. Mason rejoined Patrick at Café Luxembourg during its second and third years of operation.

Mason was executive chef for an off-premise caterer, owner of his own restaurant, and ultimately, the director and chef of a private dining club in an exclusive Manhattan condominium. Through all of the years and experiences, he considers Patrick Clark his primary mentor and is honored to have called him a friend.

It was the night before New Year's Eve in 1986. Patrick and I were engaged in complex preparations for one of the exotic menus he liked to present for such occasions. (He was downtown at Odeon, and I was uptown at Café Luxembourg.) The item that required the most care was a ballottine of foie gras with morels. There were many phone calls back and forth between us (mostly him checking on me). By late night we were down to the actual cooking of our eighteen or so ballottines apiece.

At 11:15 P.M. dinner service ended and I had the kitchen to myself. I placed three chafing pans on the stove, filled them half full with veal stock, and brought them up to temperature. I gently placed nine ballottines in the pans and cooked them for the prescribed time, watching them carefully.

During this process Patrick called to check on my progress. "Chief, how's it going?" he asked. "Not too bad, chef," I replied. "I'm making progress." "Really!" he exclaimed. "I'm going to be here all night." "Well, I don't know Pat," I said, "but I think I'll be finished soon." He just sort of groaned and said we'd talk later. I repeated the process, jumped into my street clothes, and left.

I hailed a taxi to take me to Odeon. It was 1:00 A.M. when the bartender told me Patrick was still downstairs in the prep kitchen. I ran downstairs to see if I could help out. There he was, sitting in an office chair in front of the stove, two pots on the stove, one ballottine in each pot, and a portable television up on the shelf. The chef was staring blankly at the television and carefully watching his creation at the same time. He looked at me, smiled and said, "Chief, what are you doing here?" I told him I was finished and had thought he might need some help. **He just laughed that generous laugh and made me confess my rapid technique for foie gras ballottine poaching.**

I will remember that moment in that basement prep kitchen in New York City with happiness and warmth for as long as my memory will allow.

Serves 6

1 cup butter

8 ounces
semisweet chocolate

4 eggs

4 egg yolks

½ cup sugar

½ cup all-purpose flour

2 tablespoons creamy
peanut butter

Vanilla ice cream

To prepare the cake:
Melt the butter and chocolate together in a mixing bowl set over a pot of simmering water. Remove the bowl from the double boiler and keep warm.

In a medium bowl, beat together the eggs, yolks, and sugar with an electric mixer on medium speed until light in color and very thick. Fold one-quarter of the egg mixture into the melted chocolate. Fold the remaining egg mixture into the chocolate, sprinkle the flour over the batter, and fold in gently.

Ladle the batter into the buttered tins, ring molds, or muffin pans. Place 1 teaspoon of peanut butter in the center of each tin. (Give the peanut butter a little push if necessary to position it into the center of each cake.) Bake for 7 to 8 minutes. The cakes should still be very soft and liquid in the middle. Remove the pan from the oven and let the cakes cool before unmolding.

To serve, unmold the cakes carefully onto a microwave-able plate. Reheat in a microwave oven for 15 to 20 seconds. (Don't overdo it or the cakes will be dry!) Place a cake on each plate and place a scoop of ice cream next to the cake.

Bits of broken peanut brittle or chopped peanuts sprinkled over the plate make a great garnish.

217

Gray Kunz

At age sixteen, Kunz followed his older brother into the kitchen where he began a career path that has taken him around the world. Trained in the classic European tradition, Kunz began with a three-year apprenticeship in Bern, in his native Switzerland. He went on to work at Restaurant des Parc Eaux-Vives in Geneva, the Beau-Rivage Palace Hotel, Laussanne and the Baur au Lac Hotel in Zurich and then to Girardet, where he worked for five years at which point he left to become executive chef at Hong Kong's Plume. In 1988, Kunz joined the Peninsula Hotel in New York as executive chef.

Kunz was named chef of Lespinasse in New York City in 1991. Lespinasse in Washington, D.C., opened in the Carlton Hotel in 1996 and earned the title of Best New Restaurant in America by *Esquire* in 1997.

Patrick was the father of great black chefs and of those yet to emerge. He was inspirational for young African-American chefs striving to succeed and continue the tradition of great chefs in America. **His presence has been a marking stone for individuals who see cooking not just as a vocation but as a lifelong love affair.** *The smile, the goodness, the truth. Patrick, you had it all, and more.*

Chilled Strawberry Soup

with Elderflower Ice Cream

This light, refreshing dessert is a perfect ending to a summer luncheon.

Serves 10

6 cups strawberries

¼ cup elderflower syrup

3 tablespoons plus
1 teaspoon sugar

¼ cup plus 3 tablespoons
freshly squeezed orange juice

Elderflower Ice Cream
(recipe follows)

To prepare the soup:
Purée half of the strawberries with the elderflower syrup, sugar, and orange juice. Strain through a chinois and chill on ice. When the soup is cold, slice the remaining strawberries and then chop one-quarter of the slices.

To serve, ladle the soup into shallow bowls and form a circle on the soup with the sliced strawberries. Place some of the chopped strawberries in the center of the circle and top with a small scoop of Elderflower Ice Cream.

Elderflower Ice Cream

YIELD: ABOUT 2 CUPS

3 tablespoons butter

1 tablespoon plus
2 teaspoons sugar

3 tablespoons
elderflower syrup

⅔ cup Moscato d'Asti

2 egg yolks

Bring the butter, sugar, elderflower syrup, and wine almost to a boil. Put the yolks in a medium bowl, pour the liquid over the yolks, and blend together with a hand-held mixer to combine. Immediately freeze the mixture in an ice cream maker and keep frozen until ready to use.

George Morrone

George Morrone, executive chef and partner of One Market restaurant in San Francisco, spent the three years following his graduation from the Culinary Institute of America at New York's River Café. He then moved to San Francisco to work under Bradley Ogden at San Francisco's Campton Place. Eventually, Los Angeles's Hotel Bel Air tapped the twenty-six-year-old Morrone.

Five years later, Morrone's dream of opening a specialty seafood restaurant in San Francisco was realized when he and his wife, Stacey, opened the doors to Aqua. Although the restaurant's partnership recently dissolved, his talent is still reflected in Aqua's menu. Under Morrone's leadership, Aqua earned four stars from the *San Francisco Chronicle* and was voted Best Seafood Restaurant in the *San Francisco Focus* magazine Readers' Restaurant Poll for three consecutive years.

My fond memories of Patrick Clark take me back to my first experience at the Masters of Food and Wine at the Highlands Inn, in Carmel, California. My first memory was seeing this big man with a demanding persona who spoke softly, yet confidently—until all hell broke loose around us. He then became the field general, barking orders left and right, controlling the situation until order was restored. It was brilliant! **This image of the immovable force amongst the chaos will be my enduring memory of the man.**

Serves 6

2 cups whole milk

2 cups heavy
whipping cream

2 Tahitian vanilla beans

9 egg yolks

1 cup sugar

2 teaspoons pure
vanilla extract

¼ teaspoon salt

Caramel Sauce
(recipe follows)

Malted Fudge Sauce
(recipe follows)

Strawberry Sauce
(recipe follows)

To prepare the ice cream:

In a medium saucepan, bring the milk, cream, and vanilla beans to a boil. Remove the pan from the heat and let the mixture steep for 20 minutes. Return the pan to the heat and bring the cream to a boil again. Whisk together the egg yolks and sugar. Slowly pour in some of the hot cream to temper the eggs. Add the egg mixture to the cream in the pan and cook over medium-low heat for 2 to 3 minutes, or until the mixture coats the back of a wooden spoon. Strain the mixture through a fine-mesh sieve and add the vanilla extract and salt. Place over an ice bath to chill, and freeze in an ice cream machine. Keep frozen until ready to use.

Spoon some of the ice cream into brandy snifters and place 1 of the snifters on each plate. Pour each sauce into 6 individual ramekins or small dishes and arrange 1 dish of each sauce around the base of the snifters.

Caramel Sauce

YIELD: ABOUT 2 ½ CUPS

1 cup sugar

¼ cup corn syrup

½ cup water

2 tablespoons butter

1¼ cups heavy
whipping cream

Pulp of 1 vanilla bean

1 teaspoon salt

Combine the sugar, corn syrup, and water in a stainless steel pot. Bring to a boil over medium heat and cook, covered, for 3 minutes. Remove the lid and continue to boil until the sugar begins to caramelize. Lower the heat and allow the mixture to darken to an amber brown. Slowly add the cream, whisking continuously. Add the butter and scraped vanilla bean and bring to a simmer. Remove the pan from the heat and strain the mixture into a bowl through a fine-mesh sieve. Add the salt, cover, and refrigerate for up to 1 week or until ready to use.

Malted Fudge Sauce

YIELD: ABOUT 2½ CUPS

1 cup sugar

2 tablespoons butter

1 cup heavy whipping cream

¼ cup unsweetened cocoa powder

3 tablespoons malt powder

½ teaspoon salt

Caramelize the sugar in a stainless steel pot. Add the butter, cream, cocoa, malt, and salt. Whisk for 5 minutes over low heat and strain into a bowl through a fine-mesh sieve. Refrigerate for up to 1 week or until ready to use.

Strawberry Sauce

YIELD: ABOUT 1½ CUPS

2 cups fresh strawberries

½ cup sugar

2 tablespoons freshly squeezed lime juice

Combine all of the ingredients in stainless steel pot and cook, uncovered, over low heat for 20 to 30 minutes, or until the fruit is soft. Purée until smooth and strain into a bowl through a fine-mesh sieve. Refrigerate for up to 1 week or until ready to use.

Tahitian Vanilla Bean Ice Cream

with Caramel Sauce, Malted Fudge Sauce, and Strawberry Sauce

The signature desserts of One Market Restaurant are the made-to-order ice creams. They are frozen individually and served soft with the sauces on the side.

221

Bradley Ogden

Bradley Ogden is chef and co-owner of One Market in San Francisco; The Lark Creek Inn in Larkspur, Marin County, California; and the Lark Creek restaurants in Walnut Creek and San Mateo, California. Bradley is widely acclaimed as a pioneer and inspiration to many in the culinary field, transforming traditional American food into superbly updated fare.

The forty-five-year-old native of Traverse City, Michigan, has been inducted into the Who's Who of American Cooking by *Cooks* magazine. He was chosen as one of the Great American Chefs by the International Wine and Food Society and has received many honors including the Golden Plate Award by the American Academy of Achievement and being named Best Chef: California by the James Beard Foundation.

One of my fondest memories is an annual ritual that began in 1984, after one of the first Meals on Wheels fundraisers in New York. A group of us would get together to celebrate and wind down after each successful James Beard event. This group of chefs—Larry Forgione, Jonathan Waxman, Mark Miller, and Jimmy Schmidt, to name a few—would go to Odeon for a late-night meal of burgers, fries, and champagne. Patrick was chef there at the time, and he would join us in our merrymaking. **His burgers and fries were some of the best I've ever tasted.** *They hit the spot after a long, grueling day.*

Pear Skillet Cake

with Bourbon Ice Cream

If you don't have an ice cream machine, you can serve the cake with a bourbon anglaise.

Serves 6 to 8

1 cup brown sugar

½ cup butter

6 to 8 whole pears

3 cups grated pear (with skin)

2 cups sugar

2 cups flour

4 eggs

1½ cups corn oil

1 tablespoon ground cinnamon

2 tablespoons allspice

1 tablespoon salt

2 tablespoons baking soda

Pulp of 1 vanilla bean

Bourbon Ice Cream (recipe follows)

To prepare the cake:
Preheat the oven to 350°. Place the brown sugar and butter in a 12-inch cast iron skillet and heat in the oven until the butter is melted. Remove the pan from the oven and stir until combined. Set aside. Peel the pears and slice each one into 6 wedges, discarding the cores. Place the pear wedges in the skillet, starting from the outside edge and working in toward the center in a circular flower pattern.

Place the remaining ingredients in a mixing bowl and beat with an electric mixer until fully incorporated. Gently pour the batter into the skillet. Bake in the oven for 45 minutes to 1 hour, or until a knife inserted in the center comes out clean.

Cut the cake into 6 slices and invert 1 slice in the center of each plate. Place a scoop of bourbon ice cream on the pears and serve immediately.

Bourbon Ice Cream

YIELD: 1 QUART

8 egg yolks

2 cups heavy whipping cream

1 cup half-and-half

¾ cup plus 2 tablespoons sugar

Pinch of salt

1 cup Jack Daniels whiskey

Lightly beat the egg yolks in a 2-quart stainless steel saucepan. Add 1 cup of the heavy cream, the half-and-half, sugar, and salt. Cook over medium-high heat, stirring occasionally, for 10 minutes, or until the mixture coats the back of a spoon. Strain into a bowl through a fine-mesh sieve and chill over an ice bath. Light the Jack Daniels on fire and add to the custard with the remaining 1 cup heavy cream and ¼ cup uncooked Jack Daniels. Cover and refrigerate for several hours, or overnight. Freeze in an ice cream machine and keep frozen until ready to use.

Francois Payard

Francois Payard is a third-generation French pastry chef, born in Nice. Francois cultivated his passion for pastry as a child; growing up surrounded by classic French pastry in the tradition his parents and grandparents had kept alive for over fifty years in his grandfather's renowned shop, Au Nid des Friandises.

In 1988 Payard held his first position as a pastry chef at La Tour d'Argent in Paris. The following year, he moved to the kitchens at Lucas Carton. In 1990 he moved to New York to be the pastry chef at Le Bernardin. In 1993 he joined Chef Daniel Boulud in opening Restaurant Daniel. In 1997 Francois opened his own patisserie, Payard, in New York.

My most immediate recollection of Patrick is that it was always a pleasure to work with him on big events. **He was a master of organization of parties** *such as the Masters of Food and Wine and various large-scale events in New York. He will be sorely missed.*

Drizzle a bit of chocolate sauce around the plate for a more intense chocolate flavor.

Serves 10

4 eggs, separated

1½ teaspoons all-purpose flour

3½ tablespoons granulated sugar

6 ounces extra bitter chocolate, finely chopped

½ cup plus 2 tablespoons butter, melted and kept warm, plus 1 tablespoon at room temperature

Juice of ¼ lemon

2 tablespoons extra-fine granulated sugar

To prepare the soufflé:
Preheat the oven to 375°. Beat the egg yolks in a mixing bowl with a wire whisk. Gradually incorporate the flour and add 2½ tablespoons of the sugar, one spoonful at a time. Beat the mixture until it becomes light and fluffy and turns a lemony color.

Place the chocolate in a small bowl and add the melted butter. Whisk until completely smooth. Add the chocolate mixture to the egg yolk mixture and blend well.

In a large mixing bowl, beat the egg whites and lemon juice until soft peaks form. Add the remaining 1 tablespoon of the sugar and beat until stiff. Gently fold the egg whites into the chocolate mixture until fully incorporated.

Butter ten 3-inch-diameter soufflé cups with the remaining butter and coat with the extra-fine granulated sugar. Using a pastry bag, fill the cups three-quarters of the way full. Place the filled cups in a water bath and bake in the oven for 5 to 6 minutes.

Unmold immediately onto a serving plate and serve warm.

Jacques Pépin

Jacques Pépin, celebrated host of award-winning cooking shows on national public television, master chef, food columnist, cooking teacher, and author, was born in Bourg-en Bresse, near Lyons. His first exposure to cooking was in his parents' restaurant, Le Pelican. At thirteen, he began his apprenticeship at the Grand Hotel de L'Europe. He subsequently trained under Lucien Diat at Hotel Plaza Athénée. From 1956 to 1958 Jacques was personal chef to three French heads of state: Felix Gaillard, Pierre Pfimlin, and Charles de Gaulle.

Jacques moved to the United States in 1959. He worked first at New York's Le Pavillon restaurant, and then for ten years as director of research and new development for the Howard Johnson Company. His sixteen cookbooks have earned him a place in the James Beard Foundation's Cookbook Hall of Fame in 1996.

I was privileged to see Patrick Clark in action several times. In 1996 I was a guest chef at the annual Masters of Food and Wine event at the Highlands Inn in Carmel, California. Patrick was in charge of the kitchen, responsible for directing all of the celebrity chefs, synchronizing their food—and dealing with their egos. Calm, confident, and efficient, he went about his business with a smile, gently nudging all the other chefs into position for photographs and declining any of the credit for himself. I was impressed!

I also met him on several occasions when I was invited to announce the winners of culinary scholarships from the New York City Public Schools for the Careers Through Culinary Arts Program (C-CAP), at a brunch they held each spring at Tavern on the Green, where Patrick officiated as executive chef. **I was amazed and touched to see how much the young candidates for these awards looked up to Patrick and admired him.** *There was no doubt that he cared for them, too, as evidenced by the love, time, and effort he gave on behalf of C-CAP. This was Patrick—a giant of a man in body, soul, and spirit. He is greatly missed.*

Cherry-Raspberry Pillow

This is a perfect dish for a large gathering. It can be made well in advance and served at room temperature.

Serves 8 to 10

Processor Pâte Brisée
(recipe follows)

1 pound Bing cherries, pitted

²⁄₃ cup cherry preserves
(preferably containing
pieces of cherries)

1½ tablespoons cornstarch

8 ounces raspberries

2 tablespoons
unsalted butter

1 egg

1 tablespoons crystalline or
pearl sugar (optional)

Confectioners' sugar,
for dusting

To prepare the dough:

Roll out the dough on a lightly floured surface to a ¹⁄₁₆-inch-thick rectangle measuring about 14 inches wide by 22 inches long. Roll the dough lightly around a rolling pin and unroll it over a baking sheet so the width of the dough is almost the length of the baking sheet. Let almost half the length of the dough extend beyond the baking sheet; this will be folded over the filling.

To prepare the pillow:

Preheat the oven to 400°. Combine the cherries, cherry preserves, and cornstarch in a medium bowl. Spread the cherry mixture on top of the dough on the baking sheet to within about 1½ inches of the edges of the dough in the pan. Sprinkle the raspberries on top of the cherry mixture, and dot the fruit with the butter.

Fold the excess pastry over the fruit mixture to encase it. Press on the dough at the edges to seal them well and trim the corners with a sharp knife to round them slightly. Press gently on the top of the pillow to evenly distribute the fruit inside. Break the egg into a small bowl, remove about half of the white, beat the remaining egg, and brush the entire top of the dough with the egg. Press the tines of a fork around the perimeter of the pastry to create a decorative edge about 1½ inches deep. If a crispy surface is desired, sprinkle the top of the pastry with the coarse crystalline sugar. Using a sharp knife, mark a crisscross pattern in the top of the pastry, cutting through the dough here and there to allow the steam to escape during cooking.

Bake the pillow in the oven for 45 minutes. Remove the pan from the oven and cool the pillow to room temperature. If any of the juices from the filling have leaked out onto the baking sheet during baking, slide a knife under the pastry while it is still hot and move it slightly before the juices harden and cause the pastry to stick to the pan.

Sprinkle the pillow with confectioners' sugar and cut it into segments. Arrange the segments on a serving platter.

Processor Pâte Brisée

3 cups all-purpose flour

½ teaspoon salt

1½ cups cold unsalted butter, cut into ½-inch pieces

²⁄₃ cup ice cold water

Put the flour, salt, and butter in the bowl of a food processor fitted with the metal blade, and process for about 10 seconds. (The butter should crumbly.) Add the cold water, and process for about 10 seconds more, just long enough for the dough to start gathering together. (Little pieces of butter should still be visible in the dough.) Remove the dough from the food processor, and gather it into a ball. The dough can be made ahead and refrigerated for up to 2 days, or frozen for up to 1 month.

Judy Schmitt

Judy Schmitt was born and raised on her family's farm in rural Wisconsin. She attended the University of Wisconsin-Madison, studying art and advertising, and then, after several cooking jobs in the Madison area, she realized her ambition. She attended the Culinary Institute of America, graduating at the top of her class. Judy moved to Washington, D.C., where she worked at Red Sage, the Willard Room, and later, at the Hay Adams Hotel. She worked with Patrick Clark for two years as his pastry chef before his entire management staff moved to New York's Tavern on the Green. Judy was pastry chef there for more than two years before moving to her current position at Manhattan's "21" Club.

My favorite Patrick story comes from a birthday party for Barbara Walters at Tavern on the Green. Warner LeRoy, the owner, decided on a truly spectacular dessert—a purple gorilla jumping out of a six-foot birthday cake fitted on top with a real cake with frosting. In the words of Warner, there would be cake and frosting flying everywhere and then the gorilla would come out and kiss Ms Walters and join in singing "Happy Birthday." As ridiculous as this may sound now, at the time it was no joke. It involved weeks of meetings, rehearsals, and staging that surpassed even the biggest of Broadway shows. After the second practice with the spewing cake, I felt confident there would be no problems.

The dinner progressed as planned. The cake was wheeled in and the cue was given. Again, the cue was given. Ms Walters, unsure of what was to happen, started singing her own birthday song while the banquet captains nervously fought with the top of the cake, pulling out the cowering gorilla. In that moment, the weeks of practice were lost to an awkward-looking man in a purple costume looking as confused as the rest of the guests.

Soon after, I found myself in the middle of a heated argument between the banquet manager and Patrick about the faulty cake. What a sense of emotion overcame me as Patrick, never one to be accused of having an impish voice, bellowed, "Judy did nothing wrong! Why don't you look at your gorilla?" They were so anxious to find a scapegoat for what turned out to be a major miscommunication between the gorilla and the service staff. I will never forget the way he fought off the "wolves" that evening.

I miss Patrick both as a boss and as a mentor. *He could move you to try so hard with few words; it was an honor to work with such talent. I will remember our first meeting at the Hay and last good-bye, at Tavern and I will always miss him. But I believe that he is still fighting battles for me, and I use that knowledge to drive me where I am today.*

Meyer Lemon Sabayon Tart
with Blackberry Sorbet

Meyer lemons are slightly sweeter than other lemons, but if Meyer lemons aren't available, other lemons will work just as well.

Serves 10

DOUGH

1½ cups unsalted butter

3 cups confectioners' sugar

3 eggs

¾ teaspoon vanilla extract

Scant ½ teaspoon salt

5⅔ cups cake flour

Scant ¼ teaspoon baking powder

SABAYON

1⅓ cups freshly squeezed Meyer lemon juice

1½ cups sugar

4 eggs

5 egg yolks

¾ cup plus 1 tablespoon and 1 teaspoon butter, melted

¾ sheet gelatin, soaked in cool water

MERINGUE

⅓ cup egg whites (about 3 whites)

¾ cup confectioners' sugar

Blackberry Sorbet (recipe follows)

To prepare the dough:
Cream the butter and confectioners' sugar. Add the eggs one at a time, mixing until fully incorporated after each addition. Add the vanilla. Sift together the dry ingredients, add to egg mixture, and mix until just combined. Wrap the dough in plastic wrap and refrigerate for at least 30 minutes, or until workable.

Preheat the oven to 350°. Roll the dough out to ¹⁄₁₆ inch thick and cut into 10 five-inch circles. Line 10 four-inch-diameter by 1½-inch-high tart rings with the dough and refrigerate for 30 minutes. Bake for 12 to 15 minutes, or until golden brown. Remove the tart shells from the oven and set aside to cool.

To prepare the sabayon:
Combine the lemon juice, sugar, eggs, and egg yolks in a large stainless steel bowl set over a pot of barely simmering water. Whip continuously with a balloon whip until the mixture becomes thick and pudding-like. Whisk in the melted butter, and add the gelatin. Pour into the tart shells and let cool to room temperature.

To prepare the meringue:
Preheat the oven to 400°. Put the egg whites and confectioners' sugar in a bowl set over a warm water bath until just warm. Whip the mixture with an electric mixer until soft peaks form. Pipe the meringue onto the tarts to cover the entire top and bake for 10 minutes, or until lightly browned.

To serve, remove the tarts from the rings and place a tart in the center of each plate. Spoon some of the Blackberry Sorbet next to the tarts.

Blackberry Sorbet

YIELD: ABOUT 1½ QUARTS

1 cup water

1 cup plus 2½ tablespoons sugar

1 vanilla bean, split

1 quart fresh blackberry purée, strained

1 tablespoon freshly squeezed lemon juice

Combine the water, sugar, and vanilla bean in a large saucepan and simmer until the sugar is dissolved. Remove and discard the vanilla bean and add the blackberry purée and lemon juice to the pan. Remove the pan from heat and chill in an ice water bath. Freeze the mixture in ice cream machine and keep frozen until ready to use.

229

Nancy Silverton

230

Nancy Silverton

Nancy Silverton attended the Cordon Bleu in London and then returned to California to be an assistant pastry chef at Michael's, in Santa Monica. Soon after completing a series of pastry courses at the École Le Notre in Plaiser, France, Silverton was appointed head pastry chef at Wolfgang Puck's Spago restaurant in Los Angeles, where she was responsible for developing the highly acclaimed desserts. In 1985 she and her husband, Mark Peel, moved to Manhattan and spent six months revamping Maxwell's Plum before returning to Los Angeles to open La Brea Bakery, in January 1989, and Campanile, in June 1989.

Nancy is also the author of *Desserts*, and *Nancy Silverton's Breads from the La Brea Bakery*.

Patrick Clark had a magic touch—and not just with food. This I learned the first time we worked together at the Masters of Food and Wine at the Highlands Inn, in Carmel, California. A torrent of unexpected nervousness had just swept over me when Patrick suddenly appeared behind me and put his hand on my shoulder. "You'll be fine," he said, in that way of his that made people feel bolstered by his confidence. "I will make sure."

I chose this dessert because it's just like Patrick— warm and comforting.

Serves 6

1 pound dark red, thin, firm stalks of rhubarb, cleaned

2 cups strawberries

1/4 cup plus 2 tablespoons sugar

2 tablespoons water

1 cinnamon stick

3 to 4 gratings of fresh nutmeg

2 peppercorns, crushed

Pulp and pod of 1 vanilla bean

1/4 cup Riesling

Brown Butter Biscuits (recipe follows)

2 tablespoons heavy whipping cream

2 tablespoons cornmeal

Vanilla ice cream

To prepare the rhubarb:
Cut the rhubarb into 3-inch lengths and then cut each piece lengthwise into thirds or fourths. The pieces should be about the size of a pencil. Remove the stems from the strawberries and cut into 1/4-inch-thick slices. Bring 1/4 cup of the sugar and the water to a boil in a large stainless steel saucepan over medium-high heat. Add the cinnamon stick, nutmeg, and pepper, and vanilla pulp and pod. When the sugar mixture begins to color, swirl the pan gently to ensure an even caramel color. Add the rhubarb and stir to combine. Add the wine and continue to cook over high heat for 5 minutes, or until the rhubarb just begins to soften. Stir in the strawberries and cook for 4 to 5 minutes, or until the fruit is tender and the mixture is slightly thickened. Ideally, the rhubarb and strawberries will be completely cooked yet still be intact and have texture. Set aside to cool. When cool, transfer the mixture to an 8-inch round or square pan.

To prepare the cobbler:
Preheat the oven to 375°. Place the biscuits in a ring pattern on top of the fruit, with the edges just touching. Leave a border of at least 1 inch from the edge of baking dish. Brush the tops of the biscuits with the cream and sprinkle with the cornmeal and the remaining 2 tablespoons sugar. Turn the oven temperature down to 350° and bake the cobbler for 25 minutes, or until browned.

To serve, scoop the warm fruit and 1 biscuit into the center of each plate and place a scoop of vanilla ice cream next to the cobbler.

Brown Butter Biscuits

YIELD: 6 BISCUITS

1/4 cup plus 1 tablespoon unsalted butter

Pulp and pod of 1 vanilla bean

1 1/4 cups all-purpose flour

2 tablespoons sugar

1/4 cup white cornmeal

2 teaspoons baking powder

1/4 teaspoon salt

2 hard-boiled egg yolks

1/2 cup heavy whipping cream

Melt the butter in a saucepan over medium-high heat. Add the vanilla bean pulp and pod and cook for 2 to 3 minutes, stirring occasionally, until the butter begins to brown and has a nutty, toasty aroma. As soon as the bubbling subsides, remove the pan from the heat. Remove and discard the vanilla bean, pour the butter into a bowl, and refrigerate for 1 hour, or until firm.

Combine the flour, sugar, cornmeal, baking powder, and salt in a food processor fitted with a metal blade. Push the egg yolks through a mesh strainer into the bowl of a food processor and pulse the mixture a few times, just until combined. Cut up the chilled butter, add to the food processor, and process into a fine meal. Add the cream and mix until just combined.

Turn the dough out onto a lightly floured surface and knead gently 3 or 4 times until it forms a smooth ball. Roll out the dough to 1/2 inch thick and cut out 6 biscuits using a 2- to 2 1/2-inch biscuit cutter.

Strawberry-Rhubarb Cobbler

with Brown Butter Biscuits

This warm cobbler is the perfect dessert for a chilly fall evening.

231

Bill Yosses

Bill Yosses is the pastry
chef at Bouley Bakery and
restaurant in New York City.
He was pastry chef at New
York's four-star Bouley restaurant for a decade prior this
position. Bill trained at New
York City Technical College
and at restaurants and bak-
eries in France, including
La Maison du Chocolat,
Fanchon, Restaurant La Fout,
and Le Pré Catélan.

Patrick, Michael Romano, and I were all graduates from New York Technical College (back then, in the dark ages of cuisine, it was called the New York City Community College).

Patrick was a hero of mine. At a young age he was the most successful of the past graduates. After all, he was the hand-picked sous chef of Michel Guerard, a chef who was the peak of the French culinary Mount Everest at the time. It was 1979. We culinary students knew Monsieur Guerard had created this new cuisine called "nouvelle cuisine," which we all felt sure was more than small portions on big plates, the derisive phrase that skeptical media used at the time. We were sure it was a pivotal moment in food culture.

I remember a benefit I worked with Patrick to earn contributions for our cooking school alma mater, and all my professors and mentors were there. There were also some celebrities, big-name contributors, a Trump or two, and Patrick and Michael were the chefs. Michael sent out a beautiful appetizer and Patrick had just sent out the main course, veal chop with wild mushrooms. I made a white chocolate mousse Charlotte, strawberry brunoise, and a coconut tuile with sorbet. I was set and starting to send out two hundred desserts, the most I had ever tried. I was very nervous. Patrick suddenly appeared next to me. It was the first time I had seen him all night, and the first words he spoke to me were, "I knew you would be ready. Looks great. I hope you made a few extra." **And then with a wink, he pulled a plate out of the line of desserts being sent out, grabbed a spoon, and dug in. Now that's gastronomy.**

White Chocolate Mousse

This smooth, creamy mousse is always a hit with guests.

Serves 6

1½ cups heavy whipping cream

2 egg yolks

2 tablespoons confectioners' sugar

12 ounces white chocolate, finely chopped

To prepare the mousse: Bring ½ cup of the cream to a boil in a medium saucepan over medium-high heat. In a small bowl, whisk together the egg yolks and sugar and slowly pour in some of the hot cream to temper the eggs. Pour the egg mixture into the cream in the pan and cook over medium-high heat for 30 to 45 seconds, or until the mixture thickens. Do not allow to boil or the eggs will curdle. Add the chopped chocolate, stir until smooth, remove from heat and cool to room temperature. Whip the remaining 1 cup of cream with an electric mixer until soft peaks are formed. Fold the whipped cream into the chocolate mixture, spoon the mousse into individual bowls, and refrigerate for at least 2 hours before serving.

NAME INDEX

235

RECIPE INDEX

237

239

Copyright © 1999
by the Patrick Clark Family Trust
and Charlie Trotter.

1⊖ Ten Speed Press
Box 7123
Berkeley, California 94707
www.tenspeed.com

Distributed in Australia by Simon
& Schuster Australia, in Canada by
Ten Speed Press Canada, in New
Zealand by Tandem Press, in South
Africa by Real Books, in Southeast
Asia by Berkeley Books, and in the
United Kingdom and Europe by
Airlift Books.

**PROJECT COORDINATOR
AND GENERAL EDITOR**
Judi Carle, Charlie Trotter's

TEN SPEED PRESS EDITOR
Lorena Jones

COPYEDITOR
Suzanne Sherman,
Healdsburg, California

**GRAPHIC DESIGN AND
TYPESETTING**
Three Communication Design,
Chicago

FOOD PHOTOGRAPHY
Tim Turner

Library of Congress Cataloging-in-
Publication Data on file with publisher.

Printed in Hong Kong
by C&C Offset Printing Co. Ltd.

First printing, 1999

1 2 3 4 5 6 7 8 9 10—04 03 02 01 00 99